**The World's
Hieroglyphic Beauty**

The University of Georgia Press
Athens

The World's Hieroglyphic Beauty

Five American Poets

PETER STITT

© 1985 by the University of Georgia Press
Athens, Georgia 30602
All rights reserved

Designed by Sandra Strother Hudson
Set in Linotron 202 Trump Medieval and Gill Sans types

The paper in this book meets the guidelines for
permanence and durability of the Committee on
Production Guidelines for Book Longevity of the
Council on Library Resources.

Printed in the United States of America

90 89 88 87 86 85   6 5 4 3 2 1

Library of Congress Cataloging in Publication Data

Stitt, Peter.
   The world's hieroglyphic beauty.

   Includes index.
   Contents: Introduction—The sacramental vision of
Richard Wilbur—Interview with Richard Wilbur—
[etc.]
   1. American poetry—20th century—History and
criticism—Addresses, essays, lectures. 2. Poets,
American—20th century—Interviews. I. Title.
PS323.5.S75 1985   811'.5'09   84-24056
ISBN 0-8203-0772-6 (alk. paper)

For Pete and Jon

le migliori creazioni del fabbro

Contents

Acknowledgments

●

I wish to thank the American Council of Learned Societies and the University of Houston for their generous financial assistance. By combining the fellowship awarded by the former and the faculty development leave provided by the latter, I was able to free myself from teaching for a year to complete the writing of this volume. Through its Limited-Grant-in-Aid program, the University of Houston also provided assistance with travel and typing expenses. For help in filing various applications for assistance, I wish to thank the staff of the Office of Sponsored Programs at the University of Houston.

My interviews with Richard Wilbur and James Wright originally appeared in the *Paris Review*. I am indebted to George Plimpton and three of his managing editors—Molly McKaughan, Fayette Hickox, and Hallie Gay Walden—not just for permission to reprint the interviews here, but for financial and literary assistance as well. Another debt is less direct: I learned how to interview poets by reading the work of Donald Hall, whose conversations with T. S. Eliot, Ezra Pound, and Robert Frost (all published in the *Paris Review*) remain models of the genre. An earlier version of my interview with Robert Penn Warren appeared several years ago in the pages of the *Sewanee Review*; for permission to reprint whatever remains of that version, I wish to thank George Core. My greatest debt with regard to the interviews is of course to the poets themselves, who gave generously of their time, energy, and ideas. Without them and their work, none of this would have been possible.

The essays were all newly written for this volume. However, portions of them have appeared, generally in much different form, in the pages of various magazines. For permission to reprint such material, I wish to thank the editors of the *Georgia Review*, *Kenyon Review*, and *Southern Review*. Similarly, a portion of my essay on James Wright was originally published in *The Pure, Clear Word: Essays on the Poetry of James Wright*, edited by Dave Smith; I thank Mr. Smith and the University of Illinois Press for permission to reprint.

I want also to thank Stanley W. Lindberg, editor of the *Georgia Re-*

view; Howard Munford, professor emeritus of American literature at Middlebury College; Robert Fredrickson, associate professor of English at Gettysburg College; and Philip Church, editor of the *Kenyon Review*, for reading all or part of the present manuscript and offering constructive suggestions toward its revision. Whatever errors remain (and I am sure there are many) reflect not their failure to read critically but my inability to heed their excellent advice. For assistance of other kinds I wish to thank Joel Conarroe of the University of Pennsylvania, Laurence Lieberman of the University of Illinois, and Terrell Dixon, James Pickering, and Susan Kaplan of the University of Houston.

My thinking on the poets studied here has been sharpened over the years by the many excellent students whom I have taught at Middlebury College and the University of Houston, and I thank them for their wise counsel. For the wisest counsel of all, and for support of every kind, my thanks to Marion Munford. Finally, I wish to thank my sons, Pete and Jon, who endured—and triumphed over—life with a single parent, too much of whose attention, for all too long a time, was concentrated upon the writing of this book.

Selections from "As Birds Are Fitted to the Boughs," "Carentan O Carentan," "The Peat-Bog Man," "On the Lawn at the Villa," "American Dreams," "Indian Country," "Sacred Objects," "Adam Yankev," and "The Foggy Lane" from *People Live Here: Selected Poems, 1949–1983*. Copyright © 1983 by Louis Simpson. Reprinted with the permission of BOA Editions, Ltd.

Excerpts from the following works by Richard Wilbur are reprinted by permission of Harcourt Brace Jovanovich, Inc.: *Advice to a Prophet and Other Poems*, copyright © 1961 by Richard Wilbur; *Things of This World*, copyright © 1956 by Richard Wilbur; *Ceremony and Other Poems*, copyright © 1950, 1978 by Richard Wilbur; *The Beautiful Changes and Other Poems*, copyright © 1947, 1975 by Richard Wilbur; *Walking to Sleep*, copyright © 1967, 1969 by Richard Wilbur; and *The Mind-Reader*, copyright © 1973, 1974 by Richard Wilbur.

Selections from *Stories That Could Be True: New and Collected Poems* by William Stafford. Copyright © 1977 by William Stafford. From *A Glass Face in the Rain: New Poems* by William Stafford. Copyright © 1982 by William Stafford. Reprinted by permission of Harper and Row, Publishers, Inc.

Selections from the following works are reprinted by permission of Random House, Inc.: from *This Journey* by James Wright, copyright © 1982 by Anne Wright; from *Selected Poems, 1923–1975* by Robert Penn Warren, copyright © 1976 by Robert Penn Warren; from *Now and Then: Poems, 1976–1978* by Robert Penn Warren, copyright © 1978 by Robert Penn Warren; from *Being Here: Poetry, 1977–1980* by Robert Penn Warren, copyright © 1980 by Robert Penn Warren.

Excerpts from *At the End of the Open Road* by Louis Simpson: "The Cradle Trap," copyright © 1961 by Louis Simpson; "On the Lawn at the Villa," copyright © 1963 by Louis Simpson; "Walt Whitman at Bear Mountain," copyright © 1960 by Louis Simpson; "Summer Morning," copyright © 1963 by Louis Simpson. Reprinted by permission of Wesleyan University Press.

Selections from *Collected Poems* by James Wright: "Father," copyright © 1957 by James Wright; "A Fit Against the Country," copyright © 1957 by James Wright; "The Accusation," copyright © 1959 by James Wright; "The Assignation," copyright © 1957 by James Wright; "At the Executed Murderer's Grave," copyright © 1958 by James Wright; "Saint Judas"; "A Message Hidden in an Empty Wine Bottle That I Threw Into a Gully of Maple Tree One Night at an Indecent Hour," copyright © 1961 by James Wright; "Three Stanzas From Goethe," copyright © 1961 by James Wright; "Lying in a Hammock at William Duffy's Farm in Pine Island, Minnesota"; "Eisenhower's Visit to Franco," copyright © 1962 by James Wright; "In Memory of A Spanish Poet," copyright © 1963 by James Wright; "American Wedding," copyright © 1959 by James Wright; "Two Hangovers," copyright © 1961 by James Wright; "Snowstorm in the Midwest," copyright © 1960 by James Wright; "Today I Was So Happy, So I Made This Poem," copyright © 1961 by James Wright; "March," copyright © 1961 by James Wright; "A Blessing," copyright © 1961 by James Wright; "Outside Fargo, North Dakota," copyright © 1968 by James Wright; "The Life," copyright © 1968 by James Wright; "Lifting Illegal Nets"; "A Christmas Greeting," copyright © 1963 by James Wright; "Willy Lyons," copyright © 1962 by James Wright; "Before a Cashier's Window," copyright © 1965 by James Wright; "Late November in a Field," copyright © 1969 by James Wright; "Old Age Compensation," copyright © 1968 by James Wright; "Three Sentences for a Dead Swan," copyright © 1966 by James Wright; "To the Muse," copyright © 1968 by James Wright; "The Quest," copyright © 1957 by James Wright. Reprinted by permission of Wesleyan University Press.

"An Interview with Robert Penn Warren" by Peter Stitt was first published in the *Sewanee Review* 85 (Summer 1977). Copyright © 1977 by the University of the South. Reprinted by permission of the editor.

Introduction

●

Because the present volume takes an unusual form in approaching its subject matter, I would like to begin this introduction by contrasting *The World's Hieroglyphic Beauty* with a few other critical studies of twentieth-century American poetry. Such works seem to group themselves into three broad categories. First are the many volumes that collect essays written by several different critics, either on a single poet or on several poets. No matter how penetrating the individual essays, these volumes never aim at the kind of thematic coherence that is my goal. One such work deserves mention here, however. *Contemporary Poetry in America: Essays and Interviews*, edited by Robert Boyers (New York: Schocken Books, 1974), is unusual in that it contains both essays on and interviews with various poets. To my knowledge it is the first volume to incorporate such a combination. However, it contains only three interviews, none of which is with a poet whose work is also the subject of an essay in the book. The distinguishing feature of the present volume, of course, is the pairing of the essays and interviews.

The best-known studies of twentieth-century poetry are those that I am placing in my second category—collections of individual essays on various poets written by a single critic, but without a single, unifying thesis. Whatever coherence such volumes achieve generally results either from the historical scope of the collection or from the consistency of the author's approach to various poets. Perhaps the best-known of such volumes are Richard Howard's *Alone with America: Essays on the Art of Poetry in the United States since 1950* (1969; reprint, New York: Atheneum, 1980) and Helen Vendler's *Part of Nature, Part of Us: Modern American Poets* (1980). Howard's book is a historical survey of the work of a great many poets; most of the essays in the volume began life as reviews written for literary magazines. Vendler's book is somewhat less systematic—in the Foreword she notes: "This collection includes both book reviews and essays on modern American poets."[1] While the essays were written on subjects of her choosing, the reviews were written on books assigned by a wide variety of editors. What dis-

tinguishes the present volume from these excellent collections is that
the writers were specifically chosen for study here because they embody my thesis.

Closest in conception to the present work are volumes in a third
category—those in which a single critic studies a number of different
poets from a single perspective. It is interesting that, unlike this volume, virtually all such books adopt a formal rather than a thematic
approach to the poetry. This fact is obvious in the titles of some of
these studies—for example, *Modern American Lyric* (New Brunswick,
N.J.: Rutgers University Press, 1978) by Arthur Oberg and *The Rhetoric of the Contemporary Lyric* (Bloomington: Indiana University
Press, 1980) by Jonathan Holden—while with others we must turn to
the opening pages to learn the specific approach. In the preface to *The
Fierce Embrace,* Charles Molesworth states: "This book's main assumption . . . holds that American poetry since the Second World War
has grown increasingly immersive in its *strategy,* abandoning the defensive irony that was largely prevalent in the wake of the modernist
era" (emphasis added). Similarly, David Kalstone describes his *Five
Temperaments* as "a book about the *ways* poets find to write about
their lives" (emphasis added).[2] Comparable statements appear in recent
studies by Jerome Mazzaro, Robert Pinsky, Charles Altieri, and James
Breslin.[3]

While issues of form are occasionally raised in the following pages,
my primary concern is to trace a thematic preoccupation—also manifested as a thematic strategy—through the work of five contemporary
American poets. Generally speaking, what we see in the work of each
of these writers is a quest through the physical world in search of an
essence of meaning that is felt but never quite seen, desired but never
quite defined. By its very nature, a quest is dynamic—the person who
undertakes it wishes to move from one place to another, wishes corre-
spondingly to move from a position of ignorance to a position of
knowledge. The poets studied in this volume all love the physical
world to such a degree that they sense within it some transcendent
meaning, some hovering aura of belief. Roughly speaking, the quest
each undertakes is to discover that hidden meaning by reading the "hieroglyphic" nature of the physical universe.

That these writers each read the universe differently goes without
saying; they are not members of an organized school of thought. That
they are at times reading different universes also goes without saying;
they are human, after all. They do, however, share the general movement that I have described, a movement that proceeds from the concrete toward the abstract, from the physical toward the spiritual, from
the body toward the mind. I say "toward" in each case to indicate some-

thing we must remember: none of these poets is didactic by nature, none is doctrinaire in belief. In their search for meaning, none of them would choose to make the world more meaningful than it actually is; none would choose to impose, deductively, a preformulated set of truths upon a reality that achieves much of its beauty from its teasingly ambiguous nature. The method they prefer is to draw inductively from within the fabric of the real whatever meaning may be found.

Beyond these shared methods and beliefs, the writers immediately begin to diverge from one another. Of the five, Richard Wilbur and Robert Penn Warren are most at home in the physical world; interestingly, they are also the most explicitly sacramental of these writers. Wilbur's poems are elaborate, elegant celebrations of the created world, art works as carefully and harmoniously constructed as the reality they praise. Even as he recognizes the existential primacy of material reality, however, Wilbur recognizes a spiritual reality as well. His goal as a poet is to bring these two realms together—a feat that is achieved through the use of metaphor. Because it expresses ideas through things, metaphor is the poetic device most able to live in two realms at once. Wilbur's images of the physical thus transcend the limitations of reality to enter the realm of suggestion and abstraction. It is in this way that he finds intimations of the sacred within the real.

Robert Penn Warren's ability to express the uglier side of physical life—the human capacity for evil, the primacy of the power of death—is greater than that of Richard Wilbur. This dark knowing is the basis for one of the two related quests undertaken in Warren's later poems. Without flinching from any aspect of the naturalistic universe, Warren seeks to understand its enduring beauty; his search is for the meaning of "life's instancy." In his other quest, Warren, using an aged speaker, addresses the problem of death, searching for the possibility of transcendence from the purely material realm into something else, something like "the astrolabe of joy." Robert Penn Warren is also the most prolific of the writers studied here. Because these quests have emerged most clearly in his later poetry—written since 1955—I will deal only with that portion of his work.

The three other writers under consideration here—William Stafford, Louis Simpson, and James Wright—have a less affectionate relationship with the world of material reality. This fact makes the quest pattern even more emphatic within their work than it is in the work of Wilbur and Warren. Because Wilbur and Warren believe that something sacred is to be found *within* reality, they do not feel required to abandon the physical in order to find the spiritual. Stafford, Simpson, and Wright are not nearly so comfortable with the possibilities of materiality; thus they are more driven in their searching. Over and over we see them traveling, escaping, questing away from the here-and-now toward a vague something—a something felt and passionately desired but never quite known; a something never quite found.

Although he rejects the categorization, William Stafford is the only western American writer considered here. His work embodies the quest for the wilderness found in so many American authors whose characters engage the reality of the American frontier. In outlook, Stafford is the most traditionally pastoral of these five poets—we always find within his work a sense of the moral superiority of life as it is lived in nature rather than in society. The quest we find in his work expresses a strong desire to escape from the city to the small town, from the small town to the farm, and from the farm into the uncharted wilderness. Somewhere out there, Stafford's speaker feels, is a distant and isolated place where a spiritual essence might be found. But though he is able to sense this presence in a number of ways, he is never quite able to pin it down; his is another quest with only vague findings.

In the work of Louis Simpson we find expressed another venerable American theme—the sense of alienation experienced by the sensitive, artistic, and spiritually oriented individual living in an explicitly materialistic society. In the first phase of his work, Simpson defines both this individual and the society against which he is pitted. The poems of Simpson's middle period are his most alienated—because of the Vietnam War, it is assumed that no bridges can be built between the sensitive individual and the war-loving public. In the later poetry, however, Simpson's speaking protagonist comes to realize not just that others were opposed to the war but that all mankind shares a common enemy—death. In the third phase of his work, then, Simpson writes poems expressing sympathy for the average sufferings of average American citizens. Thus, his quest ultimately takes him to a sense of human community not so different from that earlier expressed by his spiritual mentor, Walt Whitman. Moreover, because Simpson recognizes throughout his career, both implicitly and explicitly, that poetry is by its very nature akin to a spiritual activity, we realize that his ultimate devotion is to the unseen.

The relationship with material reality expressed in the poetry of James Wright is even more tenuous than that found in either Stafford or Simpson. In his first book, *The Green Wall* (1957), Wright set up a tension between the real world of suffering and death and an ideal world, a world existing perhaps within a wall, a world something like the walled garden of paradise. Within that volume, Wright chooses to escape from the ideal into the real, joining his brethren in the vale of tears. However, the other realm never leaves his work—and late in his career it seems to reassert itself in a way not to be denied. Thus James Wright's ultimate desire is to rejoin the "earliest garden," the lost "Kingdom of God," which was so powerfully felt during childhood.

As one would expect, the interviews in this volume are not as thematically pointed as the essays. However, they were conducted with many of the above ideas in mind, and thus contain an oblique commentary by the poets themselves on the thesis of this book. In them the reader will also find material of a more relaxed sort, material designed to provide a fuller introduction to the writers as poets, as thinkers, and as human beings. The reader will also find there a good deal of intentional crafting. Since the interview with the living writer became a submode within the field of literary criticism, two schools of thought have developed concerning how interviews should be produced. One school believes that the printed text should reproduce as exactly as possible the spoken conversation, down to its laughter and its grunts. The other school believes that the interview ought to be edited, not just to remove irrelevancies and redundancies, but to create a felicitous prose style as well.

These interviews were produced according to the second method. My approach was always the same. After asking the poet if he was willing to participate in this process, I would immerse myself in all materials written by him—poems, reviews, essays, memoirs, whatever—along with everything written about him by others—reviews, critical essays, earlier interviews. While doing this reading, I would take notes from which I would later formulate my questions. For an average interview, I would prepare between fifty and one hundred questions, organized into categories for easy reference. Often the first thing that would happen during an interview was that the poet, answering an opening question, would take off in an unanticipated direction. Like all interviewers, I had to be ready to follow the poet's lead, making up questions as we went along.

After the conversation, the next job was to transcribe the tape recordings. The average transcription ran more than two hundred pages and was edited down to thirty to forty. During the editing process, many answers were thrown out as redundant or irrelevant. In other cases, two or more answers were combined into a single statement. In still other cases, a single answer might be divided into two or three shorter statements—with appropriate new questions invented to fit the situation. After this detailed editing, the interview was sent to the poet, who was free to make any changes he saw fit. In no case were these changes substantial; revisions generally involved the tidying up of grammar and punctuation, the correcting of proper names.

A final point about my approach to the writing of literary criticism.

Just as the poets I am writing about prefer to draw meaning from within the world rather than to impose meaning upon the world from without, so I as critic prefer to move outward from the work itself *toward* the ideas that might explain it. The love of these poets is for the world of physical reality; as I have suggested, they express this love by recreating the world in words, intending to reveal a pattern of meaning that may not be immediately obvious to another viewer. Similarly, literary criticism for me can have validity only if it is an act of love—in this case having as its object the poetry being discussed. I attempt to express this feeling by recreating, in prose, what I see as the poet's deepest intention—thereby making clear a pattern of meaning that may not be immediately obvious to every reader.

Richard
Wilbur

The Sacramental Vision of Richard Wilbur

●

The central polarity in American poetry was established virtually at the moment the first white man, carrying his European heritage with him, stepped onto this continent. His baggage was not of much immediate value; the qualities most necessary for survival had little to do with civilization and nothing to do with high culture. Instead, early settlers of this land were forced to cultivate traits like ingenuity, adaptability, self-sufficiency, self-reliance. Once an indigenous American literature began to establish itself, roughly fifty years after the revolutionary war, these were the qualities that appeared in its heroes—meaning first the characters created by our authors (James Fenimore Cooper's Natty Bumppo, for example) and later the authors themselves, once they had become their own heroes. And yet the old fealty to the European intellectual heritage (to something, that is, outside the self-reliant self) held on strongly—more strongly in some cases than in others.

When he came to commenting on this issue, specifically in reference to American poetry in the mid-nineteenth century, William Cullen Bryant used the words "imitation" and "originality" to characterize the opposing impulses. Writing somewhat later, T. S. Eliot spoke of essentially the same dichotomy as being between "tradition" and the "individual talent." Still other terms have been used in more recent times—Philip Rahv wrote (in his 1949 volume *Idea and Image*) of the "paleface" poets and the "redskins," and of course we also have the "academics" and the "Beats." The more the terms are multiplied, however, the less certain it becomes exactly what is being talked about, though it remains obvious that a fundamental division within the tradition of American poetry is indicated by this persistent pattern of language.

The issue might be clarified somewhat by resorting to another pair of terms more general in their application—"classic" and "romantic." According to standard critical usage, the classic impulse in poetry is, in terms of form, more traditional and more imitative than it is innovative and, in terms of content, more likely to aim at a general truth than an individual one. The most important characteristic of the romantic impulse in poetry is its subjective nature—the central consciousness of the poem is likely to seek a unique form for his utterance and is likely to speak both from and of his own being. Thus the personality—the individuality, the originality—of the speaking character is brought very much to the fore by the romantic poet; in fact, this speaker is most likely to be either the poet himself or a version thereof. The classic poet, on the other hand, is likely not to emphasize his own vision of things but to operate on the assumption that that vision is collective—our shared vision. He attempts, in short, to speak, not just for himself, but for all of us.

Scholars are in general agreement that the romantic impulse, emergent nearly two hundred years ago, is still dominant in English and American poetry. It used to be thought that Eliot's doctrine of the necessary "impersonality" of the poet signified a reversion to the classical impulse. More recently Stephen Spender and others have argued persuasively that Eliot's idea should be seen more accurately as an elaborate defensive system masking what is, in reality, highly personal poetry.[1] Certainly this is true of Eliot's earlier work. Most recently—since the Second World War—we have seen in American poetry the near-complete dominance of what Louis Simpson calls "the cult of sincerity"; the demand for the "authentic" and the "sincere" has resulted in the confessional movement as well as in less radical forms of personal poetry.[2]

Richard Wilbur was trained in a classic type of poetry; he began his writing career when the new metaphysical style was in vogue and has since been consistently committed to that way of writing. It is because of the very strength of this commitment that his poetry has elicited such extreme and partisan responses from critics, responses that show clearly the classic or romantic inclination, as the case may be, of the individual critics. Robert Boyers, for example, concluded that "the voice that pulses ever so lightly in Wilbur's verse suggests a refinement of sensibility and a soundness of judgment so satisfying that one is hard-put to discern in it the contours of a man as we have been accustomed to men in our experience."[3] The bias is quietly, subtly stated, of course, but this comment still places Boyers in the same camp with Wilbur's army friend who demanded that he "join the human race." (See "Interview with Richard Wilbur.") The emphasis is on the personal element, of which Boyers does not see enough in Wilbur's poems. On the other side of the battle line we find Anthony Hecht, who as thoroughly approves of Wilbur's classic, objective stance as he disapproves of the opposing romantic tendencies. Hecht writes: "In this poetic era of arrogant solipsism and limp narcissism—when great, shaggy herds of poets write only about themselves, or about the casual workings of their rather tedious minds—it is essential to our sanity, salutary to our humility, and a minimal obeisance to the truth to acknowledge, with Wilbur, in poem after poem, . . . the vast alterity, the 'otherness' of the world, that huge corrective to our self-sufficiency."[4]

Of the poets under consideration in this study, Wilbur is certainly the most classical, traditional, and academic in most senses of those words. The stance taken in his poetry is predominantly objective: his gaze is directed outward rather than inward; his interest is in the external world, in both its material and its spiritual manifestations; he is concerned to place mankind generally within that cosmos and is unconcerned with singing either the tragedies or the triumphs of his individual life. As Wilbur has said: "It is the thing, and not myself, which I set out to explore." (See "Interview with Richard Wilbur.") All of this clearly sets him apart from most of the poets of the age.

It is of interest to note that Richard Wilbur and Robert Lowell were almost contemporaries. Wilbur is the younger, a detail surprising in view of his greater poetic conservatism. Lowell was born in 1917, Wilbur in 1921; *Lord Weary's Castle* was published in 1946, *The Beautiful Changes* in 1947. In these early works, the similarities between the two are more conspicuous than the dissimilarities; it was not until the publication of Lowell's *Life Studies* in 1959 that they began to diverge radically—Wilbur continuing in his objective way, Lowell turning toward the confessional. Another characteristic that sets Wilbur apart from his age is evident in this comparison: the personal poetry of confessionalism is permeated by doubt and despair, while Wilbur's work tends toward optimism. In his review of *Advice to a Prophet*, James Dickey praised Wilbur for "the thing that should eventually make him . . . truly important: . . . the quietly joyful sense of celebration and praise out of which [he] writes."[5]

That Wilbur has maintained his classical commitment to traditional forms in the face of the free-verse revolution also makes him exceptional among contemporary poets. It is in this area that the most serious reservations about Wilbur's work have been expressed by critics. Robert Boyers, for example, seems to emulate in his own style what he decries in Wilbur's: "Richard Wilbur's poetry has consistently provided us with so many pleasures that one must feel almost ungrateful to question the premises upon which he has founded his art. So serene and altogether orderly a style would hardly seem possible to us today were it not for his exemplary presence, and the epithet 'classical' inevitably forms at the lips when one thinks of his characteristic virtues . . . : poise, tact, formal and metrical regularity, musicality of diction, ingenuity of phrasing."[6] Central to Boyer's argument is his belief in the notion of expressive form: if the world has become, for twentieth-century man, chaotic, deprived of philosophical order, then our poetry should be similarly disordered, formally unpredictable.

In an essay written in 1966, "On My Own Work," Wilbur seems to agree both with this assessment of the modern world and with the idea of a narrowly expressive form: "Most American poets of my generation were taught to admire the English Metaphysical poets of the seventeenth century and such contemporary masters of irony as John Crowe Ransom. We were led by our teachers and by the critics whom we read to feel that the most adequate and convincing poetry is that which accommodates mixed feelings, clashing ideas, and incongruous images. Poetry could not be honest, we thought, unless it began by acknowledging the full discordancy of modern life and consciousness."[7] That Wilbur's poems do indeed contain these stylistic characteristics does not make them formally expressive of disorder; rather, the orderliness seems raised to an even higher level of patterned sophistication.

A comment made in an earlier essay, "The Bottles Become New, Too" (originally published in 1948), seems to express Wilbur's position more accurately: "The relation between an artist and reality is always an oblique one, and indeed there is no good art which is not consciously oblique. If you respect the reality of the world, you know that you can approach that reality only by indirect means. . . . So that paradoxically it is respect for reality which makes a necessity of artifice . . . rhythms, formal patterns, and rhymes."[8] The fact is that, in terms of its effect upon most readers, Wilbur's poetry is formally distanced, ritualistic in the best sense of the word, elegant, elevated. In short, it exists within, or creates, a world of its own, somewhat different from the world we habitually live in, certainly different from the relatively casual everyday world relied upon by more informal writers. In order to appreciate Wilbur's poetry fully, the reader must enter *its* world, and this requires more of a willing suspension of disbelief than is the case in reading most contemporary poetry. Wilbur is less immediate, less direct, less emotional—more oblique, more allusive, more intellectual—than most poets, and thus his work makes special demands on its readers.

In the present chapter, I will approach Wilbur's work thematically, with only an occasional sidelong glance at matters of style. Rather than proceed chronologically, I will treat the poems according to topics raised within them, topics generally recognized by the poet himself: "there are certain matters to which I keep coming back. I would rather not name them because I think they are clear enough in the poems. The funny thing is that I often won't know that I have reapproached a subject until a new poem has been finished. Then I will say, oh yes, this turned out to be that question again" ("Interview with Richard Wilbur"). My approach seems invited by the poems themselves. Not only has Wilbur never worked in extended forms—his longest poem, "The Mind-Reader," stretches for only a scant five pages—but he also does not think in terms of poem sequences: "The unit of my poetry, as I experience it, is not the *Collected Poems* which I may some day publish; nor is it the individual volume, or the sequence or group within the volume; it is the single poem."[9] This practice sets Wilbur apart from most of the other poets considered here—from Robert Penn Warren, who tends to write long, carefully integrated sequences, and from Louis Simpson and James Wright, whose books tend to be carefully designed in the direction of unity and coherence. Only William Stafford shares with Wilbur the desire to keep individual poems separate from one another.

Richard Wilbur, then, stands apart from his poetic age in a number of ways—he is an optimist among pessimists; he has a classic, objective sensibility in a romantic, subjective time; he is a formalist in the midst of a relentless informality. The underlying worldview that predetermines these characteristics is traditional and religious; admitting the existential primacy of material reality, Wilbur yet believes in a spiritual reality as well, and his goal as a poet—and, one feels, as a man—is to bring these two realms together into a unified whole. There are a few poems scattered throughout the corpus in which Wilbur toys with the idea that dreams may be more substantial than reality, but in general he does not seriously question the actuality of the material world as something that may be objectively perceived and understood. It is concretely there, though observers may interpret it differently from one another. In one of his most recent poems, "Lying," Wilbur addresses this very issue in the course of considering the function of factual untruth, myth and simile, in mankind's attempts to comprehend the world: "In the strict sense," he says, "of course, / We invent nothing, merely bearing witness":

> All these things
> Are there before us; there before we look
> Or fail to look; there to be seen or not
> By us, as by the bee's twelve thousand eyes,
> According to our means and purposes.[10]

That passage was written in 1981 or 1982; in 1948 Wilbur had stated essentially the same idea in prose, in his lecture "The Bottles Become New, Too": "poets can't afford to forget that there is a reality of things which survives all orders great and small. Things *are*. The cow is there. No poetry can have any strength unless it continually bashes itself against the reality of things."[11]

Set against absolute physical reality—the created world—for Wilbur is the world of the Creator, the spiritual realm, which he feels exists just as certainly as does the physical. In his poems, Wilbur is always reaching "Beyond the faint sun, / Toward the hid pulse of things," as he says the fire-bush does in another of his most recent poems, "Alatus."[12] In a prose comment, Wilbur has affirmed his belief in—and explained his concept of—the unseen realm of spirit:

> To put it simply, I feel that the universe is full of glorious energy, that the energy tends to take pattern and shape, and that the ultimate character of things is comely and good. I am perfectly aware that I say this in the teeth of all sorts of contrary evidence, and that I must be basing it partly on temperament and partly on faith, but that is my attitude. My feeling is that when you discover order and goodness in the world, it is not something you are imposing—it is something which is likely really to be there, whatever crumminess and evil and disorder there may also be. I don't take disorder or meaninglessness to be the basic character of things. I don't know where I get my information, but that is how I feel. ("Interview with Richard Wilbur")

That Wilbur is a Christian, a lifelong Episcopalian, is important information for anyone wanting to understand his poetry fully; a sacramental view of things is at the heart of everything he says.[13] *Advice to a Prophet* may well be his least attractive book, dominated as it is by a wasteland kind of thinking. In its moral attitudes, the volume resembles the "Fire Sermon" section of Eliot's poem, so concerned is Wilbur to point up the ethical and spiritual failings of mankind. Many of the poems swerve uncomfortably close to unalloyedly negative satire, thus straying from the poet's strongest vein, that strain of praise that James Dickey described so well. And yet *Advice to a Prophet* concludes with the beautiful "Christmas Hymn," which supplies a spiritual corrective to all that has gone before in the book. The final stanza:

> But now, as at the ending,
> The low is lifted high;
> The stars shall bend their voices,
> And every stone shall cry.
> And every stone shall cry
> In praises of the child
> By whose descent among us
> The worlds are reconciled.[14]

The basic Christian idea on which this poem concludes is a crucial one in Wilbur's thinking. Through Christ, the Christian God gave physical manifestation to pure spirituality, thus uniting the two contrasting realms. And this is the way Richard Wilbur would have the two appear in his poetry, as in the universe he inhabits—together, in interaction with one another, neither one alone. He no more desires a pure spirituality, divorced from the physical, than he desires a pure materiality, divorced from the spiritual. The satirical poems in *Advice to a Prophet* are specifically directed against those who would deny the presence of anything sacramental within the concrete world: there we find lust without love ("Loves of the Puppets"), work without workmanship ("Junk"), ownership without possession ("A Summer Morning"), action without life ("The Undead"), shame without guilt ("Shame"), dream without belief ("In the Smoking Car"), acquisition without fulfillment ("Ballade for the Duke of Orleans"). Indeed, the entire volume seems almost to be constructed to reaffirm Eliot's point in *The Waste Land*—that all of man's frenzied physical activity only acts to hide his lack of spiritual belief.

Similarly, a complete abstractionism, divorced from contact with all physicality, is also of no value to Wilbur. In the essay "On My Own Work," Wilbur comments on three of his poems, "A Baroque Wall-Fountain in the Villa Sciarra," "Two Voices in a Meadow," and "Love Calls Us to the Things of This World." One of the general points he makes is this: "The three poems . . . all have to do (a critic might say) with the proper relation between the tangible world and the intuitions of the spirit. The poems assume that such intuitions are, or may be, true; they incline, however, to favor a spirituality that is not abstracted, not dissociated and world-renouncing."[15] In several other poems, Wilbur deals with the cast of mind that prefers to deny the real in favor of the abstract. In *The Poems of Richard Wilbur*, two poems on this topic, both from *Ceremony and Other Poems*, face one another across the page. The second of them, "Epistemology," consists of two epigrams that seem to argue against the solid existence of the real world:

I

Kick at the rock, Sam Johnson, break your bones:
But cloudy, cloudy is the stuff of stones;

II

We milk the cow of the world, and as we do
We whisper in her ear, "You are not true."

(*PRW*, 121)

What the poet himself thinks of this is indicated clearly in a comment he has made on the American attitude toward the world; even his choice of words suggests this poem: "I think that, like most Americans, I have considerable respect for the actual and physical. We are all kickers of stones, you know, and we are not as likely to get enchanted with abstract thought systems as some Europeans, especially the French, are" ("Interview with Richard Wilbur"). "La Rose des Vents," which faces "Epistemology," is one of Wilbur's dialogue poems; an airy-headed "Poet," who longs for the imperishable, the ideal, speaks first, and is conclusively answered by a "Lady":

> Forsake those roses
> Of the mind
> And tend the true,
> The mortal flower.
>
> (*PRW*, 120)

Wilbur's most important poem in this regard is another from *Ceremony*, the justly famous " 'A World Without Objects Is a Sensible Emptiness' " (*PRW*, 117). The title is taken from Meditation 65 in the *Second Century*, where Thomas Traherne speaks of the necessity of love for the fulfillment and completion of life. The passage concludes: "The whole world ministers to you as the theatre of your Love. It sustains you and all objects that you may continue to love them. Without which it were better for you to have no being. Life without objects is sensible emptiness, and that is a greater misery than Death or Nothing."[16] Wilbur's poem begins by positing the existence of abstractionists, metaphorically identified as "tall camels of the spirit," "connoisseurs of thirst," who

> . . . move with a stilted stride
> To the land of sheer horizon, hunting Traherne's
> *Sensible emptiness*, there where the brain's lantern-slide
> Revels in vast returns.

Most of the poem consists of an apostrophe to these devotees of emptiness, and Wilbur makes his point through light imagery. We note that the light source for the "brain's lantern-slide" is self-generated and abstract, unattached to corporeal reality. Rather, says Wilbur, "auras, lustres, / And all shinings need to be shaped and borne." He concludes by admonishing the abstractionists to "Turn, O turn"

> Back to the trees arrayed
> In bursts of glare, to the halo-dialing run

Of the Country creeks, and the hills' bracken tiaras made
    Gold in the sunken sun,

  Wisely watch for the sight
Of the supernova burgeoning over the barn,
Lampshine blurred in the steam of beasts, the spirit's right
    Oasis, light incarnate.

The words chosen to describe light—"auras, lustres," "halo-dialing,"
"tiaras"—all suggest the connotations of spirituality that Wilbur wishes carried by the light. And of course he much prefers that this spirituality not be abstract and disembodied, but indisolubly linked with
quotidian reality. Thus, the halos hover over creeks, the tiaras crown
hills, the supernova glows about the barn, and the lampshine (final
answer to the "brain's lantern-slide") is projected through the sweat-
steam rising from farm animals—all of these are "the spirit's right /
Oasis, light incarnate."

    Insisting that these two realms, the physical and the spiritual, be
seen as coexisting, comingling, interpenetrating, may be said to be
Richard Wilbur's central thematic concern—a theme that has, of
course, been widely recognized by his critics. William Heyen perhaps
has stated it best: "One of the consistent and unifying themes of
Wilbur's poetry is what he has called 'the proper relation between the
tangible world and the intuitions of the spirit.' Since the Enlighten-
ment man's mind has begun to tell him that things are things; his
spirit has felt more, needed more, believed that the objects of this
world were involved, somehow, with a greater truth, an encompassing
truth. . . . Throughout his career, it has been Wilbur's genius to invest
the quotidian with holiness, to conceive of reality . . . as, in Scott's
words, a 'sacramental economy,' a world of presence, possibility, beauty; a world shimmering with reciprocity."[17]

    In order to understand more fully what Wilbur means by a reality
invested with the aura of spirituality, we must first define what an
unmediated reality is in his view. In line with Christian thought,
Wilbur pictures an unsanctified reality essentially as chaos, in which
darkness and death are dominant. Wilbur is consistent in the use and
significance of his primary images; one facet of the meaning of light (to
suggest spirituality) has already been mentioned, and others will be
dealt with later. Water imagery is similarly complex; Wilbur's most
consistent image for pure chaos—the threatening nothingness that existed before the creation—is the darkened or untamed ocean. In "For
Dudley," a beautiful elegy that appears in *Walking to Sleep*, the ocean is
clearly associated with the realm of death that always waits close to
mankind. The poem defines civilized human life in this way:

As if we were perceived
From a black ship—
A small knot of island folk,
The Light-Dwellers, pouring

A life to the dark sea—
All that we do
Is touched with ocean, yet we remain
On the shore of what we know.

(WS, 24)

The lines emphasize the tenuous, threatened nature of life itself, and
identify chaos, darkness, and death with the ocean. In "The Beacon,"
from *Things of This World*, we read of "the sea-in-itself," which is "the
night-fouled sea," "Gordian waters" that compose "the blinded waves":

. . . we hear their
Booms, rumors and guttural sucks
Warn of the pitchy whirl

At the mind's end.

(PRW, 81)

Wilbur establishes the sea—deathly and unmeliorated—as his locus and
emblem for chaos.

In Richard Wilbur's dualistic view of the universe, chaos is always an
implicit possibility in external, material reality. Pure spirituality—the
other extreme—is both unavailable and undesirable for mankind.
The best that we can know on this earth is a physical paradise, wherein
the material is invested with the spiritual so that neither one is entirely dominant. Wilbur's ideal is a union of the two realms, a mingling
of them, so that we deal with a spiritualized reality. The tension that
exists in a Wilbur poem is between these two poles; what the poet
seeks is a point of balance between them, where neither is slighted or
lost. From Wilbur's perspective, the easy thing for twentieth-century
man is to see base reality, the tendency toward chaos, darkness, and
death. The sacramental view was easy for Traherne, Herbert, Crashaw,
Vaughan, but for modern man the spiritual is hard to see. Thus an
effort of some kind is always required to keep it in view, and we seem
always on the verge of losing it. Wilbur is essentially in agreement with
Frost's definition of poetry as "a momentary stay against confusion."
His own statement of this principle is fuller: "One does not use poetry
for its major purposes, as a means of organizing oneself and the world,
until one's world somehow gets out of hand. A general cataclysm is not
required; the disorder must be personal and may be wholly so, but po-

etry, to be vital, does seem to need a periodic acquaintance with the threat of chaos."[18] An effort is required; the tension in Wilbur's kind of poetry inheres in the attempt to maintain a sense of order, a sense of spiritual underpinnings, against the ever-present possibility of ultimate chaos.

Wilbur's poetry has a dynamic, kinetic quality to it. His concern, crudely stated, is to discover and use whatever channels, corridors, connectors there may be that will link the physical world that enmeshes us to the spiritual world that hovers so elusively within and beyond. Thus his desire to reach "Beyond the faint sun, / To the hid pulse of things"; thus too his definition of "the imagination, which when in best health neither slights the world of fact nor stops with it, but seeks the invisible through the visible."[19] It is this desire to reach, seek, connect, balance that gives Wilbur's poetry its dynamic quality. As Anthony Hecht has pointed out, "most characteristic of all, his is the most kinetic poetry I know: verbs are among his conspicuously important tools, and his poetry is everywhere a vision of *action*, of motion and performance."[20] Wilbur's poetry exhibits motion in many ways, but most centrally in his attempt through it to unite, comingle, the worlds of materiality and spirituality.

Earlier I quoted Wilbur to the effect that the spiritual, the principle of order, exists out there, apart from man—"My feeling is that when you discover order and goodness in the world, it is not something you are imposing—it is something which is likely really to be there." For a discovery to be made, of course, there must be a discoverer—which is why the word *discover* works in two ways, meaning both to realize something outward and to reveal something inward. We are never far from this paradox when reading Wilbur's poetry. The plain fact is that, however much Wilbur may want order and spirituality to exist outwardly and independent of man, without man to perceive and note that order, its existence is either in doubt or irrelevant. Thus the relation between subject and object, between the viewer and the viewed, is crucial for a poet like Wilbur, as he himself implicitly recognizes in this comment on how his poems are triggered:

> It seems to me that there has to be a sudden, confident sense that there is an exploitable and interesting relationship between something perceived out there and something in the way of incipient meaning within you. And what you see out there has to be seen freshly, or the process is not going to be provoked. Noting a likeness or resemblance between two things in nature can provide this freshness, but I think there must be more. For example, to perceive that the behavior of certain tree leaves is like the behavior of bird's wings is not, so far as I am concerned, enough to justify the sharpening of the pencil. There has to be a feeling that some kind of idea is implicit within that resemblance. ("Interview with Richard Wilbur")

In this statement, it is the intellect or the imagination of the perceiving poet that provides what we may call the "spiritual" half of the equation; materiality is what is seen "out there." We must consider the location and reality of what I have been calling the spiritual element in Wilbur's vision and art. Wilbur's own language, in many of the passages quoted above, locates the spiritual outside of man—"the hid pulse of things" is "Beyond the sun." Similarly, the God in which he, as an Episcopalian, believes, is generally located outside of man. But God is posited as an internal entity as well—the godly or godlike part of man being his soul. For our purposes it will be most useful to define God through one of his primary attributes—creative intelligence—for through this term we can define also that which is divine in mankind. We may say, then, that through its perceiving ability—its intelligence—and through its creative power—its imagination—the soul or mind of man palely resembles God. Or, to put it another way, through his intellect and his imagination, man is able to see the "spirituality"—that is, evidence of the creative intelligence of God—inherent within outward reality. Most of Wilbur's statements ("when you discover order and goodness in the world, it is not something you are imposing—it is . . . likely really to be there") would lead us to conclude, to recur to an old formulation of this problem, that even if there is no one to hear the tree falling in the forest, it still makes a sound. Looking specifically at what Wilbur says and does in his poems, however, we can be sure that, unless someone is there to hear the sound the tree makes, there will be no poem. For the spirituality that exists within the universe to be both recognized and expressed, what is required is a perceiving creative intelligence within the observer that can somehow faintly match that of God.[21]

In *Things of This World*, Wilbur has three poems concerned specifically with the mind of man. "Lamarck Elaborated" (*PRW*, 75) develops from one of the central evolutionary ideas of the French naturalist ("The environment creates the organ") and thereby comments almost directly on the issue we have been exploring. Lamarck's idea suggests that outward reality (things to be seen, sounds to be heard) literally demanded the development of the senses in organisms. The existence of reality was prior to the observer's ability to perceive it. The idea is analogically close to one extreme of the reality/perceiver question—reality is there first and creates its perceiver. In several delicately ironic lines, Wilbur playfully presents this notion:

The Greeks were wrong who said our eyes have rays;
Not from these sockets or these sparkling poles
Comes the illumination of our days. . . .

It was the song of doves begot the ear
And not the ear that first conceived of sound.

Wilbur does not necessarily agree with Lamarck's idea, which was, after all, rather quickly modified, then rejected altogether by other scientists even before Darwin's *Origin of Species*. Rather, Wilbur is using Lamarck to introduce a concept of considerable interest to him; thus the word *Elaborated* in the title. Whatever their origin, the five senses serve a strictly physical function for man—they allow him to gather data about the material universe. What matters to Wilbur is what happens after this evidence has been collected. It is at this point that the intellect, working in conjunction with the imagination, comes into operation:

Out of our vivid ambiance came unsought
All sense but that most formidably dim.
The shell of balance rolls in seas of thought.
It was the mind that taught the head to swim.

Newtonian numbers set to cosmic lyres
Whelmed us in whirling worlds we could not know.

The word *know* is used in a primary sense—we can actually know only that which we have physically observed using the five senses. Any further knowing demands that the raw materials gathered by the senses be processed by the intellect through thought. Newton's physical perception of an apple falling, we may say, provided the raw material that allowed him to conceive of the law of gravity. This idea he projected outward, thereby coming to understand the movements of the planets around the sun. Wilbur thus suggests that reality *is* out there—not created by its human observer—but that any order present within that reality must be conceived of by the mind, man's creative intelligence. Lamarck's statement serves only as a pretext for this train of thought, and it is ultimately irrelevant, both to Wilbur and to the reader of the poem, whether Lamarck was correct or not.

In a second poem concerned with the function of man's mind, "The Beacon" (*PRW*, 81-82), Wilbur imagistically accepts the idea of the Greeks "who said our eyes have rays," which Lamarck rejected. The beacon shines from a lighthouse on the sea, and as Kenneth Johnson has pointed out, it represents "man's mind, [which] not only reveals the sea but creates an order . . . out of it. But once the beacon's light is turned away, we have only the chaotic 'sea-in-itself,' a reality that is beyond our knowledge. We may sometimes sense hidden layers of reality . . .; but . . . all that nature clearly reveals is 'death's kingdom.' "[22] The poem begins by defining the function and significance of the light:

Founded on rock and facing the night-fouled sea
A beacon blinks at its own brilliance,
Over and over with cutlass gaze
Solving the Gordian waters,

Making the sea-roads out, and the lounge of the weedy
Meadows, finding the blown hair
As it always has, and the buxom, lavish
Romp of the ocean-daughters.

These things, of course, are not available to be seen strictly by the senses alone; it is the mind of man that has invested the sea with its mythology, a way of imposing order upon chaos or perceiving order within chaos.

When the light moves away, order and knowledge, even life itself, depart from the scene as well. Now, "Watching the blinded waves," we hear only their

Booms, rumors and guttural sucks
Warn of the pitchy whirl

At the mind's end. All the sense of the sea
Is veiled as voices nearly heard
In morning sleep; nor shall we wake
At the sea's heart.

Beyond the limits of the reach of the mind, the meaningfulness of the sea, its "sense," is lost. Chaos remains, along with the threat of a final death ("nor shall we wake"). Then the beacon swings round again to turn "The face of darkness pale":

And now with one grand chop [it] gives clearance to
Our human visions, which assume
The waves again, fresh and the same.
Let us suppose that we

See most of darkness by our plainest light.
It is the Nereid's kick endears
The tossing spray; a sighted ship
Assembles all the sea.

Wilbur's use of light in this poem is traditional. Primarily it provides an image for the organizing, meaning-giving intelligence of man, which is projected outward from him onto reality. The image also carries spiritual undertones; Wilbur implicitly alludes to God's attempt to banish chaos with the imperial dictum, "Let there be light." Man's creative intelligence (manifested in his creation of the many sea myths alluded to in the poem) is thus implicitly linked with God's creative intelligence: God originally created the order that man's God-given or godlike intelligence is able to perceive.

The third poem in *Things of This World* that deals directly with the subject of human intelligence is aptly titled "Mind" (*PRW*, 72). The poem is brief and to the point, but more complicated than it looks at first glance because of the way it opens into further layers of Wilbur's thought. The first stanza introduces the poem's central trope:

> Mind in its purest play is like some bat
> That beats about in caverns all alone,
> Contriving by a kind of senseless wit
> Not to conclude against a wall of stone.

It is primarily the word *senseless* that expands these lines: like the bat, the mind performs its purest functions essentially without the assistance of the five senses, which allow a direct connection with the world of physical reality. Of course Wilbur allows for the bat's use of echolocation, a sixth "sense" unavailable to man, through his qualification "*a kind of* senseless wit." This also admits that the mind does rely on the five senses to an extent, though it also, when operating at its highest level, goes well beyond them. Thanks to these abilities, both units in the figure—mind and bat—are able to chart a successful course through the darkness, danger, relative chaos, of the surrounding reality:

> Darkly it knows what obstacles are there,
> And so may weave and flitter, dip and soar
> In perfect courses through the blackest air.

In the third and concluding stanza, Wilbur questions the truth of his own poetic method:

> And has this simile a like perfection?
> The mind is like a bat. Precisely. Save
> That in the very happiest intellection
> A graceful error may correct the cave.

The lines focus specifically upon the creative aspect of man's intelligence, his ability to alter reality through the creation of myth, through artistry generally conceived, by shining a "beacon" upon it. It is perhaps this creative function that defines the closest parallel between man and God.

In the course of talking about these three poems, the focus of our interest has undergone a subtle, inevitable shift from mind narrowly conceived as pure intellect to mind more broadly conceived as intellect working in concert with imagination, which Wilbur defines as "the very happiest intellection." Indeed, imagination is the most important of the faculties of the mind for a poet like Wilbur, for it is imagination that allows him to perceive the relationship between a bird's wings and the leaves on a tree, or, more importantly, the relationship between those things observed in external reality and some idea within the mind. It is the imagination, in short, that specifically allows the poet to perceive the spiritual inhering within the physical.

A tension does exist in Wilbur's work between what we may call the describing process, which reproduces and appreciates the sheer physical beauty of the scene before one, and the poeticizing process, which insists upon comparing that scene with something else imagined within the mind. So great is Wilbur's love for the physical universe, "the world's body," that he sometimes wonders if anything more than accurate description is needed. "Praise in Summer" (*PRW*, 225), an ars poetica that appears in Wilbur's first book, *The Beautiful Changes*, begins by recounting figures he had invented to express his sense of praise:

> I said
> The hills are heavens full of branching ways
> . . . .
> I said the trees are mines in air.

This metaphorizing, he realizes, takes attention away from the here and now, the summer scene before his eyes, and since that is so beautiful by itself, he wonders why it isn't enough for the poet simply to describe literal truth:

> To a praiseful eye
> Should it not be enough of fresh and strange
> That trees grow green, and moles can course in clay,
> And sparrows sweep the ceiling of our day?

The answer seems present in the question, the language of which embodies at least two metaphors, the "sparrows *sweep* the *ceiling*," and perhaps a third, the moles "course" through the ground. We must also note that the resemblances dwelt upon in this poem are like that between the bird's wings and tree leaves—both elements in all equations are drawn from the world of materiality. It is only when one of the elements is a concept drawn from the mind that the spiritual may truly be said to enter the poem.

Another poem, "C Minor" from *The Mind-Reader* (pp. 25–26), comments directly on the order-making function of art, which feels false and unnecessary to the poem's speaker early in the day:

> Beethoven during breakfast? The human soul,
> Though stalked by hollow pluckings, winning out
> (While bran-flakes crackle in the cereal-bowl)
>   Over despair and doubt?
>
> You are right to switch it off and let the day
> Begin at hazard.

The role that art plays with regard to the quotidian chaos of the real is clearly defined here—but the poet feels that this function does not need to be served at the start of day, before reality has had its chance to complicate things. There follow several stanzas that project what may happen that day and thus require harmonizing by nightfall. The poem concludes:

> There is nothing to do with a day except to live it.
> Let us have music again when the light dies
> (Sullenly, or in glory) and we can give it
>   Something to organize.

Lying beneath the surface of this poem is another of Wilbur's concepts—that sleep is allied with the spiritual realm, or provides a way into it, and waking is allied with the material, the everyday. Thus, by the end of a busy day, the speaker is far from his earliest experience of the orderly spirituality of sleep and much more in need of the organizing, the harmonizing, power of music than he was in the morning.

A poem that depicts even more strikingly the effect of art, the process of imagination, upon reality, is "L'Etoile," from *The Beautiful Changes*. The poem describes a ballet dancer at the very end of her practice, as the last note of music hangs still in the air. "Toward her dance's flight," the woman "aspires in loudening shine" while the music plays and she dances, but once silence takes over, she is returned to the realm of an untransformed reality, bordering almost on chaos:

> . . . some ancient woman will unmesh
> Her small strict shape, and yawns will turn her face
> Into a little wilderness of flesh.

> (PRW, 208)

It is the dance that animates the dancer, the art that elevates her from bare reality. "A Plain Song for Comadre," from *Things of This World*

(*PRW*, 76), makes a similar point, but with an important difference. The poem begins with a rhetorical question:

> Though the unseen may vanish, though insight fails
> And doubter and downcast saint
> Join in the same complaint,
> What holy things were ever frightened off
> By a fly's buzz, or itches, or a cough?

The poem carefully locates the "holy," not as an entity separate from the everyday, but as an intimate and inseparable part of it. Bruna Sandoval, the *comadre* ("cleaning woman") of the title, has worked in "the church / Of San Ysidro" for seventeen years "And seen no visions but the thing done right." The poem ends with this image:

> Sometimes the early sun
> Shines as she flings the scrubwater out, with a crash
> Of grimy rainbows, and the stained suds flash
> Like angel-feathers.

It is once again through the agency of simile that the spiritual is inserted into the mundane. We aren't sure whether the *comadre* sees this or not, but clearly the poet, whose simile it is, has seen the "angel-feathers." It is the richness of his imagination, his creative intelligence, that allows him glimpses of the spiritual within the real.[23]

It is no accident that motion is an important attribute of most of the poems so far cited showing the presence of the spiritual within the material. It is true that chaos, in Wilbur's view, does possess motion—the death-threatening, uncontrollable heaves and surges of the sea. The middle realm in his work—the ordinary, everyday reality of nature especially—which stands between utter chaos and a pure spirituality, may or may not possess motion, however. In fact, a careful reading of several poems shows that Wilbur's injection of motion into a scene is his way of imagistically indicating the presence of the spiritual within the material. This is why Wilbur's most important formulation of the idea of motion is through the concept of "grace." Wilbur means to retain both of the most important senses of this word—using it to refer, that is, to a beautiful, harmonious (graceful) motion and to "the unmerited love and favor of God toward man" (*Webster's New World Dictionary*, 2d ed.). In some of Wilbur's poems, this kind of motion is specifically human—as with the dancer in "L'Etoile" and the "Juggler" in the poem so titled. It is poems like these that Anthony Hecht was thinking of when he wrote: "Wilbur has been from the first a poet with a gymnastic sense of bodily agility and control, a delight in the fluencies we all admire in a trained athlete, in the vitality and importance of stamina and focused energy. . . . again and again in Wilbur's poems this admirable grace or strength of body is a sign of or symbol for the inward motions of the mind or condition of the soul." More important in this regard are poems dealing with nature or natural images in motion—reality itself somehow on the move. Hecht was also aware of this dimension, and went on to show what in Wilbur's poems resembles the techniques of "cinematic film: the observation of things in motion from a viewpoint that can, if it cares to, move with an equal and astonishing grace. But what these poems can do so magnificently . . . is . . . a dissolving of one realm of reality into another."[24]

Which is precisely what happens in one of the simplest of such poems, "Fern-Beds in Hampshire County," from *Walking to Sleep* (pp. 11–12). Wilbur is here operating basically at that level of imagination that finds a striking resemblance between two physical realms, but that does not invest either of them with an idea or the concept of spirituality. The poem is organized not in stanzas but in four sentences. The first establishes the relative simplicity of the ferns by comparison to the more complex, highly developed trees that grow above them. In the second sentence, Wilbur allows "a trifling stir / Of air" to pass over the ferns, which then alternatively "dip," "switch," and are "still"— "Sporadic as in guarded bays / The rockweed slaps a bit, or sways." The simile is much less casual than it looks, more studied, for in the third sentence Wilbur proceeds to turn the swaying ferns into a sea:

Then let the wind grow bluff, and though
The sea lies far to eastward, far below,
These fluent spines, with whipped pale underside,
Will climb through timber as a smoking tide
Through pier-stakes, beat their sprays about the base
Of every boulder, scale its creviced face
And, wave on wave, like some green infantry,
Storm all the slope as high as eye can see.

It is the motion caused by the wind upon the ferns that allows for the metaphorical transformation of them from plants into sea. We note too that there is an apocalyptic undercurrent to the poem; as the ferns become the sea, they implicitly take on the destructive function served by ocean as chaos. Thus, in the final sentence:

These airy plants . . .
Dwell in the swept recurrence of
An ancient conquest, shaken by first love
As when they answered to the boomed command
That the sea's green rise up and take the land.

The reference, of course, is to the biblical flood, a watery apocalypse that is here presented more in seductive than in destructive terms; what results is, not ruination, but marriage between sea and land.

A poem that accords a more precisely spiritual function to motion is "From the Lookout Rock," which appears in *Ceremony and Other Poems* (*PRW*, 159–60). The poem begins with the wind "faltering, / In long cessation dying down." A frightening calm ensues, primarily over the sea that lies before the poem's observing consciousness, but extended elsewhere as well; thus, "Haphazard stand the weather-vanes, / Unrocked the cradles of the vales"; "Appalled are all the sagging sails" and "cities fill / With space as barren as their snow." The language here distinctly suggests both the loss of order and the emergence of death—states that we have come to associate in Wilbur's work with chaos, a reality devoid of all spiritual infusion. All this is background to the stanza-long prayer that concludes the poem:

> Gods of the wind, return again,
> For this was not the peace we prayed;
> Intone again your burdened strain,
> And weave the world to harmony,
> Voyage the seed along the breeze,
> Reviving all your former trade,
> Restore the lilting of the trees
> And massive dances of the sea.

Again, it is motion, handmaiden to spirituality, that allows for the existence of order ("harmony"), art ("dances"), even life itself ("seed"), within quotidian reality. The metaphorical extension is here not just from one physical realm (flora) to another (sea) but from physicality to idea within the poet's head (motion in nature suggests the presence of the spiritual).

The spiritualizing effect of motion—and, in this case, of light—upon the everyday is made even more explicit in another poem from *Ceremony*, "Part of a Letter" (*PRW*, 119). The setting is apparently a French bar, with tables placed outdoors in a grove of trees. In his description of the setting, Wilbur is again speaking primarily of flora—the trees in this instance—and again makes a comparison to water:

> Easy as cove-water rustles its pebbles and shells
> In the slosh, spread, seethe, and the backsliding
> Wallop and tuck of the wave, and just that cheerful,
>   Tables and earth were riding
>
> Back and forth in the minting shades of the trees.

Light and shade are set in motion by the wind, which agitates the
leaves on the trees, creating the resemblance to the pebbles and shells
moving in the clear water of the wave (and we note how essential,
though unexpressed, is the presence of sunlight for this ocean scene to
have its effect). Eventually one of the "dazzled" drinkers asks, "Comment s'appelle cet arbre-là?" The answer comes from a girl with "gold
on her tongue": "Ça c'est l'acacia." The mythological reference is to
Arcadia, a simple, naturalized version of paradise, where the material
and the spiritual spontaneously coexist.[25]

The literary device that allows Richard Wilbur's poetry to encom-
pass, in its very texture and imagery, these two different realms is metaphor, here used in the broad sense of the word (the sense, that is, that
includes both simile and exact metaphor). Metaphor is the "doubling"
device, an effect achieved through comparison, analogy, equivalency. It
allows the poet to point out a close physical resemblance (wings and
leaves), to transform one thing into another (ferns into ocean waves), or
to suggest the presence of the unseen within the seen (Arcadia within
an ordinary grove of trees, the Neriads within the sea). It is thus
through the use of metaphor that Wilbur's poetry technically accomplishes what he has conceived as true of the world in a philosophical
sense. It is at this point that form and content come most profoundly
together in his work.[26]

A poem in which a remarkable physical transformation is achieved
through this kind of imagery is "A Storm in April," from *The Mind-
Reader* (p. 3). Wilbur defines this late-spring snowstorm, not as a "last,
hard blow" from winter, a harsh and final goodbye, but as winter's
"way of leaving / So as to stay." How is such a wonder to be accom-
plished? Through nature's (and Wilbur's) use of sympathetic imagery:

> The light flakes do not weigh
> The willows down, but sift
> Through the white catkins, loose
> As petal-drift,
>
> Or in an up-draft lift
> And glitter at a height,
> Dazzling as summer's leaf-stir
> Chinked with light.
>
> This storm, if I am right,
> Will not be wholly over
> Till green fields, here and there,
> Turn white with clover,
>
> And through chill air the puffs of milkweed hover.

The poem accomplishes a unification through imagery of all four sea-
sons—the white snowflakes of winter resemble the "petal-drift" of
spring, resemble "summer's leaf-stir," resemble spring's "clover," resemble "chill" late autumn's "puffs of milkweed." The degree of unity
is remarkable, deftly achieved through a subtle form of buried extended
metaphor.

Wilbur's most complex, subtle, and perhaps most successful love
poem is "The Beautiful Changes" (*PRW*, 226); the first stanza begins
with a transformation of a sort we are by now quite familiar with, and
moves to something deeper.

> One wading a Fall meadow finds on all sides
> The Queen Anne's Lace lying like lilies
> On water; it glides
> So from the walker, it turns
> Dry grass to a lake, as the slightest shade of you
> Valleys my mind in fabulous blue Lucernes.

In the last line and a half we are carried from resemblances perceived in
external reality into the pure realm of the imagination; or, to put it
another way, in the first four and one-half lines, imagination is the
agency through which the comparison is achieved and expressed, while
in the last line and a half, imagination is both the activating agent and
the subject. We also see in this stanza how the title of the poem works
in two different ways. That is, in the first complex of images, "the
beautiful changes" is used in the sense that one beautiful image (Queen
Anne's Lace) turns into another (water lilies). At the end of the stanza,
it is the beautiful as essentially an abstract entity that causes something else to change—in this case, a perception is called up in the mind
of the speaker.

The final stanza extends these notions even further, in language that
is enticingly abstract, allowing Wilbur to suggest many things at once
and causing the reader to be fruitfully puzzled over the exact significance of the lines:

> Your hands hold roses always in a way that says
> They are not only yours; the beautiful changes
> In such kind ways,
> Wishing ever to sunder
> Things and things' selves for a second finding, to lose
> For a moment all that it touches back to wonder.

The woman is implicitly identified as "the beautiful"; her way of hold-
ing the roses changes them in a conceptual way, apparently separating

their strictly physical manifestation from their Platonic essence. Thus, the speaker is enabled to see the relationship between those two things—basically, the material and the spiritual—differently. The spiritual is most directly represented in this poem by the underlying feeling of love that brought the poem into being in the first place. When all that is touched is "lost" "back to wonder," a spiritual intensification is taking place: the inherent loveliness of the woman intensifies and is intensified by the inherent loveliness of the roses. Such a reading is anticipated in the poem's middle stanza, where:

> . . . a mantis, arranged
> On a green leaf, grows
> Into it, makes the leaf leafier, and proves
> Any greenness is deeper than anyone knows.

There is an alliance established in this poem between various essences that inhere within and give life to outward elements of reality: beauty, love, greenness, wonder, imagination. Thus the poem affords a dense revelation of various forms of spirituality either already existent or potentially so just beneath the veil of external, material reality.

The ordering, harmonizing, unifying power of the imagination is itself specifically the subject of "An Event," from *Things of This World* (*PRW*, 106). The poem begins with another intricate metaphorical description:

> As if a cast of grain leapt back to the hand,
> A landscapeful of small black birds, intent
> On the far south, convene at some command
> At once in the middle of the air, at once are gone
> With headlong and unanimous consent
> From the pale trees and fields they settled on.

The movement in these lines is remarkable. The action of the birds is described twice, and in reverse chronology, according to the effect that these actions have upon the composition and appearance of reality: first we see them gathering in air, then we see their earlier departure from the trees. Adding to this movement is the metaphorical extension of the first line. The tension established is between the orderliness of grouping, of collective activity, and the relative chaos of a scattered individuality. The eye of the poet sees an example of an orderly gathering-together within nature and matches this by creating a similar (though physically impossible) image in the mind. At this point in the poem, imagination and reality are in a harmonious relationship to one another, and the poet goes on to revel, briefly, in his triumphant vision—until reality dispels it:

> What is an individual thing? They roll
> Like a drunken fingerprint across the sky!
> Or so I give their image to my soul
> Until, as if refusing to be caught
> In any singular vision of my eye
> Or in the nets and cages of my thought,
>
> They tower up, shatter, and madden space
> With their divergences, are each alone
> Swallowed from sight, and leave me in this place
> Shaping these images to make them stay:
> Meanwhile, in some formation of their own,
> They fly me still, and steal my thoughts away.

The collective action of the birds was orderly, a self-justifying outward manifestation of the poet's inward, imaginative vision of harmony. But when the birds break apart, their individual action is a challenge to the poet's ideal conception, and he is left behind by reality—somewhat chagrined, but trying nobly to adjust his inner view of things to the outer evidence provided by his senses.

It is in the concluding stanza of the poem that Wilbur specifically considers the division between reality and the poet's inner vision of things; we discover that the incident, and his attempt to capture it in words, has not left him defeated after all. Instead, he admits the tension and is appreciative of the power each realm possesses:

> Delighted with myself and with the birds,
> I set them down and give them leave to be.
> It is by words and the defeat of words,
> Down sudden vistas of the vain attempt,
> That for a flying moment one may see
> By what cross-purposes the world is dreamt.

Wilbur is no polemicist for the spiritual; he does not preorder the evidence so that a sacramental view of things will always emerge triumphant. Rather, he admits the fertile tension that inevitably is going to exist between reality itself and an ideal view of reality. What results is poetry, for Wilbur the most productive activity possible for the active, engaged imagination.

We are now in a position finally to understand Wilbur's definition of the concept "grace" as it applies to his poetry. We began by asserting that grace for Wilbur encompasses both a sense of graceful motion and

God's freely given love. His own definition, which appears in the poem "Grace" from his earliest book, *The Beautiful Changes*, links these concepts directly with the activity of poetry: "flesh made word / Is grace's revenue" (*PRW*, 219). It is the reversal that makes this definition tricky—the standard Christian view is that grace is word made flesh. True—but it is the poet's function, in his attempt to read God's mind, as it were, his attempt to match God's creative intelligence with his own pale version of the same thing, to change that manifest grace back into words. The principle of the beautiful—which in this context is the perceiving, the recording, the altering, the ordering creative imagination of the poet—we may say, changes the raw materials of reality into a version of the ideal, while ever admitting the uncertainty, even the impossibility, of the task.

Wilbur's critical writings on Edgar Allan Poe are both penetrating and appreciative, and yet he has said, referring to his own poetry: "A good part of my work could, I suppose, be understood as a public quarrel with the aesthetics of Edgar Allan Poe."[27] What he quarrels with specifically is apparent in the essay "Edgar Allan Poe," where Wilbur defines Poe's approach to his materials in this way: "His only means of escape is the suspension of outward consciousness, and a deliberate retreat from the temporal, rational, physical world into the visionary depths of his mind. There, in the immaterial regions of dream, he can purge himself of all earthly taint, and deliver himself to visions of that heavenly beauty which is the thought of God."[28] We are already well aware of Wilbur's own suspicious attitude towards a pure and disembodied spirituality and are therefore not surprised by the opinion reflected here. And yet Wilbur does share Poe's desire to catch a glimpse beyond the veil of reality to the spiritual underpinnings of the universe. And there is an area in which his practice bears an interesting resemblance to Poe's. One of the primary ways in which Poe's characters are able to transcend the limitations of ordinary reality in order to peer into eternity is through a disordering of the mind. Poe achieves this in many ways—through drugs, as in "Leigia"; through terror, as in "A Descent into the Maelstrom"; through illness, malnutrition, spiritual withdrawal, as in "The Fall of the House of Usher." Poe's longest and most artistically chaotic piece of prose fiction is *The Narrative of Arthur Gordon Pym*, which provides almost a casebook study of the kinds of disorientation Poe uses to get his characters as close to the spiritual—as far removed from the ordinary, the real, the everyday—as possible. Pym, a teenager, has a friend whose father is captain of a sailing ship; the friend is about to go on a voyage with his father and wants Pym along for company. The father, however, refuses permission, so the friend stows Pym away in the far recesses of the ship's hold, promising to return as soon as they are safely away from shore. There is no fresh air in the hold, and it is permeated by narcotic fumes from some part of the cargo or from some previous cargo. Pym falls into a deep, drugged sleep. When he awakens, his candle has completely burned down and the hold is pitch black—he is removed from the ordinariness of light; his food has rotted and his water turned rancid—showing the passage of considerable time and increasing his mental confusion through malnutrition; his watch has run down—removing him from the ordinary realm of time; the noxious fumes remain—continuing the mental disorientation that first put him to sleep; and he can feel by the movement of the ship that it is far out at sea—removing him from the ordinary, stable reality of solid land. At this point Poe is ready to begin his quest for the "supernal," for "the glories beyond the grave"—for, that is, the realm of pure spirituality—in earnest.

Wilbur is not so extreme, neither in his ultimate goal nor in the methods used to approach it. His longing is not for an unmeliorated spirituality but for an awareness of how the spiritual is delicately inherent within the material. When Richard Wilbur alters the mind of the perceiving consciousness in his poems in order to achieve an easier entry into the magical realm of the spiritual, he generally does so through that willing suspension of control, or of disbelief, that comes to us chiefly in sleep. (Another such avenue is used in "The Mind-Reader," where the speaker is able to float his awareness into the minds of others—but that is the exception in Wilbur's work, and trickier than is necessary.) The poems "In Limbo" (also from *The Mind-Reader*) and "Marginalia" (from *Things of This World*) are both explicitly concerned with the state of mind one is in while falling asleep. Sleep is an appropriate choice for a poet like Wilbur, who places so much emphasis upon the art-making process, for it is while in the dream state that man is most spontaneously and obviously creative; it is then that he is most likely to make his own connection to the spiritual.

"The Ride" is a recent poem and perhaps the only poem Wilbur has written devoted entirely to one dream experience. The speaker rides a magnificent, strong horse through a vicious snowstorm to an inn—and then wakes up. It is the concluding two stanzas of this poem that are the most interesting, for it is there that Wilbur indicates his attitude towards the dream as a dream:

How shall I now get back
To the inn-yard where he stands,
Burdened with every lack,
And waken the stable-hands

To give him, before I think
That there was no horse at all,
Some hay, some water to drink,
A blanket and a stall?[29]

We catch the speaker at a point of transition here, as he grows more awake, more a part of the literal world of the everyday. As this process continues within him, he is anxious to complete the action of the dream—before he loses entirely his belief in the reality of the horse. The poem again provides us with a measure of the inherent tension within Wilbur's worldview, a tension that results from the very tenuousness of the sacramental vision in the face of stark, uncompromising, reality.

"Love Calls Us to the Things of This World" (*PRW*, 65–66), Wilbur's best-known, most-admired poem, is built upon the same point of transition from sleep to wakefulness and reveals a similar tension between the realms of the spiritual and the material. The poem is narrated from the third-person point of view by someone able to perceive the split personality of a character whose "eyes open to a cry of pulleys"—one part of him is "the astounded soul," and the other is "the waking body." As the poem begins and the eyes are startled open, the soul still "Hangs for a moment bodiless and simple," apart from the body. While the body sleeps, the soul apparently romps in the spiritual world of dream; the experience transforms reality, heightens it towards the spiritual so that instead of laundry, "The morning air is all awash with angels"— "truly there they are." Two stanzas describe the wind-billowed laundry as ghostlike angels; then we see that the soul has approached close enough to the material, returning from fields of spiritual dream, to want to cry out against this coming down:

The soul shrinks

From all that it is about to remember,
From the punctual rape of every blessèd day,
And cries,
          "Oh, let there be nothing on earth but laundry,
Nothing but rosy hands in the rising steam
And clear dances done in the sight of heaven."

The waking process, which returns the soul to its material home, is irreversible, however, and as the poem ends, the soul and the "waking body" are reunited into the "man," and the soul delivers a final prayerlike speech:

    Yet, as the sun acknowledges
With a warm look the world's hunks and colors,
The soul descends once more in bitter love
To accept the waking body, saying now
In a changed voice as the man yawns and rises,

    "Bring them down from their ruddy gallows;
Let there be clean linen for the backs of thieves;
Let lovers go fresh and sweet to be undone,
And the heaviest nuns walk in a pure floating
of dark habits,
            keeping their difficult balance."

The resignation is not a bitter one. The vision here represents another
attempt to invest quotidian materiality with an aura of the spiritual.
Instead of using light as his image, Wilbur has used clothing, which
can similarly surround the real. His wearers are, of course, carefully
chosen to show the presence of the spiritual even in unlikely places—
in thieves and undone lovers. By this point in the poem, the end, the
character has completely woken up, and these clothes images represent
all that he is able to retain of the spiritual within the physical world.
We see how tenuous, and how desirable to Wilbur, is the delicate balance that is finally achieved between the material and the spiritual.
    To "Icarium Mare," a recent poem, Richard Wilbur brought many of
the best techniques, images, and ideas that appear in his earlier work.[30]
The poem could stand, in fact, as representative of much in his career,
and it is for that reason that I conclude with it here. He begins by
drawing a distinction, familiar to us by now, between the ideal, Platonic, spiritual realm above and the realm of reality here below:

    We have heard of the undimmed air
Of the True Earth above us, and how here,
    Shut in our sea-like atmosphere,
We grope like muddled fish.

Earlier we have seen how Wilbur uses the ocean to represent an unre-
deemed level of reality, chaos; here the sea is appropriately used to
indicate the relatively debased status of the real. However, it is from
that ideal realm above, Wilbur suggests next, that Icarus may have fall-
en, "to be quenched / Near Samos riding in the actual sea." Wilbur
next turns his attention to the area of the Aegean known as the Icarian
Sea and to two human events that he considers notable—this is

> Where Aristarchus first
> Rounded the sun in thought; near Patmos, too,
> Where John's bejeweled inward view
> Descried an angel in the solar burst.

These two instances of human endeavor are chosen because of their relationship to the sun, to which Icarus earlier, mythologically, had flown too close. Aristarchus of Samos was an astronomer of the third century B.C. and is thought to have been the first man to propose a heliocentric theory of the universe. The reference to St. John is to the vision of Christ bathed in light, which constituted the command unto him to write his epistles to the seven churches (Revelations 1:9-20). In both cases, Wilbur is praising human creative intelligence, the mind and imagination that allow man to transcend the limits of his senses:

> The reckoner's instruments,
> The saint's geodic skull bowed in his cave—
> Insight and calculation brave
> Black distances exorbitant to sense,
>
> Which in its little shed
> Of broken light knows wonders all the same.

The five senses present a limited world to man, no matter how glorious it also is. It is only through his intellect and his imagination that man has the ability to reach for the sun, as in the myth of Icarus; only these things allow us to "name anew / Creatures without which vision would be blind."

It is in the final two stanzas that Wilbur provides an epitomizing statement of his view of man's estate and abilities, of the world man inhabits, and of the relative possibility for seeing the sacramental within the real:

> This is no outer dark
> But a small province haunted by the good,
> Where something may be understood
> And where, within the sun's coronal arc,
>
> We keep our proper range,
> Aspiring, by our lashed and irised sight,
> To gather tokens of the light—
> Not in the bullion, but in the loose change.

This may sound like a minor achievement so stated, but for Wilbur it is a kind of miracle that, given the limitations of his senses, man's mind—his creative intelligence—can aspire to so much. Again, we conclude at a point of "delicate balance" and relative diminishment: man's vision, achieved through the employment of his creative intelligence, enables him to see the sparkling, golden "loose change," but is not quite strong enough to enable him to see this scattering assembled into the luminescent "bullion" of God's vision.

Interview with
Richard Wilbur

●

The interview was conducted at Mr. Wilbur's home in Cummington, Massachusetts, in March 1977. *The Mind-Reader: New Poems* had been published the year before.

When did you begin writing poetry?

I began writing poetry as a small child, and became a hired poet at the age of eight, when my first poem was published in *John Martin's Magazine.* As I remember it, it was a horrible little poem about nightingales, which I never could have seen or heard as an American child. Of course, I wasn't thinking of poetry as my chief activity or even chief avocation at that age. I was drawing pictures, playing the piano vilely, thinking of being a cartoonist or a painter, and imagining that I might be a journalist. Poetry was just one of the many products, and I can't be said to have done anything very prodigious.

Were you paid for the poem?

Yes, a dollar. I still have the dollar somewhere. Over there in that silo, which I cannot unlock because I've mislaid the key, there are all sorts of brown boxes full of memorabilia, and I think one of them contains the dollar.

What eventually made you decide on a career as a poet?

I really drifted into it. When I was at Amherst College, I was editor, or chairman as they called it, of the college newspaper, and I did a lot of writing and drawing for the college humor magazine, *Touchstone.* At the same time, I felt a sort of vocation for the study of English literature and thought I might want to be a scholar. During World War II, I wrote poems to calm my own nerves and to send to my wife and a few friends, a few teachers at Amherst. Then when I came back after the war and went to Harvard on the G.I. Bill to get an M.A. in English, there was a friend we made there, a well-known French poet now, named André du Bouchet. He was involved with a little magazine called *Foreground*, which was being backed by Reynal and Hitchcock as a means of discovering new talent. André heard from my wife one evening that I had a secret cache of poems in my study desk. He asked to see them, then took them away to read. When he came back about an hour later, he kissed me on both cheeks and declared me to be a poet. He sent these poems off to Reynal and Hitchcock, and they also declared me to be a poet, saying that they would like to publish them, and others if I had them, as a book.

How do you compose your poems? Do you write in longhand or on the typewriter? Do you write in bursts or long stretches, quickly or laboriously?

With pencil and paper and laboriously, very slowly on the whole. I do envy people who can compose on the typewriter, though I reject as preposterous Charles Olson's ideas about the relation of the typewriter to poetic form. I don't approach the typewriter until the thing is completely done, and whatever margins the typewriter might offer have nothing to do with the form of a poem as I conceive it. I write poems line by line, very slowly; I sometimes scribble alternative words in the margins rather densely, but I don't go forward with anything unless I am fairly satisfied that what I have set down sounds printable, sayable. I proceed as Dylan Thomas once told me he proceeded—it is a matter of going to one's study, or to the chair in the sun, and starting a new sheet of paper. On it you put what you've already got of a poem you are trying to write. Then you sit and stare at it, hoping that the impetus of writing out the lines that you already have will get you a few lines farther before the day is done. I often don't write more than a couple of lines in a day of, let's say, six hours of staring at the sheet of paper. Composition for me is, externally at least, scarcely distinguishable from catatonia.

That reminds me of a story about Flaubert. Some friends came by his house one Friday to ask if he would join them on a weekend picnic. He said no, he was much too busy. They looked at his manuscript, made some small talk, and went on their way. On Sunday night they came back to say what a wonderful time they had had. They also asked Flaubert how his work had gone. He said that he had made enormous progress. So they looked at the manuscript again, and noticed that he was at exactly the same point as on Friday—in the middle of a sentence interrupted by a comma. They chided him for making no progress at all. He replied that they didn't understand— that he had, on Saturday, changed the comma to a semicolon, and on Sunday changed it back to a comma; thus he had made wonderful progress.

What is it that gets you started on a poem? Is it an idea, an image, a rhythm, or something else?

It seems to me that there has to be a sudden confident sense that there is an exploitable and interesting relationship between something perceived out there and something in the way of incipient meaning within you. And what you see out there has to be seen freshly, or the process is not going to be provoked. Noting a likeness or resemblance between two things in nature can provide this freshness, but I think there must be more. For example, to perceive that the behavior of certain tree leaves is like the behavior of bird's wings is not, so far as I am concerned, enough to justify the sharpening of the pencil. There has to be a feeling that some kind of idea is implicit within that resemblance. It is strange how confident one can be about this. I always detest it when artists and writers marvel at their own creativity, but I think this is a very strange thing which most practiced artists would have in common, the certainty which accompanies these initial, provocative impressions. I am almost always right in feeling that there is a poem in something if it hits me hard enough. You can spoil your material, of course, but that doesn't mean the original feeling was false.

You have been a teacher for many years. Does teaching complement your work as a poet?

I think the best part of teaching from the point of view of the teacher-writer, writer-teacher, is that it makes you read a good deal and makes you be articulate about what you read. You can't read passively, because you have to be prepared to move other people to recognitions and acts of analysis. I know a few writers who don't teach and who, in consequence, do very little reading. This doesn't mean that they are bad writers, but in some cases I think they might be better writers if they read more. As for the experience of the classroom, I enjoy it; I am very depressed by classes which don't work, and rather elated by classes which do. I like to see if I can express myself clearly enough to stick an idea in somebody's head. Of course there are also disadvantages, one of which is that the time one spends teaching could be spent writing. Another involves this very articulateness of which I've been speaking. It uses the same gray cells, pretty much, that writing does, and so one can come to the job of writing with too little of a sense of rediscovery of the language. That is one reason I like to live out here in the country and lead a fairly physical life—play a lot of tennis, raise a lot of vegetables, go on a lot of long walks. I do things which are nonverbal so that I can return to language with excitement and move toward language from kinds of strong awareness for which I haven't instantly found facile words. It is good for a writer to move into words out of the silence, as much as he can.

What poets would you name as having had the most influence on your own work?

That question is hard for me to answer because it involves too many names, some of which are from other literatures and other cultures. Perhaps the most useful thing I can say is that I am not the sort of person who has derived most of his inspiration from his contemporaries. I cannot place myself at all as a member of any school or as a continuator of any trend or flow. This is not to say that people haven't categorized me as they have everybody else, but I don't think the classification has been as just in my case as it might be in some others. There are many people who are discipular types—say the Sons of William Carlos, whose poetry I also love—but I am not that kind of follower. My influences are much more scattered. I studied the Latin poets at Amherst, for example, and can still read them, though not with any facility. I have also done a lot of translation from French poetry, particularly of the seventeenth century. And I was lucky enough to go to Rome for a year, in 1954, where I picked up an ability to read Dante. I haven't read every bit of him in the original, but I have made some pretty good tries in all three departments of the *Commedia*. I think I've also taken a lot of inspiration from Milton, and from the Metaphysical poets of the seventeenth century, to whom I was introduced by my teachers at Amherst. I delight in John Keats, and at one time knew a large part of Tennyson. One of my early great excitements was Gerard Manley Hopkins, whom I discovered during World War II, and whom I toted all around Europe in a musette bag. Then there's Yeats, on whom I have taught seminars at Wesleyan and Harvard. And I know perfectly well that the first person whom I ever heard read his poetry, Robert Frost, gave me a strong impression of what poetry ought to be, what a poet ought to be. There was a time when I knew almost all of Frost by heart—not that I had memorized it, but it had just gotten stuck in my head. I don't think I know it that well now. I'n not saying that I've read everything, but the things which have influenced me are of a very scattered nature and come from many periods and many languages and represent many modes of verse.

Can you tell me which contemporary poets you most admire?

That would be a long list, and I don't think that there would be a lot of surprises on it. I could also, I suppose . . . no, I couldn't. I couldn't give you a long list of poets I *don't* want to read, because I have repressed many of their names. I do think this is a time in which there is too much poetry being published and too much of it being heard. It is hard to read poetry, I think, and if the returns are not great, then one begrudges the effort. I was made aware the other day, in the midst of a chat, that I am not really very critical of movies. Every now and then there is some movie so pointlessly violent or so tasteless that I will get up, perhaps protesting audibly, and walk out. But mostly I find something to look at on the screen. Even if the actors are no good, the scenery or props will be interesting. In poetry there are no such incidental compensations. You don't have anything in poetry save what the words give you, and therefore a bad poem is very much worse than a bad movie. There is simply no excuse for its being thrust upon one.

We have seen before us the terrifying example of many twentieth-century poets—a record of alcoholism, madness, suicide, depression. Do you have any way of accounting for this?

It is very easy for poets to feel, I think, that what they are doing is a little too lonely, marginal, and partial. Whatever sense of insecurity or instability a person may have can only be accentuated by this feeling of uselessness—even to the point of excessive drinking and self-slaughter. It would be good for poets to feel that they are as essential to the community as the mailman is, but you can't feel that way all the time. I myself am always terribly grateful for letters saying, "I just read your book and it meant something to me." A response of this sort makes me feel as if I had delivered a service to society.

And yet we have seen large audiences for poetry readings lately, which would seem to indicate that the poets are serving some sort of need within society.

Yes, but most of that has been associated either with the universities or with the protest against the Vietnam War. Many of us felt, during the Vietnam War, that we were performing a social function in resisting the war, but really those read-ins were pretty tiresome, and we went through with them, as listeners and as spouters, out of a feeling of obligation to political principle. I don't think those were occasions on which poets truly and legitimately acquired large publics. As for the universities, it is very pleasant to give readings there—you are speaking to people who have actually read your work and can catch whatever you are pitching. But it is a special sort of audience too. Some people are there because of a very temporary excitement, and some are there because their teachers have told them they must come. For me, the most exciting audiences are those you get at something like a museum or arts club, where there is a great mixture of kinds of people. To get a good response from so varied an audience is more exciting to me than to be well and knowledgably received by an audience of college students, though I don't mean to minimize the latter—any kind of good reception is pleasant.

As a young man, did you ever do what John Berryman did so consciously—visit older poets, to learn from them or to sit at their feet?

Not as a very young man, though I knew Robert Frost rather well when I was in my latter twenties and thereafter. My entrée was not so much my own merits as my wife's. Her grandfather, William Hayes Ward, was the first person to publish Robert Frost. He edited the *Independent,* a journal of literature and opinion which later turned into the *Outlook,* which later still became the *Literary Digest.* So Frost was very fond of my wife's family. He was also responsive to the fact that I knew most of his poems by heart. And then I had the luck to please him with a few of my own poems. So there is someone at whose feet I have sat, although after a while I got up off the floor and we were just friends. And let's see—I have never made pilgrimages, though I've always been delighted to meet people about whose work I cared. I loved meeting people like Stevens and Williams and Marianne Moore, usually at performances which they gave. I introduced Stevens one time when he gave a splendid reading at Sanders Theatre at Harvard. Unfortunately, I am the only person who heard the reading because the sound equipment was not working. I was sitting on the stage next to him, and it sounded wonderful, but the acoustics in that building are so bad that everyone else was forced to sit through an hour of silence. And they respected him so much that they did it gratefully. Luckily, the tape recorder was working, so we have a record of that occasion.

Did Frost seem to you the kind of man that Thompson says he was?

I think most of Thompson's evidence is undoubtedly true. But since I
take a more positive view of Frost's character than Thompson, I don't
find those books agreeable to read. I think Thompson is reacting
against the phony picture—the mellow old New England fellow—
which Frost gave of himself and which his admirers so often gave. He
was, as I well knew, a much more dark and dangerous person than that.
There was paranoia in him and a savage competitiveness. But that is
not what you felt when you were with him. Personally, he was extremely warm. You could occasionally put him off, because in eighty-
odd years he never lost his original touchiness. But he would come
back; perhaps he would even like you better for having braced him a
little. I can remember putting him off several times. Once I said to him
in Cambridge that he ought to go down to Washington and get Ezra
Pound out of the madhouse, that he shouldn't allow his old bitter-
nesses and envies against Pound to detain him. I said, "You don't want
to be a Brutus, and I don't mean the Brutus in Shakespeare, I mean that
other Brutus who was so perfect a Roman judge that he sentenced his
own sons to death." Having said that, of course, I winced, because I
remembered that Frost's son had committed suicide and that many
people, Frost included, had felt that he bore some responsibility in the
matter. Well, Frost winced too and glared at me for a bit, but he finally
felt that I and other people who urged him in that manner were right,
and acted on it. Another time, as I was leaving his cabin in Ripton, he
called me back, and said, with a very youthful diffidence, that he hoped
it was understood that we were friends. There wasn't any question of
our being enemies, of course; he was just saying that we had had a good
talk and he was sorry I was going, something like that. It came very
close to being tenderness, and it also came out of, as did so much that
he spoke, a very deep loneliness. I was tremendously touched. It seems
to me that this kind of thing is not frequent enough in the Thompson
biography—what I've read of it. People were always saying, around
Bread Loaf and Ripton, that the world did not know the real Robert
Frost. I suppose Thompson is telling the world what it never knew.
Perhaps he has lost his balance and is overtelling them. So often, I
think, a biographical study is likely to be written in a corrective spirit,
as was John Brinnin's *Dylan Thomas in America*. There were so many
damn fools who thought that Dylan was a healthy, bouncing, priapic
figure, rebuking us all for our stuffiness, whereas, although he had been
a delight to be with, he had also been a sick man drinking himself to
death. Brinnin, as Thomas's closest associate in America, had seen that

horror, and had seen the almost willful incomprehension of the many people who adored Dylan and tagged along after him and drank with him. So he had to write the book to correct a false impression, to put the horror on record, and many people didn't understand what had moved him.

You have said that "the work of every good poet may be seen in one way or another as an exploration and declaration of the self." Is this true in your own case?

I don't think that I explore myself in poetry in the way in which some so-called confessional poets do, although I must say I am getting much more garrulous and writing many more poems out of my actual experience and my relationships. But I usually have a certain sense of distance from my material, a feeling that I am not spilling my guts but arranging some materials and trying to find out the truth about them. If, in the process, I also find out something about myself, I think it is indirectly done. It is the thing, and not myself, which I set out to explore. But then, having chosen my subject and explored it, and having seen what I can say, I suppose one result of the poem is that I know myself a little better. There are certain things I find that I will not say, and there are certain matters to which I keep coming back. I would rather not name them because I think they are clear enough in the poems. The funny thing is that I often won't know that I have reapproached a subject until a new poem has been finished. Then I will say, oh yes, this turned out to be that question again. My process of self-exploration is almost as strangely indirect as that of Beau Brummell in a story that I remember hearing told about him. Somebody asked Brummell which one of the northern lakes he preferred. He turned to his valet and said, "Which one of the northern lakes do I prefer?" "I believe it is Windermere, sir," the valet replied. So Brummell said to his questioner, "Apparently it is Windermere." I see some resemblance between that process and the process by which I make discoveries about myself. I ask some poem to write itself, and once I am through supervising that process, I have discovered whether I like Windermere or not.

I do feel that the truth, especially the truth about oneself, is hard to report, and that if you set out to confess, what you are likely to do is tell lies in addition to reporting some of the truth. And the fact that you are consciously part of the material of the poem may lead you to falsify in ways that are not good. There are good fictions and bad fictions. The kind of fiction which glamorizes you is not good either for your sake or for the reader's, and I think that very often the confessional poet is drawn to glamorize himself, whether he is aware of it or not.

While we are speaking of the element of personality in poetry, I would like to get your reaction to a review of your work which I came across. While calling you "smug" and "self-indulgent," the reviewer also said: "in many of his new poems, Wilbur still addresses us as if he were the only one alive." How do you feel hearing or reading something like that?

I remember seeing that somewhere. I think the critic is reacting to the personality which he feels behind the poems he has read. We all do this, of course, but I am sorry that my critic does not like what he has seen in or through my work. Perhaps his idea of humanity in speech and in art involves a greater directness and a higher degree of blurting than he finds in me. I don't like the kind of poetry which seems to harangue the reader. D. H. Lawrence, for example, some of whose work I think is marvelous, can be a dreadful haranguer. Perhaps that reviewer would like the instancy and the insistence of Lawrence, who is indeed dealing directly with his reader, though he is also dealing carelessly with his lines in the process. Lawrence always writes at his worst when he is hectoring an imagined reader. But maybe my critic doesn't like Lawrence either. It is hard to know why these reactions happen. I remember a case that may be similar to this one. Toward the end of World War II, I had a friend—we really did like one another—who came out of a kind of ethnic, urban world. He was periodically exasperated by what he felt was my WASP cool. He would come and stand next to my cot in the barracks and say: "Wilbur, why don't you join the human race?" I would ask him what I could do in order to join the human race, but he never made any specific suggestions—he'd just tell me to loosen up, that sort of thing. I think it is possible that there are some critics for whom one's poetry just cannot work because of temperamental differences and distances.

You mentioned your admiration of William Carlos Williams earlier. In another review, I found a comment which I found puzzling. The critic said that you have failed to learn what Williams had to teach about the use of objects in poetry. I wonder how you would react to that.

Well, I am not sure what he means. I do admire Williams's objective poetry very much. His descriptions are among the best we have. I have always hoped that some of my descriptions also made things vivid to the mind's eye. You don't want description to be the whole purpose of any poem, it seems to me, but it is one of the authenticating elements in poetry. I like poetry to excite us at all points, and one thing that ought to be excited is the mind's eye. I have got a few lines which seem to me to be as precisely evocative as some of Williams, and I wonder why my critic won't agree.

Perhaps this critic perfers a poetry that is limited to the physical and is bothered by your desire to go beyond that in order to seek a balance between the material and spiritual worlds. Williams doesn't do this.

That is true, often he doesn't, and some of his poems may be a little impoverished because of that. But he has many other poems in which an idea is very much coextensive with the objects being described. As for myself, I seldom write wholly in images. At the same time, I like to stay close to the physical and close to the given situation. So maybe what that critic is doing is making a puristic and imagistic criticism of my poems, and I must say I would have to plead guilty. I am not an imagist—I enjoy some of the productions of imagism and I have tried to incorporate some of what I have found in imagism into my own work. But I have never wanted to remain on that level.

You have said, "I do think that there is nothing more dangerous to the imagination than fantasy." Many people would equate the two things. Could you elaborate on that?

To me, the imagination is a faculty which fuses things, takes hold of the physical and ideal worlds and makes them one, provisionally. Fantasy, in my mind, is a poetic or artistic activity which leaves something out—it ignores the concrete and the actual in order to create a purely abstract, unreal realm. If we think of fantasy at its least dignified, non-artistic level, this becomes obvious. Sexual revery very clearly leaves something out, and that something is the physical object of one's desire.

Edgar Allan Poe is a writer who relies a good deal on fantasy; his work and his theory of art both seem very different from yours. What, then, is the basis of your fascination with him?

I first read Poe sensitively during World War II, in a foxhole at Monte Cassino. The extreme isolation of my situation made for a great power to concentrate. I felt a tremendous symbolic or allegorical depth beneath Poe's prose, and this excited my curiosity. I have been reading him ever since, and find myself continually discovering new things. I tried to write a book on him when I was a Junior Fellow at Harvard, between 1947 and 1950, but it didn't quite pan out. I hadn't yet found a language sufficient to describe the operation of his work as I saw it. So I began to write short pieces on him. I think I have said a certain number of things about him which are true, and it is fun to have been a discoverer. Now as for our conflict, Edgar's and mine, I object to him simply because he is far too much a fantasist. Or, as Allen Tate put it, the trouble with him is that his imagination does not proceed upward through the order of nature, moving toward the invisible through the visible. Instead, he tries to destroy the visible world on the assumption that if you do that, then the invisible world will rush in to take its place. Well, I question that formula, but I think it is an exciting mistake and resulted in a number of remarkable works.

But you don't seem to care much for his poetry.

I have a strong weakness for certain of the poems—"To One in Paradise," for example. But too much of the poetry is virtually pure incantation, its substance being cloudy or predestroyed. The fiction, for my money, is far more accessible and far more defensible aesthetically. Poe's stories have a neo-Platonic or Gnostic myth for their frame, but within that frame we're also given wonderful pictures of the states and motions and conflicts of the psyche. Modern studies of the dream process are just catching up with some things which Poe noticed and, in his own way, set down.

Critics of a certain type describe your poetry as rigid in its formality, old-fashioned, etc. Apparently because we live in an age of loose forms—of free verse, the prose poem, and the plain style—your practice strikes them as odd.

It is true that I have used a metrical basis in almost every poem that I have written, and it is true that more than half of my poems rhyme. At the same time, we must recognize that meter in itself is not rigid—it depends on how you use it. I hope that in my best poems I have used meter flexibly, so that the rhythm of a given poem is appropriate to its mood and its subject. Robert Lowell wrote me a friendly note when "Walking to Sleep" came out in the *New Yorker*, praising among other things the looseness of my pentameters. I didn't know what to make of that at first; I didn't think my pentameters were especially loose. But his remark led me to see that they sometimes were and are—that in contrast to many poets I pay little heed to the decasyllabic norm. Most of my poems are put together in the way in which free verse comes about. That is to say, I start talking the poem to myself, and I wait to see what rhythmic lengths the poem naturally wants to fall into. Having let the poem have its head for five or six lines, I decide whether or not I have a stanza. By that time I also probably have discovered whether the poem wants to rhyme, whether it wants to emphasize itself or deepen its sound by rhyming. This seems to me a perfectly organic way to proceed with a poem. Very seldom has this approach gotten me into a formal straitjacket in which it was impossible to develop the thought as the thought wanted to develop. That can happen. I think one could start out in a very difficult form, like terza rima, and find that the natural drift of the thoughts and perceptions was being impeded, was being falsified, by the technical difficulties. What you do at that point is to start over, maybe, or eliminate some of your rhymes. So I would say that I approach a poem in just the way a free-verse writer does. What matters is the subject and the words which are going to be found for conveying and exploring the subject. The only difference is that I include meters and rhymes in my free-verse proceeding.

When I spoke with James Wright, he suggested that a rigorous formalism in poetry, rather than confining the imagination, as some people think it does, actually liberates the imagination. Does this make sense to you?

Oh, yes. I have argued that for years. I think it is perfectly true that if you put yourself in a position where you have to pay attention to all sorts of wild suggestions which come to you through the sound contract you have made, it can be liberating. If you are a silly person, it will ruin your poem because you will let the rhyme twist your thought, take your mind off where you were going. But if you are not silly, it can be very enriching and instructive. I don't really take an Apollonian approach to poetry. I think you have to be using your brains all the time, yes, but your brains have to be very attentive to the stupid part of you. I trust the stupid part at least as much. And one way of extorting suggestions from that part of you is through the use of formal devices such as rhyme and stanzaic patterns.

Another reviewer, perhaps referring to your use of formalism, called you "a bell too conscious of its clapper, clapper-happy." How do you react to that?

I guess that means that I am self-conscious about the sound of my own voice, and I think I would have to plead guilty in some measure.

Every line that I set down is considerably pondered, and while I try to have a colloquial and dashing movement in my poems, it does not satisfy me if they are not of a more than colloquial density or import. Now I always find self-consciousness annoying in other people—carefulness I don't. I find gaudiness annoying; richness not. All I can say in answer to that criticism is that I hope that some people find me more careful and rich than clapper-happy.

There is a good deal of attention being paid today to the poem sequence and even to the long poem, as in Warren and Berryman, for example. Do you have any inclination to work along those lines?

I'm not sure any of my poems could qualify as long. I write so slowly that anything which is, let's say, a hundred and fifty lines long seems to me like a long poem. I haven't recently counted the lines of my longer poems, like "The Agent" or "Walking to Sleep" or "The Mind-Reader," but I do know that "Walking to Sleep" takes eight minutes to read aloud. And that is about as long as I believe I am likely to get. "Walking to Sleep" has the density of any of my lyrics—every line has a certain amount of trouble in it—and I think that if I were to write a sixteen-minute poem of that same density, it would be very hard for the reader to consume. If I were to write a longer poem, I think I would have to become more open, plainer, more prosaic, for considerable stretches. Who can tell what he will do? I must say the idea is attractive to me, the idea of seeing how simple I could be and still get away with it. I believe I have been getting simpler as I have gone along. In my last book, in fact, there are some lines—I don't think I have any poems which are simple in toto—which are so simple that an unfriendly reviewer in the *Times* was able to extract them and say, look how dull Wilbur can be. But when I was putting down those simple lines—lines like "It is always a matter, my darling, of life or death, as I had forgotten"—I was excited by their very simplicity. They occur within poems which, taken as a whole, are not altogether simple, which you might have to read two or three times to consume. Every time I encounter a good translation of a Chinese poem, I am teased by the thought that it would be nice to try that sort of thing. A good Chinese poem, as Witter Bynner says in his *Jade Mountain*, makes most of our poetry look over-dressed and self-important. And a good Chinese poem is so much the poem of its moment—it is attractive in that way too.

Well, all I can say is that such things attract me, but I don't have any notion of what I am going to do next. I have written almost no poetry for about a year now, though I have translated a play of Molière's—*The Learned Ladies*. That is part of my excuse. The rest of my excuse is that I really did say to myself recently that I must escape altogether from the impulse to overachieve, which can possess you once you get into the business of producing books of poetry. I called up Stanley Kunitz the day John Berryman killed himself. We consoled one another and talked about whether his act had been predictable. One thing we agreed upon was this, that whereas Stanley and I do many things apart from poetry—we both love gardening, for example—John Berryman was such a very hard worker that he lived almost entirely within his profession. Some of the dream songs seem to drag in a good deal of the world, but they do it mainly through books and *Time* magazine and the daily newspaper. The impression one is left with is of a man who is working desperately hard at his job. Well, I admire that, but I think it can break your health and destroy your joy in life and art. I haven't got any clever hypotheses about why John killed himself, but a statement of Stanley's during that telephone conversation has stuck in my mind. He said: "In this country it is not enough just to publish a book of good poems and forever after be thanked for it. It should be possible, but it's not." As soon as you publish a book of poems, people begin to say, When is your next book coming out? And if you don't publish books at intervals of three years, they say, Why are you so slow? I have been reproached in the *Times Literary Supplement* for taking seven years to get out a book, you know. That kind of pressure is not good for you and isn't good for your work. Stanley said: "As soon as you publish a book of poems in this country, you are in the poetry prison." I think John felt himself to be in the poetry prison, and that may have been contributory to his death.

You once said—and here is another quotation for you—"there's always some impulse in the American writer to set out for the frontier in some sense, to head for the savage, the original, the uncivilized, to stand loose from whatever actual coherences people may try to thrust upon him." Have you felt this impulse, and do you think it shows up in your poetry?

Yes, I feel the impulse. I think that, like most Americans, I have considerable respect for the actual and physical. We are all kickers of stones, you know, and we are not as likely to get enchanted with abstract thought systems as some Europeans, especially the French, are. The French are always coming up with enormously boring notions which they consider *très très très interessantes*. A man like Sartre can get a whole book out of a proposition which is, on the face of it, untrue; the proposition that Jean Genet, because he is masochistic, has the humility of a saint. There isn't any point in saying that even once, but a French intellectual can get a whole book out of it. I suppose we Americans are at fault in the other direction, that we are too primitive and have too much respect for the voiceless and the unvoiceable. Maybe it is just that we are closer to the frontier than they are, and therefore are less capable of getting lost in our minds—we are surer that there is something out there.

I take it that you would not then agree with the critic who said: "Wilbur does not really care for things. For Wilbur, the call to things is equivalent to 'the punctual rape of every blessed day.' "

That is not true at all. The critic is entitled to his insight—we all have to make guesses like this about what we are reading. But that is not how I feel. I feel intensely drawn to things, I think more drawn to things than to thoughts. Since the world has to pass through thought in order to come out as poetry, it may not be immediately obvious that I am drawn to things. But I sure am.

Could I ask which of your books and which of your poems are your favorites?

I'm not sure about that. There is always the coy answer in which you say that your most recent work is your favorite because you hope so desperately that it is not a decline. I think it is possible that my best book is *Things of This World.* I have not tired of most of the poems in it, and I don't find any conspicuous failures there, whereas there are a couple of poems in *Advice to a Prophet* which I wish had never happened. Usually when I feel that way about a poem, I think it has to do with a lack of originality—sounding too much like somebody else. As for my favorite poems, I like "Walking to Sleep" very much. And I haven't gotten tired of "Love Calls Us to the Things of This World." Since I have read that so often to audiences, it seems to me that I have given it the acid test—it must for me have a lasting strength. And then I like the new poem to my daughter, the one called "The Writer." But I enjoyed that also as a formal departure; I enjoyed not rhyming for a change.

Let me conclude by asking your reaction to a comment which William Meredith made about you. He said that you "obviously believe that the universe is decent, in the lovely, derivative sense of that word."

Well, yes. To put it simply, I feel that the universe is full of glorious energy, that the energy tends to take pattern and shape, and that the ultimate character of things is comely and good. I am perfectly aware that I say this in the teeth of all sorts of contrary evidence, and that I must be basing it partly on temperament and partly on faith, but that is my attitude. My feeling is that when you discover order and goodness in the world, it is not something you are imposing—it is something which is likely really to be there, whatever crumminess and evil and disorder there may also be. I don't take disorder or meaninglessness to be the basic character of things. I don't know where I get my information, but that is how I feel.

**William
Stafford**

William Stafford's
Wilderness Quest

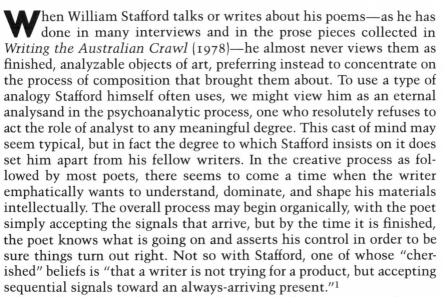

When William Stafford talks or writes about his poems—as he has done in many interviews and in the prose pieces collected in *Writing the Australian Crawl* (1978)—he almost never views them as finished, analyzable objects of art, preferring instead to concentrate on the process of composition that brought them about. To use a type of analogy Stafford himself often uses, we might view him as an eternal analysand in the psychoanalytic process, one who resolutely refuses to act the role of analyst to any meaningful degree. This cast of mind may seem typical, but in fact the degree to which Stafford insists on it does set him apart from his fellow writers. In the creative process as followed by most poets, there seems to come a time when the writer emphatically wants to understand, dominate, and shape his materials intellectually. The overall process may begin organically, with the poet simply accepting the signals that arrive, but by the time it is finished, the poet knows what is going on and asserts his control in order to be sure things turn out right. Not so with Stafford, one of whose "cherished" beliefs is "that a writer is not trying for a product, but accepting sequential signals toward an always-arriving present."[1]

In psychoanalysis, the analysand receives only one, apparently simple, instruction, intended to help him achieve free association: Say whatever occurs to you at a given moment. That something very like this is William Stafford's procedure when he composes his poems is apparent whenever he discusses how he does his writing:

> When I write, I like to have an interval before me when I am not likely to be interrupted. For me, this means usually the early morning, before others are awake. I get a pen and paper, take a glance out of the window (often it is dark out there), and wait. It is like fishing. But I do not wait very long, for there is always a nibble. . . . To get started I will accept anything that occurs to me. Something always occurs, of course, to any of us. We can't keep from thinking. Maybe I have to settle for an immediate impression: it's cold, or hot, or dark, or bright, or in between! Or—well, the possibilities are endless. If I put

down something, that thing will help the next thing come, and I'm off. If I let
the process go on, things will occur to me that were not at all in my mind
when I started. These things, odd or trivial as they may be, are somehow
connected. And if I let them string out, surprising things will happen.[2]

So committed is Stafford to this free-associative way of writing,
"This"—as he calls it—"process-rather-than-substance view of writing," that he would prefer not even to think about meaning and content
while he writes: "I cannot . . . insist on high standards. . . By 'standards' I do not mean correctness. . . . I am thinking about such matters
as social significance, positive values, consistency, etc. I resolutely dis-
regard these. Something better, greater, is happening! I am following a
process that leads so wildly and originally into new territory that no
judgment can at the moment be made about values, significance, and
so on."[3] Clearly what Stafford is trying to avoid is having his poetry
controlled by the reflective, rational, intellectual, analytical portion of
the mind. Occasionally, however, this side will gain the upper hand,
and when it does, Stafford yields, though only briefly and with great
distrust: "At times, without my insisting on it, my writings become
coherent; the successive elements that occur to me are clearly related.
They lead by themselves to new connections. Sometimes the language,
even the syllables that happen along, may start a trend. Sometimes the
materials alert me to something waiting in my mind, ready for sustained attention. At such times I allow myself to be eloquent, or intentional, or for great swoops (Treacherous! Not to be trusted!) reasonable.
But I do not insist on any of that, for I know that back of my activity
there will be the coherence of my self, and that indulgence of my impulses will bring recurrent patterns and meanings again."[4] Even in the
psychoanalytic process there are many times when free association
stops so that the analysand can participate with the analyst in an ex-
amination of what has been said. For the poet, this would mean thinking critically, intellectually, about his own work—a function that
William Stafford is most reluctant to perform. And it is in this fact that
both his greatest strength and his greatest weakness as a poet may be
found.

The strength lies in his spontaneous creativity, the ease with which
he writes. It is for this reason that Stafford is widely recognized, by
critics and fellow poets alike, as a natural writer. James Dickey, for
example, began his review of Stafford's first book, *West of Your City*
(1960), with this observation: "There are poets who pour out rivers of
ink, all on good poems. William Stafford is one of these. He has been
called America's most prolific poet, and I have no doubt that he is. He
turns out so much verse not because he is glib or empty, but because he

is a real poet, a born poet, and communicating in lines and images is not only the best way for him to get things said; it is the easiest."[5] Stafford has published a great many poems, and there is no denying that most of them are of high quality, as pleasurable to read as they were effortless to write. The problem with all this is that William Stafford's conception of his poetry is really not any larger than the scope of the individual poem, as seen—reductively, the critic has to feel—from inside the creative process.

That Stafford is himself aware of this limitation is apparent from a statement he has made in an interview. He suggested that contemporary "poetry is trapped trying to do little adventitious piddling jobs. . . . It is interesting, but it isn't overwhelming the way Pascal is overwhelming, or the way some writer like Alfred North Whitehead, who turns his first-class mind to a sustained communication project, is overwhelming. I think there are many prose projects now that are calling forth more of the talents and the serious and sustained attention of writers than the kind of crochet work many of us are doing in poetry. You can write a poem rather quickly, close it out, and publish it in a magazine. Then you put together a collection of these fragments—but it is not the same thing as a book. There may be someone who writes a collection of poems as a whole book, but I've never done it. Mine always come in pieces. My feeling is that the most interesting parts of those collections of poems are the spaces not written out between the poems. Maybe we're trying to do the wrong thing."[6] Although this observation is stated as though it were generally true of contemporary poetry, the poet who most perfectly fits the pattern is, of course, William Stafford himself. Other of today's poets may not have written *Paradise Lost,* but they have written such coherent efforts as *The Dream Songs* (John Berryman, 1969), *The Book of Nightmares* (Galway Kinnell, 1971), and *Kicking the Leaves* (Donald Hall, 1978). Indeed, even most of the more loosely constructed books of lyrics by other poets considered in this volume are more carefully structured than the tightest of Stafford's volumes. As James Wright has said, echoing Robert Frost: "If you have a book of twenty-four poems, the book itself should be the twenty-fifth."[7] About the most that Stafford is willing to do structurally is "cluster" similar poems together in a given area of a given book: "I try to choose poems that will make a chord—that would be one way to put it—with the other notes that are in this part of the book." (See "Interview with William Stafford.")

Whatever coherence, whatever thematic depth, there is within the body of Stafford's poetry has to be given its pattern by the critic (or the "analyst," if you will) to a much greater degree than is the case with most other poets. The problem is compounded by the complicated publishing history of Stafford's work. Nearly all of his published poems have appeared in magazines. Many, though not all, of them have subsequently been collected into books—some issued by small presses and some by his major publisher, Harper & Row. Because Stafford admits to having saved his best and most characteristic work for the Harper & Row volumes and because these are the volumes most readily available to readers, the present essay is based almost entirely upon those collections.[8] Finally, because of the unplanned, occasional nature of Stafford's poems, they will not be discussed in chronological order; instead, the poems will be presented here according to the thematic pattern that I see running through them.[9]

Generally speaking, William Stafford must be grouped with the other "optimistic" poets being studied in this volume—Richard Wilbur and Robert Penn Warren. If the dominant mood of American poetry from the fifties into the seventies is the pessimistic, even despairing one we find in the confessional writers and others, then these three poets are among the exceptions to the rule. As will soon be demonstrated, Stafford's poetic terrain is the village and the country; he believes in the small-town virtues and is even able to feel the presence of a vague sacredness within nature—most of which sets him apart from more pessimistic writers. And yet—although some readers have chosen to view him this way—Stafford is no Pollyanna; he is, in fact, considerably more doubting in his beliefs than is either Wilbur or Warren. Thus, the first stanza of "An Introduction to Some Poems," which opens the volume *Someday, Maybe,* turns out to be less surprising than it seems on first reading:

> Look: no one ever promised for sure
> that we would sing. We have decided
> to moan. In a strange dance that
> we don't understand till we do it, we
> have to carry on.[10]

Obviously Stafford is speaking less directly for himself than for what he perceives to be the dominant attitude of the poetic age; and yet this attitude must be recognized as a component of his own thinking as well.

During an interview conducted by Sanford Pinsker, Stafford indicated something of what might make him "moan" in some poems: "Loneliness is something you'll have plenty of without trying to induce it. You can count on it. As a matter of fact, you don't have to be a neurotic to discover that the world can be a frightening place."[11] This powerful sense of loneliness has two causes in Stafford's work: one is the hard fact of death, and the other is the absence of God. Among Stafford's best and most affecting poems are several that deal with the double kind of loss that results from an awareness both of death and of the passage of time—for example, "Stereopticon." The title of this poem refers to a double-lensed slide projector that allows one photograph to fade out while another is fading in. The title is not so specific in its usage; we are to understand simply that the act of looking at photographs of old scenes can reanimate those scenes in our minds:

> This can happen. They can bring the leaves back
> to the cottonwood trees, those great big rooms
> where our street—as long as summer—led
> to the river. From a rusty nail in the alley
> someone can die, but the street go on again.
>
> Hitler and others, those pipsqueak voices,
> can twitter from speakers. I can look back
> from hills beyond town, and every person
> and all the alleys, and even the buildings
> except the church be hidden in leaves.
>
> This can happen, my parents laughing
> because they have already won. And I can
> study and grow up and look back and call "Wait!"
> and run after their old green car
> and be lost again.[12]

The manipulation of time in this poem is very careful—it is the perspective of yesterday that reanimates things like "Hitler and others," while the perspective of today, knowledge of Hitler's ultimate defeat, robs them of fearful sting, reducing them to "those pipsqueak voices." Conversely, it is today's knowledge that makes the appearance of the speaker's parents doubly upsetting by projecting a more recent, fearful knowledge back upon the memory drawn from childhood: then they failed to see him because their eyes were on the road ahead; now they fail to see him because they are dead. In either case he is left behind, alone.

The second cause of the loneliness that Stafford finds to be so pervasive and frightening a force in the world derives from his religious beliefs. What matters most in this regard is not the fact that Stafford is a Christian, but the fact that he has been a pacifist for his entire life. During World War II he declared himself to be a conscientious objector and was incarcerated in work camps for four years. On the occasion when he and I met to finish the interview in this volume, Stafford handed me a pamphlet entitled "That Men May Live: Statement of

Purpose of the Fellowship of Reconciliation," with the words, "This explains pretty much what I believe." The organization was founded on a religious base, "with its roots in the ethic of love as found preeminently in Jesus Christ," but since has shifted to a more humanistic orientation, now welcoming the "community of Judaism" as well as those who simply "affirm their faith in man and in the unity and interdependence of the human race." In fact, it is not the religious dimension that is primary here; rather, the most important tenet of belief of this group (and, one has to assume, of William Stafford as well) is that found in the opening sentence of the pamphlet: "The Fellowship of Reconciliation is composed of men and women who recognize the essential unity of mankind and have joined together to explore the power of love and truth for resolving human conflict." The aim of all pacifist organizations is to find a positive solution to a pervasive negative threat within the world—that of war and death. It is especially important from the perspective of Stafford's poetry that the fellowship does not call upon God to intercede in the affairs of man, but upon mankind to change its own ways.

When Stafford speaks of God in his poems, as he does occasionally, the allusions are generally more convenient and predictable than suffused with a heartfelt belief. What is far more convincing than any of this are the many poems that express a sense of the absence of God, a longing for his presence—for example, "A Walk in the Country" (*STCBT,* 197–98). As is often the case in Stafford, this poem has a parablelike quality; that is, it tells a vague story—in which neither setting nor event is quite specific enough for solid, literal grounding—that seems intended primarily to deliver a generalized point. The opening stanza presents a kind of thesis by asking a question:

> To walk anywhere in the world, to live
> now, to speak, to breathe a harmless
> breath: what snowflake, even, may try
> today so calm a life,
> so mild a death?

The calm "walk"—metaphorical for "life"—is presented as a natural ideal, unfortunately thwarted somehow by factors of today. Most often in Stafford, such negative factors have to do with society, technological progress, the dangers of human conflict, but here the context is metaphysical, referring to the gradual loss of religious faith, the death of God. Thus, when the speaker of the poem goes out to walk in "the hollow night," he somehow is caused to carry the empty burden of moonlight:

> . . . a terrible thing had happened:
> the world, wide, unbearably bright,
> had leaped on me. I carried mountains.

Mountains are later identified metaphorically as "my fear and pain." Daylight, more comforting and cheerful than night, temporarily returns a semblance of faith to the speaker's world—"God had come back there / to carry the world again"—but knowledge of his loss remains ineradicable for the speaker, and the poem ends plaintively:

> Since then, while over the world
> the wind appeals events,
> and people contend like fools,
> like a stubborn tumbleweed I hold,
> hold where I live, and look into every face:
>
> *Oh friends, where can one find a partner*
> *for the long dance over the fields!*

By identifying his speaker with a rooted, a stationary tumbleweed—whose natural function ought to be to roam freely wherever the wind blows, "To walk anywhere in the world," to "dance over the fields"—Stafford is expressing the paralyzing effect that the speaker's loss of faith has had upon him. The religious hunger, the longing for "a partner" is a powerful, but all too often unrequited, desire in the modern world of Stafford's poems.

A poem with a similar message—though a somewhat different method—is "Late at Night." Here the action is concrete and specific rather than vaguely metaphorical, though an interpretation of the events is suggested at the end of the poem (which is quoted in its entirety).

> Falling separate into the dark
> the hailstone yelps of geese pattered
> through our roof; startled we listened.
>
> Those V's of direction swept by unseen
> so orderly that we paused. But then
> faltering back through their circle they came.
>
> Were they lost up there in the night?
> They always knew the way, we thought.
> You looked at me across the room:—
>
> We live in a terrible season.

(*STCBT*, 86)

The poem represents almost a twentieth-century reversal of William Cullen Bryant's "To a Waterfowl," in which the instinctive sense of direction possessed by a duck, which invariably leads it to its destination, is seen by the poet as proof of the existence of a guiding, paternalistic God:

> There is a Power whose care
> Teaches thy way along that pathless coast,—
> The desert and illimitable air,—
> Lone wandering, but not lost.

Stafford's poem, by contrast, suggests not just the death of God but also the failure of natural, instinctive processes—processes that one might expect would supply guidance (and thereby a measure of assurance and comfort) in a godless world. Furthermore, we must note that all this is an interpretation by Stafford and his speaker—migrating geese regularly break formation and circle in the process of landing for a rest. So uneasy is the twentieth-century sensibility portrayed in this poem, however, that it is apparently unable even to consider this explanation. The position of mankind generally in the modern world in Stafford's poems is probably best expressed by the title of one of his books—we are *Traveling Through the Dark,* alone and unguided, perpetually and ignorantly "In Medias Res" (as one section of that book is subtitled).

Nature serves many functions in Stafford's poetry, appears in many guises, some of which also go to show (like death, time, the absence of God) "that the world can be a frightening place." Stafford is always aware that nature has at its disposal forces far greater than any that man could summon—earthquakes, hurricanes, tornadoes, even so simple a thing as winter, which he often uses as a metaphor for the coming of death or for the death state itself.[13] Probably the best expression of this metaphor is to be found in the poem "Kinds of Winter," which tells a parablelike story of hunting:

> It was a big one. We followed it over
> the snow. Even if it made no mistakes, we
> would have it. That's what The World means—
> there are kinds of winter that you meet.
> And that big one had met us, its big winter.
>
> But there was a hill, and when we rounded
> it the tracks were gone. We had used up
> the daylight. The wind had come and
> emptied our trail, back of us, ahead of us.
> We looked at each other. Our winter had come.[14]

Winter in this poem represents the primal destructiveness Stafford always feels as a potential within nature.

However, it is also true that Stafford consistently locates whatever god or godliness may remain in the universe within nature, within the created world, within God's original physical manifestation of himself. The theology that results from this perception is not always a comforting one—as is evident in another poem, "Walking the Wilderness." Here, God is associated explicitly with nature and winter's destructiveness; Stafford speaks of "His / eye that freezes people, His zero breath / their death" (*STCBT*, 138). The poem concludes on lines that describe the ending to man's presumptuous "walk in the wilderness":

> Warm human representatives may vote and
> manage man; but last the blizzard will dignify
> the walker, the storm hack trees to cyclone
> groves, he catch the snow, his brave eye
> become command, the whole night howl against
> his ear, till found by dawn he
> reach out to God no trembling hand.

The lesson administered to man's pride here is extreme, the result not just of nature's wintry cold, but of God's volition as well, which uses nature's power to this destructive end. And that the poem is another following the parablelike pattern generalizes the lesson—this is what lies in store for all mankind.

All of which does seem to place William Stafford convincingly within the camp of the twentieth-century pessimistic poets, despite his failure to flirt poetically with mental illness, alcoholism, and suicide. But again a distinction must be made—the poets I am labeling pessimists (in this volume, primarily James Wright, though others—such as John Berryman and Robert Lowell—could be mentioned) tend to derive that attitude from contact with, immersion within, society and the city. As was said earlier in this essay, William Stafford is a poet, not of the city, but of the small town and the countryside. In fact, a case could be made for considering him to be a modern pastoralist, even though his work does not exhibit most of the conventional, external trappings of traditional pastoral poetry. Indeed, we would not expect to find in the work of any twentieth-century poet such elements as "The unhappy shepherd, the fair shepherdess, the wandering flock, the daisies and violets, the greensward dance, the flowery wreath and oaten pipe [that] represent a cluster of motifs which can be traced in the tradition from Theocritus to Pope and beyond into the nineteenth century,"[15] and none of these characteristics is found in Stafford's pastoral poetry—nor in that of Robert Frost, one of his few twentieth-century predecessors in the mode. One could argue that yet another of the traditional elements does appear in the work of both writers. I refer to the rural swain, who appears as farmer or roving handyman in Frost and as the Indian in Stafford. What is most centrally relevant to both poets, however, is none of this surface detailing but rather the moral vision that gives significance to the pastoral tradition.

At the heart of pastoralism is a contrast between two locales, two different ways of life. As John F. Lynen has pointed out, "Pastoral comes to life whenever the poet is able to adopt its special point of view—whenever he casts himself in the role of the country dweller and writes about life in terms of the contrast between the rural world, with its rustic scenery and naive, humble folk, and the great outer world of the powerful, the wealthy, and the sophisticated."[16] The moral distinction is implicit within this social or geographical contrast: "Behind all this, of course, lies the idea of innocence. Pastoral tends to merge with the myth of the golden age, because it assumes that in the rural world life retains its pristine purity. The swain, untainted by the evils of civilization, is a sort of ideal man, like the noble savage—not that he can escape from evil or is completely free from it himself, but he has not been exposed to the subtle corruptions of a complex society."[17]

Despite his preference for the natural world over the world of the city, William Stafford is not a traditional nature poet, one whose chief goal is to describe and venerate nature. He is instead a wisdom poet who uses the world of nature as a means to an end—he is in pursuit of a truth higher than those customarily perceived by ordinary men leading ordinary lives. Thus, in those poems mentioned above wherein nature's power to destroy is emphasized, the lesson is one of humility for mankind—in the face of tornadoes, earthquakes, erupting volcanoes, the numbing cold of winter, even the strongest of man's devices pale to a powerless insignificance. This truism is very much in line with the general pastoral vision, which locates delusion in man's works and cities, while the real, the elemental, the essential and true, is to be found in the less-peopled places of earth. Stafford is concerned to draw this basic contrast in many of his poems. In "Evening News," for example, he portrays the apparent power and significance of television—with its ability to show how "a war happens, / only an eighth of an inch thick"—as shallow and unimportant when contrasted to the quiet depth of nature:

In the yard I pray birds,
wind, unscheduled grass,

that they please help to make
everything go deep again.

                                                    (*STCBT,* 183–84)

An apparent irony in the work of so prolific a poet as Stafford is his
association of a shallow volubility, talkiness, with society and of a profound silence or carefully measured speech with nature. It is possible
to trace several stages in this subtheme or motif, three of them especially relevant here. The poem "Representing Far Places" (*STCBT,*
96–97) is actually concerned with the empty talkiness of society, although its first stanza dwells entirely on the silence of nature, describing the actions of fish "In the canoe wilderness":

Up through water at the dip of a falling leaf
to the sky's drop of light or the smell of another star
fish in the lake leap arcs of realization,
hard fins prying out from the dark below.

By contrast to this, the second stanza shows the generic Stafford protagonist at a party, wisely struck dumb amid the hubbub:

Often in society when the talk turns witty
you think of that place, and can't polarize at all:
it would be a kind of treason. The land fans in your head
canyon by canyon; steep roads diverge.
Representing far places you stand in the room,
all that you know merely a weight in the weather.

Although this nature-oriented man may look like a fool when keeping
such witty, dialectical company, the familiar prejudices of pastoralism
make clear that we are meant to see him (however difficult this may be)
as a wise man surrounded by fools.[18]
   What truly meaningful verbal communication might be is revealed
in another poem contrasting the social and pastoral realms. At first
glance, the title—"I Was in the City All Day"—appears irrelevant to
the poem itself. Stafford's method, however, is one of stark contrast;
the title shows how a day can be wasted, while the poem itself tells
how time might best be spent:

Into the desert, trading people for horses,
the leader rode toward a responsible act:
the having one person at the last campfire,
telling just the next thing to that one person,
with all around only the waiting night waiting,

in the shadows horses eating wild hay—
and then the last word without distraction,
one meaning like a bird slipping out into the dark.

(STCBT, 79)

Language here is significant, instructional—wisdom is being passed on
to a lone young acolyte by a knowledgeable old man—a Sam Fathers
sort of figure.

At a further extreme from the empty noise of society is the seeming
silence of nature itself, which embodies what may be the greatest
wisdom of all. In "From the Gradual Grass," Stafford again begins with
the emptiness, the hollow sound and fury, found in so much of society's noise (the effect of which is only to draw attention to itself) and
moves to the more resonant sounds of nature:

Imagine a voice calling,
"There is a voice now calling,"
or maybe a blasting cry:
"Walls are falling!"
as it makes walls be falling.

Then from the gradual grass,
too serious to be only noise—
whatever it is grass makes,
making words, a voice:
"Destruction is ending; this voice

"Is promising quiet: silence
by lasting forever grows to sound
endlessly from the world's end
promising, calling."
Imagine. *That voice is calling.*

(STCBT, 98)

Such a "sound" is always an inherent possibility, Stafford suggests, for
those with enough imagination to listen beyond the world's insistent
cacophony. The person who would hear this call, this promise, has to
seek it actively by pushing first beyond noise to silence and then beyond silence to an actually unheard, but convincingly imagined,
wisdom.

Of course it is likely to be the poet—whose primary tool of trade is
the imagination, which creates wise sound from silence—who can
best make such wonders available to the rest of us. And there is a poet
at the heart of Stafford's poems, most of which are spoken from the
first-person point of view by a character or characters who seem to

resemble closely the poet himself. It would be a naive mistake, however, to assume that this speaking character *is* William Stafford, that all details of its life belong to Stafford's as well, that all of his opinions are also Stafford's. In fact, among these details, facts, and opinions, there are subtle shifts and inconsistencies, leading one to conclude that Stafford, in order to achieve his larger goals, is willing to sacrifice a purely surface consistency. Stafford has himself commented on this procedure: "I feel like such an unreliable character in a poem that I can say something . . . and then drop it, just leave it, because I don't mean that for the rest of my life at all, I just mean that's a remark to make in order to get along to the next remark."[19] The conclusion reached by Jonathan Holden on this issue is both accurate and reasonable: "Generally, in a Stafford poem biographical content is placed wholly in the service of imagination, as material for fiction."[20]

It is curious that statements such as these carry us virtually to the borderline between an essentially traditional poetry—in which the poet's ultimate commitment is to telling the truth, in small matters as in large—and that minority movement known as postmodernism—where the spirits of play and parody are preeminent and in which the poet's commitment is to the logic of the poem's world rather than to the external truth of the world that surrounds him. Rightly understood, the term *postmodernism* describes, not a historical literary age, but this still rather specialized approach to the possibilities of literature. Despite his basic devotion to telling what he perceives as the truth, William Stafford does also have an interest in the possibilities of a freer kind of invention, wherein poetry makes its own rules and its own truth. In a short series of aphorisms collected under the title "Writing and Literature: Some Opinions" in *Writing the Australian Crawl*, Stafford says, laying the groundwork for this spirit in his poetry: "Literature is not a picture of life, but is a separate experience with its own kind of flow and enchantment."[21] Going even farther in a recent interview ("Interview with William Stafford"), Stafford chose to compare himself to John Ashbery—postmodernist par excellence—rather than to more sincere kinds of poets: "I feel a lot more harmony with someone like Ashbery and his assumptions about poetry . . . than I do with many other poets: . . . those people who seem to feel that they are corraling ultimate truth. . . . I think poetry is ultimately playful, no matter what anyone says. And Ashbery is explicit about this."[22]

Such a statement should not be applied too literally to Stafford's poetry. His words accurately indicate, however, the rich vein of playfulness that can occasionally be found in his work. His newest book, *A Glass Face in the Rain*, provides several examples. In "We Interrupt to Bring You," for instance, the speaker leaves his television set to go to

the bathroom; while he is away, a meteor is discovered speeding towards earth, everyone is evacuated into

> ... those new domes on the ocean
> floor ... and the domes
> collapse, and I'm the only one left.

(GFR, 74)

The speaker returns to his TV, and is mildly unhappy because he, the
last man on earth, cannot find his favorite show, *Perry Mason.* Another
poem, "Incident," tells a similarly apocalyptic, fanciful story:

> They had this cloud they kept like a zeppelin
> tethered to a smokestack, and you couldn't see it
> but it sent out these strange little rays
> and after a while you felt funny. They had this
> man with a box. He pointed it at
> the zeppelin and it said, "Jesus!" The man
> hurried farther away and called out,
> "Hear ye, hear ye!" Then they coaxed
> the zeppelin down into the smokestack
> and they said, "We won't do that any more."
> For a long time the box kept shaking its head,
> but it finally said, "Ok, forget it." But, quietly,
> to us, it whispered, "Let's get out of here."

(GFR, 67)

As is so often the case, Stafford invites his reader to find sequestered
meanings by casting his statement in the form of a parable or an alle-
gory. In this case the poem obviously expresses further disenchant-
ment with the age of industrialism and technology. It doesn't matter
how much antipollution equipment a factory installs, the speaker
seems to be saying; the situation is still going to be dangerous to my
health. In contrast to this rather solemn message, the story the poem
tells is amusing. Stafford is toying with the tools of his trade in an
almost mock-heroic manner, and the ultimate effect is enticingly close
to self-parody.

Such playfulness is certainly a component of Stafford's work—and
yet we must not lose sight of the fact that he is a serious poet committed to telling his version of the truth. In line with this, he is more
interested in achieving an overall authenticity of vision than he is in
harmonizing the specific details presented in separate poems. Sincerity
(a surface truthfulness) is a poem-by-poem matter in Stafford's work—
each individual poem is honest unto itself and internally consistent,

but similar poems placed side by side may well reveal contradictory details. For example, amid several poems in which Stafford's speaking character talks of his father as a kind and gentle man, there are a few poems that portray him as cold, indifferent, cruel. We must recognize that different poems may demand different fathers, just as they demand slightly different versions of the same basic central character.

It is, in fact, this central, basic character, this more or less singular speaking voice, that lends the greatest unity to Stafford's poems when they are studied as a whole. It is important that we investigate this character in order to understand something of his personality, his way of living and thinking in the world. We might begin with what he seems to have learned from his parents, proceed to a consideration of the kind of faith that seems to sustain him, and then investigate how, in several poems about poetry, he says he wants to embody this faith in verse.

Just as Stafford has accounted for his own early commitment to poetry by pointing to his parents and the storytelling atmosphere they created for him as a child ("Interview with William Stafford"), so the speaking character in the poems often points to *his* parents to illustrate the attitudes and character traits that have guided and determined his life. To the mother figure of these poems is ascribed the source of the pastoral desire to be separate from the dominant aims and values of the larger society—as in "Our Kind," which provides a wry definition of success:

> Our mother knew our worth—
> not much. To her, success
> was not being noticed at all.

> *(GFR,* 69)

The pastoral attitude is especially evident in the ironic conclusion of the poem:

> She sent us forth equipped
> for our kind of world, a world of
> our betters, in a nation so strong
> its greatest claim is no boast,
> its leaders telling us all, "Be proud"—

> But over their shoulders, God and
> our mother, signaling: "Ridiculous."

The speaker prefers his apparently lowly position because it is morally superior—humility may not walk off with the prize today, but it will be triumphant in eternity. Even in their battle against the War Department, the most effective technique available to the pacifists is patience, as the speaker is advised in "My Mother Was a Soldier":

> Tapping on my wrist, she talked: "Patience
> is the doctor; it says try; it says
> they think we're nice, we quiet ones, we die
> so well: that's how we win, imagining things
> before they happen." "No harm in being quiet,"
>
> My mother said: "that's the sound that finally wins."
>
> (*GFR,* 75)

The gaze of the mother in Stafford's poems is from a pastoral world towards society; she is defined in terms of her power of opposition. The father, contrastingly, turns his eyes towards the more mysterious, elusive world of nature, where the stories are. It is from him that the figure of the poet learns to look into things—and learns to tell his own stories. The poem "Listening" defines the character of the father well:

> My father could hear a little animal step,
> or a moth in the dark against the screen,
> and every far sound called the listening out
> into places where the rest of us had never been.
>
> More spoke to him from the soft wild night
> than came to our porch for us on the wind;
> we would watch him look up and his face go keen
> till the walls of the world flared, widened.
>
> My father heard so much that we still stand
> inviting the quiet by turning the face,
> waiting for a time when something in the night
> will touch us too from that other place.
>
> (*STCBT,* 33)

The father is, in fact, a kind of nature mystic who listens, even beyond hearing, not to the other world of religion but to something implicit within this world, nature. From him the son learns a desire to hear the same sounds, see the same signs, and this desire becomes the major quest enunciated in Stafford's poems. In "A Thanksgiving for My Father," the son indicates the strength of this inheritance by speaking his obligation almost as a lament:

> "Oh father, why
> did you ever set your son such being!

Your life was a miracle
and could build out of shadows
anything: your restless thought
has made the world haunted.

(*STCBT,* 135)

The role of the father in Stafford's poems has been accurately described by George S. Lensing and Ronald Moran, who see him as "the
high priest of the wilderness. Like Sam Fathers to Isaac McCaslin or
Natty Bumppo to the neophytes of the frontier, Stafford's father is initiator and instructor to the son, not only in relation to the wilderness
itself, but in the moral values which inhere within it. Again like Fathers and Leatherstocking, he is imbued with certain mystical, almost
superhuman, powers."[23] From the mother in these poems comes an
attitude of opposition to the false values of society, a tough pacifism;
from the father comes a sense of the mystery inherent in nature, a love
for the stories that might unlock it. Given the importance of narrative
and storytelling in these poems, it appears that most of the poetry
comes from the father.[24]

There is, however, one important area in which the father's approach
to and view of the world is significantly different from that of the
speaker. The attention of the father is so concentrated upon particulars
that he often fails to perceive the larger flow of reality. As the poem
"Parentage" explains, this makes him uneasy, an insecure and uncomfortable citizen of the world:

My father didn't really belong in history.
He kept looking over his shoulder at some mistake.
He was a stranger to me, for I belong.

There never was a particular he couldn't understand,
but there were too many in too long a row,
and like many another he was overwhelmed.

(*STCBT,* 67)

Essentially, the father attempts to know and understand the world by
trying to control it, subject it to his own categorizing mind. Underlying
such a method is an inevitable attitude of competition, opposition—
the father sets himself against the continuum of history and is
eventually overwhelmed by the volume of its never-ending flow. Rather
than frustrate himself in this way, Stafford's poet chooses instead to
become part of the world's process, its being and flow. At the end of
"Parentage," he describes what this means:

I want to be as afraid as the teeth are big,
I want to be as dumb as the wise are wrong:
I'd just as soon be pushed by events to where I belong.

The ultimate source of wisdom for any pastoral poet is of course
nature, the earth itself, and at the end of another poem, "In Response to
a Question," Stafford attributes this go-with-the-flow method for gain-
ing wisdom to the earth (the unstated question of the title is, "What
does the earth say?"):

                                        . . . join
the sparrow on the lawn, and row that easy
way, the rage without met by the wings
within that guide you anywhere the wind blows.

Listening, I think that's what the earth says.

                                        (STCBT, 76)

What has just been defined is essentially the faith of the poet in
William Stafford's poems. He may not know just where he is going or
what he will find when he gets there, but he does know how to travel
down the path he thinks will lead him there. In the many ars poeticas
that Stafford has written over the years, poetry is similarly defined, not
as an end result, a goal or product, but as a process, an ongoing method
that itself ought inevitably to lead to—or toward—the truth sought by
this wisdom poet. In the first stanza of "With My Crowbar Key," for
example, Stafford gives a basic definition of his method:

I do tricks in order to know:
careless I dance,
then turn to see
the mark to turn God left for me.

                                        (STCBT, 65)

What is described here is quite similar to the free-associative system
discussed at the beginning of this chapter. Stafford insists that he does
not know his thematic destination when he begins a poem. Rather, he
allows some more instinctive or unconscious process to guide him and
has faith that, once the poem is finished, he will be able to look back
and see how he got where he was going; the guideposts appear after the
journey, not before.

The image implicit in "With My Crowbar Key" is of a path down
which the poet dances; in "An Introduction to Some Poems" (a more
extensive and suggestive poem on the same topic), the image is of a

"line" that holds seemingly disparate things together. The final four stanzas constitute what is probably Stafford's most crucial poetic statement on his own art; he speaks for poets generally, using the first-person plural:

> Just as in sleep you have to dream
> the exact dream to round out your life,
> so we have to live that dream into stories
> and hold them close at you, close at the
> edge we share, to be right.
>
> We find it an awful thing to meet people,
> serious or not, who have turned into vacant
> effective people, so far lost that they
> won't believe their own feelings
> enough to follow them out. '
>
> The authentic is a line from one thing
> along to the next; it interests us.
> Strangely, it relates to what works,
> but is not quite the same. It never
> swerves for revenge,
>
> Or profit, or fame: it holds
> together something more than the world,
> this line. And we are your wavery
> efforts at following it. Are you coming?
> Good: now it is time.
>
> (*STCBT,* 201)

Because of its surface discursiveness, the poem is itself an interesting example of the doctrine enunciated within it. The "authentic"—metaphorically described as the "line" that unites seemingly different things—is here possessed in common by dreams, by unlocked feelings, and by poems. Poetry as a process is similar to these other things because it functions as they do—each allows entry to the subconscious portion of the mind, where the authentic, untrammeled personality (the glue that holds together all that man is and does) can be found. The key that opens this level is that free-associative process central to both dreams (in the area of the personal) and poems (in the area of art).

Implicit within these poems on the poet's faith and on his methods as a writer is the idea of a path, a road, a direction; movement; by extension a quest or a searching.[25] All these things in their turn imply an end point or goal; because he is a wisdom poet, one of the things that Stafford is pursuing in his poetry is some ultimate sense of truth, some kind of final knowledge. However, Stafford also has serious doubts about the adequacy of human knowledge. He has expressed this many times, but most succinctly in the essay "Some Arguments against Good Diction": "I saw inscribed in gold on a pillar in the Library of Congress this saying: 'The inquiry, knowledge and belief of truth is the sovereign good of human nature.' To me, such a saying is hollow; I see it as demonstrating man's pathetic infatuation with an apparent power that is essentially just a redundancy. The highest we know is high for us, but its communication is an interior, not an absolute, phenomenon. And I cringe to realize that my own saying of my kind of truth is hazardous at best."[26] Despite this reservation, it is a fact that Stafford is in pursuit of truth in his poetry—probably not, however, a human truth. The other goal to his quest is for something we may label "home"—a multifaceted concept within the world of Stafford's poetry.

The ordinary, everyday sense of a home—involving a settled place to live and a family, with plants and pets perhaps included—appears in Stafford's poetry, not as something quested for, but as something already achieved, taken for granted. The "home" for which his character searches is a much vaguer, more spiritual entity, something that can be located, in differing manifestations, in both the past and the future. In order to distinguish these adequately, we must first carry a bit farther the pastoral distinction made above between the world of the city and the world of the countryside. The latter of these two landscapes actually embodies, not just one, but two types of locales—the specifically pastoral one combining small town and farm, and the further, less pastoral, and more extreme one of the wilderness. All three places exist on a scale ranging from the relatively decadent, distant-from-God city to the most unsullied, closest-to-God wilderness. The gardenlike middle range is a kind of golden mean, participating in the advantages of both extremes, but avoiding their dangers.

One of the homes for which Stafford's character searches is located in the past, on the farms and in the small towns of Stafford's own youth. Stafford—the closest thing to a folksy poet that serious contemporary literature has to offer—uses a great many of his poems, most of them occasional in nature, to celebrate the people and scenes, the events and values, of rural America. Because such material does not fit into the more substantial, more mythic pattern we are tracing, I do not intend to deal with it here in any detail.[27] It is the other search for "home," the one that carries Stafford's character towards the wilderness and into the future, that is of greater interest.[28] In "The Gift," Stafford defines this rather specialized concept of "home" as he applies it to the poet. The poem begins, "The writer's home he salvages from little pieces / along the roads" (*STCBT*, 164) and ends with these words of prophecy and exhortation, spoken by the imagined figure of the poet:

> . . . "Some day, tame (therefore lost) men, the wild
> will come over the highest wall, waving
> its banner voice, beating its gifted fist:
> *Begin again, you tame ones; listen—the roads are your home again.*"

Again we see the image of the road, the path, the line—it is the lot of the true poet to be homeless; his "home" is on the road, on which he travels towards his destiny and the world's. (In "Vocation," another ars poetica, the poet's calling is defined this way: "Your job is to find what the world is trying to be"—*STCBT,* 107.) This road leads the poet ever westward, always away from the cities, through the small towns and across the farms, toward and into the wilderness.

Stafford attaches symbolic or quasi-symbolic meanings to two of the four compass directions. In the north is located cold, harshness, winter, death, perhaps God; in the west is located nature, the pastoral world, eventually the wilderness. In fact, in titling his first volume of poetry *West of Your City,* Stafford was indicating his commitment to moving in this direction. The introductory poem, "Midwest," is an attempt to define what the west means, what it promises to one who would travel there:

> Cocked in that land tactile as leaves
> wild things wait crouched in those valleys
> west of your city outside your lives
> in the ultimate wind, the whole land's wave.
> Come west and see; touch these leaves.
>
> (*STCBT,* 29)

The last line, of course, is the book's invitation to the reader; "these leaves" are the pages that follow. It is in the West, away from the man-made landscape of the city and all its consequent delusions, that a person can confront a greater reality, a more fundamental level of experience. Even there, however, exist delusions to be avoided. Stafford is a relentless dualizer; having divided the world into city and country, having divided the country (preferable to the city) into small town/farm and wilderness, he then proceeds to divide the wilderness (ultimately more authentic than either town or farm) into its surface and its depths. This may be seen happening in many poems, but nowhere more tellingly than in "Bi-Focal," another peom from *West of Your City:*

Sometimes up out of this land
a legend begins to move.
Is it a coming near
of something under love?

Love is of the earth only,
the surface, a map of roads
leading wherever go miles
or little bushes nod.

Not so the legend under,
fixed, inexorable,
deep as the darkest mine
the thick rocks won't tell.

As fire burns the leaf
and out of the green appears
the vein in the center line
and the legend veins under there,

So, the world happens twice—
once what we see it as;
second it legends itself
deep, the way it is.

                                                      (*STCBT,* 48)

What Stafford is ultimately searching for is this hidden "legend,"
which can be found only beyond all roads, lines, and paths—we note
that in the image of the leaf, the legend is, not the linelike vein that
appears through fire, but something further, which "veins" even "under there."[29]

In a poem entitled "Earth Dweller"—appropriately placed in the
book *Allegiances*—Stafford gives a clear indication of where he directs
his faith, where he expects sacredness to be found. The first stanza
praises the pastoral life—working on the land and the land itself. At
the beginning, "all the clods at once become / precious," and at the end
the world of the farm becomes sacred:

    . . . somewhere inside, the clods are
vaulted mansions, lines through the barn sing
for the saints forever, the shed and windmill
rear so glorious the sun shudders like a gong.

                                                      (*STCBT,* 196)

In the second and final stanza Stafford generalizes from this to a sense
of earth worship:

Now I know why people worship, carry around
magic emblems, wake up talking dreams
they teach to their children: the world speaks.
The world speaks everything to us.
It is our only friend.

The more-than-human truth that Stafford seeks is essentially a spiritual truth—located, however, not in church, but on the land.[30] It is another example of that nature mysticism so prevalent in the poetry of America—wherein the profound religious sense that our earliest settlers brought with them from the Old World combines with a sense of the mystery of the wilderness, that great empty continent out there, to produce a sense of the mystic truths resident in the far reaches of nature.

Which is why, ultimately, Stafford's poet has to leave the road behind him, wander from the path, venture away from all visible lines onto the one that legends itself beneath the surface, unseen. In William Faulkner's "The Bear," the young acolyte Ike McCaslin wishes to have a glimpse of the mythical beast in the forest. His early forays end in failure. Then Sam Fathers, figure of the priest, instructs Ike that he must leave behind him all man-made implements that would aid in his search—compass, watch, gun—and rely instead on faith. Ike, we may say, must leave all roads behind if he is to attain the mystical experience he seeks. This is precisely the requirement that William Stafford discovers must be met by the figure of the questing poet, the truth seeker, in his poetry. Stafford has many poems in which the quest is the actual subject of the poem, and always the lesson is the same—"finally in every canyon the road ends. / Above that—storms of stone," as he states it in "The Research Team in the Mountains" (*STCBT*, 68). It is only at this point, where the road ends, that the actual quest can finally begin. The method to be followed is described in an early poem, "Watching the Jet Planes Dive" from *West of Your City*, where Stafford rejects the ways of modern man as superficial, guaranteed to achieve only ignoble ends; if we are to attain the authentic, rather than travel in planes and cars, "We must go back and find a trail on the ground / back of the forest and mountain on the slow land" (*STCBT*, 44). The poem concludes with these lines:

We must find something forgotten by everyone alive,
and make some fabulous gesture when the sun goes down
as they do by custom in little Mexico towns
where they crawl for some ritual up a rocky steep.
The jet planes dive; we must travel on our knees.

As the mention of customs in "little Mexico towns" makes clear, Stafford looks for a paradigm of the kind of searching he advocates, not in contemporary society, but in earlier, more primitive societies, where the people were closer to and therefore more in touch with nature and the land. Most often he locates these qualities in the society of the American Indians: "I've always liked their way of life, living in the woods, close to the animals. And the sense of freedom—I like a lot of space and plenty of chance to let the impulses I have be predominant over impulses imposed on me. Maybe that's a definition of freedom. I take a step when I want to, not when the escalator tells me to. I'd like to be able to go to the edge of town and just keep going, the way the Indians did" ("Interview with William Stafford"). In many of his poems Stafford uses the Indian as a kind of paradigm for the man who is fully in touch with his environment, for reasons noticed by Robert Coles: "The sense of continuity, the faith in the ways of nature and at least a certain kind of man (themselves) which Indians unselfconsciously have as a psychological possession and as elements in their cultural tradition."[31] William Stafford commits himself imaginatively to the Indian way of life in a great many poems, perhaps most fundamentally in "Returned to Say," where he envisions joining a young chief on what seems a mystical quest. Much of the language of the poem echoes statements on this topic we have already looked at.

> When I face north a lost Cree
> on some new shore puts a moccasin down,
> rock in the light and noon for seeing,
> he in a hurry and I beside him.
>
> It will be a long trip; he will be a new chief;
> we have drunk new water from an unnamed stream;
> under little dark trees he is to find a path
> we both must travel because we have met.
>
> . . . .
> We will mean what he does. Back of this page
> the path turns north. We are looking for a sign.
> Our moccasins do not mark the ground.

(STCBT, 102–3)

The journey begins with a path that eventually disappears, leaving them to look "for a sign" on unmarked ground. We might speculate that when "the path turns north," it is turning from west; north is the ultimate direction in Stafford, the final direction, and leads into even more wild, more authentic territory than does west, leading at the end, in fact, both to death and to God.

The mystical thing sought for in Stafford's poetry may be meta-physical or spiritual, but it is not to be found in airy realms of ethere-ality. The quest for it carries Stafford's poet to the most basic, most physical, most elemental, even the most primitive realms. It is never quite attained in the poetry; the spiritual in Stafford's poems—as in those of the other "optimists" examined in this book, Richard Wilbur and Robert Penn Warren—is ultimately ungraspable by physical man within a material world. But he can gain glimpses of it, glimpses that foster and reinforce his faith that it does in fact exist and may some day be reached. In Stafford, such glimpses are gained in three different ways, each progressively less physical and more spiritual than the one before it—through touch, through sound, and somehow through the air. There is, of course, something frustratingly—but inherently, un-avoidably—nebulous about a quest for a goal that can only be sensed, never reached. Stafford has, however, written several poems in which his speaker's goal is at least vaguely defined. "How to Get Back," a recent poem, appears in *A Glass Face in the Rain*. The first stanza describes the possibility of penetrating beyond time to a still moment of eternity:

> By believing, you can get there—that edge
> the light-years leave behind, where no one
> living today survives. You can get there
> where the lake turns to stone and your boat
> rocks, once, then hangs tilted a long time:
> in that instant you don't want to leave,
> where talk finds truth, slides near
> and away; where music holds its moment
> forever, and then forever again.
>
> (*GFR*, 29)

What Stafford describes is a frozen instant within time, which seems to open onto eternity; though the context is not specifically religious, the description resembles accounts of moments in which mystical union was achieved by such writers as St. Teresa and St. John of the Cross. The second, and concluding, stanza of Stafford's poem closes the opening to eternity and comments upon the process:

> You are only a wandering dot that fails—
> that has already failed, but you can get
> there. And you can come back—the boat
> moves; talk turns ordinary; music
> is hunting its moment again.
> Around you people don't know how you

and themselves and the whole world
hover in belief. They've never been gone.

Again we see the dualistic view, probably based on the pastoral contrast. Although such perceptions are universally available, Stafford believes, most people in the modern world do not achieve them—the
falseness of their lives isolates them from such profundity.

While commenting upon the importance of nature imagery in his
poetry during an interview, Stafford alluded to a myth that emphasizes
the importance of touching, of establishing physical contact with elemental reality: "nature . . . is important to me. I think about the Greek
hero, Antaeus—every time he touched the earth he got stronger. For
me, this myth is part of my life—to touch something outside, to have
things in your poetry, is a healthy move. The world can save you, it can
make you strong. This . . . is a faith I live by" ("Interview with William
Stafford"). The language used, with its talk of faith and hints of salvation, does seem to promise that the avenue of touching the physical
world will lead somehow to a further world, a more than physical
world. For those specific connotations we will have to wait, however;
although what is ultimately felt in the poems about "touching" does
seem to hint at something more essential than mere matter, the hints
are teasingly vague. In "Touches," for example, the speaker feels the
wall of a real cave and imagines a more elemental one, closer to the
essence and source:

> You put a hand out in the dark of a cave and
> the wall waits for your fingers. Cold, that stone
> tells you all of the years that passed without knowing.
> You think of caves held in the earth, no mouth,
> no light. Down there the years have lost their way.
> Under your hand it all steadies,
> is the world under your hand.

(STCBT, 223)

"In the Deep Channel," an earlier poem, is even more indirect. It tells
of "Setting a trotline after sundown" to catch a "secret-headed channel
cat"; in the morning:

> We would come at daylight and find the line sag,
> the fishbelly gleam and the rush on the tether:
> to feel the swerve and the deep current
> which tugged at the tree roots below the river.

(STCBT, 31)

Here the speaker's sense of touch puts him in contact with a tension caused by movement, the current of the river that is pulling on the dead weight of the fish. Again, physical reality is as far as the poem reaches, but something seems alive, as though the speaker's hand felt the motion of nature's lifeblood.

While what we touch can be perceived in most cases by four senses—those of touch, sight, smell, and taste—sound is perceived only through the sense of hearing. It is for this reason that the "other" that is present in Stafford's poems based on sound seems a more spiritual "other" than that seen above in poems relying on touch. However, the sound in "A Sound from the Earth" still has only a physical origin:

> Somewhere, I think in Dakota,
> they found the leg bones—just the
> big leg bones—of several hundred
> buffalo, in a gravel pit.
>
> Near there, a hole in a cliff
> has been hollowed so that
> the prevailing wind
> thrums a note so low and persistent
> that bowls of water placed in that
> cave will tremble to foam.
>
> (*STCBT,* 172)

Nevertheless, there is an implication that this hole somehow picks up the sound of mourning the earth makes over the death of the buffalo. Such a reading is reinforced by the rest of the poem, where "The grand-father of Crazy Horse" makes a sound in mourning for his grandson that in turn makes

> . . . that thin Agency soup that they
> put before him tremble. The whole
> earthen bowl churned into foam.

In other poems a sound emanates from earth that seems to have a more distinctly mystical or spiritual source. In "Tornado," for example, Stafford describes the destructive passage of a storm through a town, and concludes with this observation:

> We weren't left religion exactly (the church
> was ecumenical bricks), but a certain tall element:
> a pulse beat still in the stilled rock
> and in the buried sound along the buried mouth of the creek.
>
> (*STCBT,* 71)

The "pulse" emanates from silent sources and is also loosely associated with religion; at the least it would seem to represent the spirit of power within nature, which we earlier saw manifested as winter. The poem "Believer" is both a subtle consideration of various levels of truth and a cunning testament of faith. In the first and third stanzas, Stafford suggests that even lies and tall tales tell a certain kind of truth:

> A horse could gallop over our bridge that minnows
> used for shade, but our dog trotting would splinter
> that bridge—"Look down," my father said, and there
> went Buster to break that bridge, but I called him back
> that day:—whatever they ask me to believe, "And
>   furthermore," I say.
> . . . .
> And scared as I am with my blood full of sharks, I lie
> in the dark and believe that whistle our dog's ears could hear
> but no one else heard—it skewers my dream; and in crystals
> finer than frost I trace and accept all of the ways
> to know:—they tell me a lie; I don't say "But"—
>   there are ways for a lie to be so.
>
>   (*STCBT,* 122)

Stafford is essentially a narrative poet, though most of his important poems also function almost as parables, verging on homily. He clearly believes that the most important truths are best communicated through stories, narratives. At the level of literal fact, these may seldom be "true"—but at a higher, more illustrative, analogical, even allegorical or symbolic level, they are likely to be very true. This is why Stafford called his collected volume of poems *Stories That Could Be True;* it also clarifies why he has explained the authenticity of the material in his Indian poems in this way: "Well, it's authentic, but I make it up. In other words, it is authentic because I am an Indian, I have that Indian feeling, and not because I read it in some book" ("Interview with William Stafford"). If the spirit is authentic, then the story will be true whether the facts are right or not.

In the above stanzas from "Believer," then, Stafford is not so much saying he believes in the literal truth of everything he is told, but that there is a deeper level to every story, a level where the spirit of the story may always be said to be true. The "whistle our dog's ears could hear / but no one else heard" thus functions as an image for this deeper, this less easily seen, narrative level. The poem itself goes suddenly deeper in its fourth and concluding stanza, the meaning of which is structured upon the image of sound:

You don't hear me yell to test the quiet or try to shake
the wall, for I understand that the wrong sound weakens
what no sound could ever save, and I am the one
to live by the hum that shivers till the world can sing:—
May my voice hover and wait for fate,
    when the right note shakes everything.

                                      (*STCBT,* 123)

The aggressive sounds of the first two lines go against the nature of things, wherein an ultimate harmony is both desired and forthcoming. The language and imagery here associate that "song" and "note" with the millennium, when all things will hum in concert. The connotations of these lines seem distinctly religious. Meanwhile, "the hum that shivers" corresponds to the sounds the speaker now hears, the truthful notes residing in the "lies" he is told, the harmonic lyricism of the stories he himself tells in poems.

We now come to the third of three realms in which Stafford's quest for the absolute, the elemental, the spiritual seems to find its goal. And in line with the progression we have been following, this realm is the one in which the balance between physical and spiritual is most heavily dominated by the spiritual. In the realm of touch, the images carrying mysterious connotations are the most certainly corporeal, available to as many as four of our physical senses. In the realm of sound, those images are available to only one of our senses—though often the connotative sounds themselves are located by Stafford in convincingly physical places—stone, mountains, water. In poems relying upon the realm of air for their spiritual suggestion, the appeal is again to one sense—that of feeling, a more vague version of the sense of touch. Even more uncertain than the sensing of such images is their source. In the poem "Things That Happen" (*STCBT,* 177–78), Stafford begins by talking about the anticipation of "great events," when an average person might say to himself, "A great event is coming, bow down." The speaker, again a "believer," differentiates himself: "And I, always looking for something anyway, / always bow down." He then proceeds to narrate one such great event—not the arrival of a president, a pope, or Halley's comet, but something that

    . . . turned an unseen corner
and came near, near, sounding before it
something the opposite from a leper's bell.

The speaker and a companion are hiking in the mountains when "one little puff of air touched us, / hardly felt at all." The final two stanzas consist of a comment on this event:

That was the greatest event that day;
it righted all wrong.
I remember it, the way the dust moved there.
Something had come out of the ground
and moved calmly along.

No one was ahead of us, no one
in all that moon-like land.
Oh, I thought, how hard the world has tried
with its wind, its miles, its blundering
stumbling days, again and again, to find my hand.

This seeking world, of course, is not the everyday surface world in which we all live, but the same world that, in "Bi-Focal," is said to "legend" itself "deep, the way it is"; it is the world that, in "Earth Dweller," is said to speak "everything to us. / It is our only friend." Despite this distinction, this first puff of air definitely originates in the earth, comes "out of the ground"; its spiritual connotations are thus no stronger than those of the sounds thought to emanate from rocks or the strange vibrations with which a river current pulls on a fishing line.

Because the similar event that takes place in the poem "Space Country" does not originate with the earth, but comes instead from "out there" somewhere, its effect is more ethereal, its implications more spiritual. In fact, this event is not just a perturbation of the air, but also involves a change in light:

As usual the highest birds first
caught it, a slow roll even the air
hardly felt; then the thick gold haze
that many filters of eyes found
fell deep in the desert country. Wells filled
and rocks—pooled in their own shadows—
lay at ease. People did not know
why they stood up and walked, and
waited by windows or doors, or leaned
by fences to look at far scenes.
The surface of all weathered wood relaxed;
even gravel and cactus appeared soft.

The world had passed something in space
and was alone again. Sunset came on.
People lay down, and the birds forgot
as they sleepily clucked and slept, close
on boughs, as well hidden as could be
in the air again clear, sharp, and cold.

(*STCBT*, 181–82)

The source of this event is left purposefully vague—indeed, it really does not matter exactly what has happened—the lie is both more interesting and more important than the truth. There was a moment of magic; something sacred came our way; somehow the world once again reached out to try and touch Stafford's speaker.

Stafford's goal in all of his poems is ultimately to achieve a sense of union with something absolute. In his cagey way, he will not define this something as being explicitly either spiritual or religious, nor does he refer to God when he is most serious in his quest. As I have said before, God usually appears in Stafford's poems at moments of convenience, times when God is what nearly anyone would rhetorically allude to. And yet the union that Stafford seeks sounds a lot like the sense of union with the godhead sought by mystics in more specifically religious texts and traditions. In the poem "Uncle George," Stafford is concerned once again to define life on a farm—now abandoned and falling to ruin—but in the midst of this he also defines the ultimate goal his questing poet figure seems to have as he journeys through the world:

> . . . Trapper
> of warm sight, I plow and belong, send breath
> to be part of the day, and where it arrives
> I spend on and on, fainter and fainter
> toward ultimate identification, joining the air
> a few breaths at a time.
>
> (*STCBT,* 120)

Air is specifically used here as the connecting medium, the means of achieving union ("ultimate identification") with the world. Once again the context is entirely physical, but the language and narrative pattern together suggest the sacred mythology of mystical union with the spiritual realm.

Interview with
William Stafford

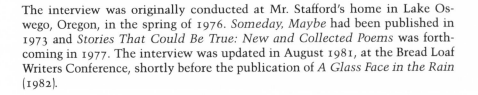

The interview was originally conducted at Mr. Stafford's home in Lake Oswego, Oregon, in the spring of 1976. *Someday, Maybe* had been published in 1973 and *Stories That Could Be True: New and Collected Poems* was forthcoming in 1977. The interview was updated in August 1981, at the Bread Loaf Writers Conference, shortly before the publication of *A Glass Face in the Rain* (1982).

When did you begin writing poems?

It's not so much a question of when did you start for me as why did other people stop? I began to write when I was in school and I just didn't stop. Other people stopped, most of them. In our family, we liked to read and talk and write things down. My parents always encouraged us to do that—in fact, when we were young they would read all sorts of things to us—Kipling, Robert W. Service, anything. Later, after I learned how to read, I stuck my own nose into the anthologies—my father had all sorts of anthologies around the house, like *Elbert Hubbard's Scrapbook*. I suppose no one's heard of that recently, but it was very big in the old days, the kind of book you had around the farm. I read the anthologies, read poems about kids in foreign lands, *The Jungle Book*, things like that. All kinds of verses—I was interested in stories, and some of the stories were in verse. I still feel not just like a poet, but like an all-purpose writer. When I start to write something, I don't know whether it is going to become a poem or something else.

Although you began writing much earlier, your first book of poems was not published until 1960. Why did you wait so long?

I just never got around to it. I began sending poems out to magazines in about 1948, and was published in magazines people would know about, like *Poetry* or the *New Yorker*. By 1960 I had this great bunch of poems that had appeared in magazines. Just about then, a fellow in San Jose, where I was teaching, Robert Greenwood, started the Talisman Press. He said, "Bill, why don't you send us a set of poems?" So he published the first book, *West of Your City.*

So you weren't seriously gathering things together, you were just producing poems?

Even now it is true that when I write I just think of sending them to magazines, and it is only after some decent interval that I think of putting some together. Sometimes a signal comes from the publisher— you know, "It has been a while." I always have a lot of ungathered poems—always have had. Most of the poems that have been published haven't been in books, they are just scattered around in little magazines.

You have a new book coming out, A Glass Face in the Rain. *Does it consist entirely of new work?*

Yes—it is made up entirely of poems written since the publication of *Stories That Could Be True* in 1977. There has just been a flood of poems since then, published during these last few years, including another book already out, *Sometimes Like a Legend.*

It seems that you have always had that luxury of so many poems to choose from. What principles guide you in choosing, say, one poem over three others for inclusion in a book?

Well, I don't want to put down poems that I haven't included in my books, because sometimes they interest me. They might even be crucial, might save my life even, but that's not crucial for the book. For the book, I have to feel that a poem will fly, that a reader can pick it up from the page. He won't have to study to get it, won't have to be interested in anything like my career. That's part of it, but there are other things. Because I write many poems, I might have several that are fairly satisfactory, but that overlap each other, are notes too close together. I try to choose poems that will make a chord—that would be one way to put it—with the other notes that are in this part of the book. So it is not as simple as just deciding on the best poems. I might even include some poems that I think are not as strong as some others, but they belong in this book—there are some little notes as well as some big notes. I do try to do my best on the Harper and Row books—I don't hold back anything, except those poems that have been in my small press books. I have a long string of these little books going way back into the sixties, but I've never collected them, mostly because I figure that whoever is nice enough to publish a little collection of mine deserves a chance to sell it. But I have made an exception with the new book—I've taken the title poem, "A Glass Face in the Rain," from a little book called *Smoke's Way,* which was done by Scott Walker of Greywolf Press.

How much of this selecting involves thematic considerations? In assembling a book, are you aiming at a larger thematic statement?

It would be easier for me to talk about if I were more sure about thematic significance, which is a little bit slippery to me. I find that the negative way usually prevails, cutting out poems that clutter up what's happening. I wish I could write a book with a positive thematic stride to it, but I haven't done it. I just sort of grope around and try to keep one poem from getting in the way of another poem. But there are usually divisions in my books, and this allows me to keep in mind a whole section, a smaller selection of poems, so each part can sort of have a chord in it. I've tried that from the very beginning—*West of Your City* has three parts, and so on.

Can you give any kind of general characterization of the poems in A Glass Face in the Rain? *I wonder, for example, about the significance of the title.*

The title is a little clue to me that the book contains a number of very serious, even overwhelming, poems. I gave a poetry reading recently and at the end I read a poem called "A Walk in the Country." My son Kim, who is a poet himself, was in the audience, and he said afterwards, "Daddy, don't ever read that poem at the end again." The poem finishes up by asking, "*Oh friends where can one find a partner / for the long dance over the fields.*" It is a very serious poem, and I have done a lot of them like that lately—I think "A Glass Face in the Rain" is one. But these poems are scattered throughout the collection—not all the poems are thematically dismal, or serious, or full-scale poetic statements, but a number of them are, and some are quite direct.

The poems that you mentioned earlier as possibly having saved your life—are they also very serious? What did you mean by that?

There is a distinction. Some poems that I think of as having "saved my life" wouldn't even sound serious to other people. A few will appear in this book—one called "Yellow Cars," for example, a strange combination of seriousness and not-seriousness. It ends—"Hope lasts a long time if you're happy." Some of these lighter poems are as crucial to me as a really serious one like "A Walk in the Country," but what I feel delicious about them is that they reach in both directions, the very serious and the vigorously good-humored. Another one like this is "Serving with Gideon," which is going to appear in a book Marvin Bell and I have done together. It ends, "I walk with my cup toward the elevator man," which in the context of the poem takes a stand.

There is a run of poems scattered through your work that I think ties in with the idea of poems that might have saved your life—poems like "The Little Ways That Encourage Good Fortune." What they do is posit a truth about living, being in harmony with one's own life and one's own environment. They represent almost a therapeutic art, though I hesitate to use that term. Are you conscious of that?

I think we shouldn't shy away from thinking those thoughts, verbalizing those thoughts, even living with the actuality of those thoughts. I feel no hesitation at all about having a poem be as direct and luminously meaningful as possible. The justification for poems that aren't clear to all readers is that sometimes you can't have everything. I mean, in order to get intensity you've got to risk some obscurity. But when you can have both, I would certainly have both, myself. I don't feel at all jumpy about poems that overtly say, "Let me save your life." Of course I don't take them entirely seriously either; after all, life is more complex than that. "The Little Ways That Encourage Good Fortune" is a brief arpeggio of this sort, but I realize that all those big mountains are still out there to climb.

Why were you a conscientious objector during World War II?

Partly it goes back to those poems we talked about. I can remember my father reading me poems about a little German boy, a little Japanese child—from all over the world. I think without being very doctrinaire about it, my family had this sort of world citizenship idea, and it never occurred to me that people from Germany ought to be shot or people from Japan ought to be shot or anything like that. I suppose that was part of it. There was also a strong peace movement in the thirties, before the war. And other people changed.

You stayed the same and they changed?

I felt so. I've had that gyrocompass feeling all my life.

What about your religious background, does that enter into this?

Well, my parents were not at all orthodox, but I often went to Sunday school. In a little Kansas town that's one of the social things to do. If someone asked, "Where's the action in this town?," you'd answer, "Church!" So there I'd go, for ice cream socials, folk dancing, expeditions, picnics, and so on. But as for doctrine, it never occurred to me to believe or disbelieve. So I wasn't orthodox. In fact, when I was drafted, one of my problems was that I wasn't a member of any church. I was called up before the draft board in Lawrence, Kansas, where the university is, and they asked me for any witnesses from my hometown. I got a letter from the commander of the American Legion, who had been the Sunday school teacher in the Methodist Church in El Dorado, Kansas. He wrote and said, "Bill's been this way for years!" So that proved it.

You are or were associated with the Church of the Brethren?

Yes, that's true. My wife's father was a minister in the Church of the Brethren. When I was drafted you would give your option and I opted for a Friends' camp, because I'd heard about the Quakers and their work. But there were just certain openings and I was sent to a Church of the Brethren camp at Magnolia, Arkansas. And I liked it, it was a fine place, lots of good people, so when I was transferred I went to another Brethren camp in California. Dorothy's father came out to our camp to preach, and she came along. We were both in our twenties, and we met and got married.

You seem to have spent much of your life in quiet opposition to the dominant attitudes of this country. Are you comfortable being an American?

I am uncomfortable, like many people, about what America has done in the sixties and early seventies. But I would have to say that, essentially, yes, I am comfortable being an American, in that the alternatives are not all that great either. I've traveled abroad, and the French foreign legion doesn't look any better to me than commandos of any kind. The Iranian army is not any more humane than the United States Army, and so on. I feel that my country is in the backroads of all countries, and we're responsible for many things, but I have never felt anti-American and I've never felt like leaving. I would rather keep on trying here.

You've written very few outwardly political poems, but is there a more subtle level on which you feel your poems have a political significance?

I do feel this way. I take a breath because I don't want to sound arrogant about this, but I have a feeling of great confidence that the poems are a steady tide of subliminal political significance. I have a little poem called "B.C.," and it begins: "The seed that met water spoke a little name." Then all sorts of great things happen, and at the end this little seed says: "Sequoia is my name." I've always felt that the conscientious-objector beliefs—all the alternative life-style ways of dealing with society—are like that little sequoia seed. They're quiet, but they're going to last. My political position is nonagressive, and it makes me jumpy to have doctrinaire positions and forensic stances. I think my poems are consistent with this—I would rather have them be nonapparently political than apparently political. To have implications, that I am very much in favor of. For me, poetry is best when it's subliminal.

Outwardly, political poetry in general has a very short life.

I have a feeling that it can't stay intellectual, it's gotta hustle you. Maybe there would be those that have very strong political feelings who'd feel that my poems are too weasel-worded or wishy-washy, but I don't worry about that.

What do you think is the role of the poet in contemporary America?

This question for me factors into two parts. One is the actual things that poets do in America. They go around to schools and do poetry readings and so on. And—especially since the start of the war in Vietnam—poets are often rallying occasions for students and citizens in various ways. They are spokesmen for the things that people want to hear but that very few people get a chance to announce publicly. So they are voices for incipient or actual movements in society. I recognize this in poets around me, and lots of times I like it. But the reason I say I'd like to factor the subject into two is that I think the role of poetry in society is a lot bigger than the role of poets in society. Wherever people are responding with their whole selves to new experiences in terms of their total feeling, I believe they are in the area of poetry. And so those that call themselves poets are a small part of what poetry is happening in the country. Poetry is happening many places where they scorn poets, is my feeling. To assign yourself the role of poet is an odd thing to do. I think it's a necessary thing and I'm willing to do it, but I don't stencil it on the outside of my car or anything like that, because it does seem odd. Wherever real liveliness of emotion and intellect is happening, I feel poetry is near.

Is this something that is common in the country or something that's needed in the country?

I think it's common. I also think it's needed more. Instead of feeling that, as I've heard even some poets say, too many people are writing poetry, I think there will never be enough poetry until everybody is involved in this kind of activity and this way of feeling and living. I think it is commoner than it used to be, but until it's part of the air we breathe, I don't think there'll be enough of it.

One last semipolitical question. In Allegiances *you have two poems, and in* Someday, Maybe *you have one poem, about "the governor." Nice poems, but normally you write of people who fail or who live close to the earth or about your family. Why the governor in these cases?*

It is not through policy that these are scattered around, but that they just happened to surface in my consciousness when I was writing and they seemed all right when I was putting the books together. So far as I know, no governor has ever read one of these poems. I think they got in there for the same reason that the poems about failures and troubled people got in there. Governors are failures and troubled people. I mean, it's impossible for a governor to do everything right, but he's expected to. Governors and other public officials who seem to have control but don't have had a tough time, and I just feel sympathetic. In Oregon the governors have prevalently been very congenial people, and I have felt in my imagination sorry for them and for their burdens. It may be natural for me to defend them because they're being attacked. Just part of that pacifism, I guess.

For many years, you were a professor of English at Lewis and Clark College. What did you normally teach?

Literature. When I had my druthers, I would teach nineteenth-century British lit—the Romantics and Victorians. But because of the way our school was organized and the size of the department, we all would swap around a lot, so I've taught from the Greeks to T. S. Eliot and beyond. Mostly I didn't teach creative writing.

Was that a deliberate choice?

It was deliberate. I think the job is hard, and if people like to do it I'm in favor of their doing it. I always felt competent in a writing course, but the way it's done in colleges is often competitive. It's usually done in the upper division and it is heavy work. So if they're willing to pay me for something lighter, I'd just as soon do something lighter, and literature seems lighter.

Does your interest in nineteenth-century literature have any influence on your own writing? Would it perhaps have been more productive for you to have taught contemporary poetry?

I don't think I was influenced by nineteenth-century literature, but that I was putting some distance between my writing and my job. I think it would have been harder for me to teach absolutely current poetry and to write poetry. I read current poetry the way you eat olives at a party—you start nibbling and pretty soon you're addicted, and I never wanted to make my addiction be a part of my work. I feel congenial with nineteenth-century literature—I like those big, long, slow novels; I love Walter Scott, all that stuff—so it's not that I have to make an effort to read that stuff. It's just that, while it's pleasant to me, it is also distant from current writing. I've heard people say it's dangerous to teach and write. I say, well, it's not dangerous if you teach the nineteenth century. Push it off a little bit.

Do you feel that there is such a thing as a distinctively Western American poetry today?

I don't think so. It's an interesting topic and I'm often involved in it from living out here. In fact, I've been in collections where the person who writes the introduction has done a heroic job of identifying Western literature. But I never have been convinced. The country is too mobile, and people aren't limited by their region. David Wagoner lives up in Seattle—is he a Western poet? "Ha, ha," he says if you ask him. He was born in the Midwest and has become a world-culture sort of person. Has he traveled abroad? Yes. Has he been to Greece? Yeah. That sort of thing.

What about indigenous factors though, like the use of the Western landscape, the use of Western dialect, that kind of thing?

Well, because poetry is done with words, and because words can be so distinctive out here—Indian words, for instance, or even the kind of lingo they use about landscape (instead of a ravine, it is a gulch), I suppose I do recognize that kind of distinction. But when I said I didn't think there was a Western school, I was thinking about more subtle things—habits of thought or stances about world affairs. I don't think there is that difference. But because it is done with words, the syllables can be different. The poems aren't different, but the syllables are. Say Richard Hugo writes a poem and mentions the Kapowsin tavern. Of course, Kapowsin is somewhere other than New York City, so that seems Western, but I would say, don't let the syllables fool you.

So much of our recent poetry has been dominated by anguish and a kind of suicidal despair. Many of these poets—Berryman, Lowell, Plath, Sexton—can be associated with the East and perhaps with the city rather than with nature. Yours is much more a poetry of joy, and you write about nature, the land, and the West. Is there any validity to this regional distinction?

Well, don't forget Roethke, who brought his anguish from Michigan and domesticated it in Seattle, where it thrived. The anguish I sense in a number of poets—like Berryman, Lowell, and Roethke—I have a feeling that it is natural to these people, and not a matter of region or environment. These poets are so pessimistic. My own feeling is that human beings are too fallible to be confident about what the future will bring. To be pessimistic—that's like saying you know the future and it's going to be bad. I think that's too arrogant—people don't know that much. We're too ignorant to be sad. But this is not a regional matter, it is probably a personal matter. We're talking about a very few individuals, and maybe there are life circumstances we don't understand that would make them write prevalently anguished poems. But you also mentioned nature, and that is important to me. I think about the Greek hero, Antaeus—every time he touched the earth he got stronger. For me, this myth is part of my life—to touch something outside, to have things in your poetry, is a healthy move. The world can save you; it can make you strong. This is maybe a Western superstition, maybe not Western, but it is a faith I live by.

You have sometimes been compared to the Beats. How do you feel about that group of poets?

In many ways I had sympathy for the Beats—a lot of them came right out of alternative life-styles in World War II. People like Kenneth Rexroth, who had an anarchist impulse; very much Brother Antoninus, who was a conscientious objector. Or a whole bunch of people in Berkeley who were doing a dance around the edge of society, all through those years. They were by no means locked into the mainstream of American nuclear superiority—far from it. So that part makes me very sympathetic about a lot of those poets. You know—did we need something else? You bet we did! Were they something else? Yes they were. But then there's a part of the Beats that I've always felt very much alienated from, including the people I've mentioned. A lot of the time the Beats were quite aggressive in their dislike of America. I myself favored reconciliation and redemption. So I felt the same unrest as those people, but preferred different tactics.

What contemporary poets do you most admire?

Neruda. I can't help feeling pretty well persuaded by that fellow. I've always felt he was a cut above what we have to offer. You start there and where do you go next? Well, a few years ago I read *The Collected Poems of Thomas Hardy*. Great! His mind rolled around everywhere, busily turning out all sorts of surprising things. All I knew were the poems in anthologies—but he's got hundreds of them, just as good. But that's a long way back. Current? Mostly I like to read prose now. I think I prefer prose to poetry. I think there are more talented people writing prose than poetry in our country today. Besides, poetry is trapped trying to do little adventitious piddling jobs, even today when it seems to be flourishing. It is interesting, but it isn't overwhelming the way Pascal is overwhelming, or the way some writer like Alfred North Whitehead, who turns his first-class mind to a sustained communication project, is overwhelming. I think there are many prose projects now that are calling forth more of the talents and the serious and sustained attention of writers than the kind of crochet work many of us are doing in poetry. You can write a poem rather quickly, close it out, and publish it in a magazine. Then you put together a collection of these fragments—but it is not the same thing as a book. There may be someone who writes a collection of poems as a whole book, but I've never done it. Mine always come in pieces. My feeling is that the most interesting parts of those collections of poems are the spaces not written out between the poems. Maybe we're trying to do the wrong thing. I realize I've done a dance around your question. Well, I feel a lot of affection and respect for many current poets, but Neruda is the last one who overwhelmed me.

When you sit down to write a poem, how do you go about it? What is your method of composition?

I have a definite thing to say about this; the diffidence I feel is not from difficulty in framing it but from wondering how it will fare in the big world. I get up early and start to write the first thing that occurs to me, anything, and go on from there. Things always occur to me. This morning I got up—mostly I can't remember what I write on a given morning, it's like remembering your dream. But I remember today simply because as the day went along I harked back to it a few times. I began to write something like "My life is a present participle becoming a past participle" or "This poem is a present participle." This doesn't mean anything yet for the poem, but I was making the poem be the construction rather than the content. I have a feeling I could do a poem in which the reader gradually comes to realize that it is the constructions in this poem that are the plot, not the content. So I could substitute all kinds of words, nouns or even verbs, just so I had them in the present- or past-participial form. This began to interest me—it's like a juggling act. That is just what occurred to me this morning. Anything can occur—yesterday it was something different.

And you just follow it out when it occurs?

I think a poem starts to be something, and you help it become whatever it started to be. If it is leaning in one direction you push it farther. I don't know if this makes sense, but the process is less like putting into words a thought or position or concept that you have than it is like picking up on the opportunities that emerge as you write things down. That's the way I think of a poem.

Do you revise heavily?

I go through it again, if it interests me. I go back, and sometimes things get drastically reversed and left out and rephrased. Not only reversed in place on the page, but I reverse my position about what I'm talking about. In order to get more zing or just more valence out of the words, almost anything can happen. So I feel the poem is like taffy; I can do anything with it. But it is still very tentative; the revision may be even more of a guess-timate than the first time.

You've said elsewhere that "poetry is a process and not a product." What do you mean by that?

Poetry is a creative process, and it's not done by imitating somebody else's product. The poet's problem is, not worrying about the accomplishments of other writers, but learning to accept what occurs to him, to give it the dignity and worth it deserves. I have written for a long time in this accepting way and always been surprised by the product rather than aiming at the product. I guess the main thing that I have learned from writing almost every day for so long is that, miraculously, something new occurs to me. Even when I feel the cheapest and poorest, all sorts of things I couldn't possibly have anticipated come as a result of my inviting them to come. I feel grateful. It is that kind of process that I am trying to emphasize.

I was also wondering when I came across that word product *whether you were thinking of the way some people try to "make it" in the world through poetry. The poem becomes a kind of hula hoop—you want to sell as many as possible, in competition with the rest of the world.*

Yes, that's in my mind. I think the first thing you have to learn is that you're not going to turn out a hula hoop, it's not like that. Writing is not a manufacturing process, but a getting-with-yourself kind of process. You can sell hula hoops or poems, but that isn't what should interest us. We should be finding our way forward into this new territory, not studying examples or competing with somebody else in a certain kind of poem. No, you have to give that up to do creative work. Recently I tried to get some writing students to realize that they should not try to avoid their bad poems—go ahead and write them. You shouldn't be afraid. Hardy did it; everybody did it. The critics point out how terrible some of these poems are—how can you think you're not going to write any bad ones? You are, and you should. You must go ahead and write the things that are in your way. So it is the opposite of being competitive, even with yourself. I don't think you should try to write a better poem today than you wrote yesterday. You should write today's poem, whatever it is. You can be your own worst censor, and then you've got writer's block. That's real anguish.

Do you pay attention to the critics and reviewers of your work?

Recently someone asked me, "Has the work of any critic ever helped you?" I took a breath and began to think, and this pause went longer and longer and longer as the old computer went back through the years. Finally, I just had to say no. I can't think of anyone who has done any good. The process of writing that I am involved in cannot be preaimed even by myself, let alone a critic. The critic can be right—he can clobber some poem and say it is terrible—but that is not the same thing as saying I shouldn't have written it. And it is not the same thing as saying if I change it the way he's thinking of, it won't be even worse. Because to see that it is bad is not the same as being able to make it better. What I'm looking for when I write is unpredictable and unprogrammable, and I've got to forget the critics when I start to write. I see merit in the work of lots of critics, but it is irrelevant for me. To me, writing is done by letting the whole current and tide of your life determine what you write, and if you are writing as part of a program or part of a learned literary movement, by that very fact you are excluding a part of your life. Writing poetry is so total that to do it for an editor, for a movement, or as part of a critical program is an inhibition, a distortion. Mark Vinz, as an epigraph to one of his poems, quoted St. John of the Cross, who said: "If a man would be sure of his road, he must close his eyes and walk in the dark." That struck me. I think writing is like that. To peek to see whether you are in line with the critical demands, to that degree you are doing something mechanical, and this troubles me. Tolstoy said the arts come from living the way common people live. If you adopt the line of some critical school, you're just not going to get there, and I feel like Daniel Boone—I'm gonna find Kentucky myself.

You have said elsewhere: "I think I prefer prose to poetry and I'm forced into poetry by various considerations that don't really have a lot to do with my feeling of the quality or the value of the two kinds of discourse." What are the various considerations that have forced you into poetry?

For one thing, there are the conditions of my life. I have always liked to get up early and do something that I can finish in a small amount of time before the activities of the day take over—teaching or whatever. Poetry can be rewarding in intermittent dashes of effort. To write a big, sustained prose work would require a devoted effort over a long interval, writing out things that had occurred to me as much as a week ago, and I'd like to give up a week ago. What I said was bad about reading books of poetry is what is good about writing books of poetry—you can do it in intervals and you can feel these little, local satisfactions, which I have a lot of gusto for—I like to feel the completion. For another thing, doing books of sustained prose seems more like work and more like being responsible to somebody else. I never like to be responsible except to myself. And in poetry I can do that.

You use a lot of Indian material in your poetry. Why are you so attracted to the Indians?

I've always liked their way of life, living in the woods, close to the animals. And the sense of freedom—I like a lot of space and plenty of chance to let the impulses I have be predominant over impulses imposed on me. Maybe that's a definition of freedom. I take a step when I want to, not when the escalator tells me to. I'd like to be able to go to the edge of town and just keep going, the way the Indians did.

When you use Indian lore in a poem, is it authentic, based on study, or do you make it up?

Well, it's authentic, but I make it up. In other words, it is authentic because I am an Indian, I have that Indian feeling, and not because I read it in some book. An Indian today who copyrights legends is a faker unless he has that feeling. You know, a poem like "The Animal That Drank Up Sound" is authentic not because the Indians told it to me, but because I was up there at that lake where the animal drank up sound. I was camping up at Green Lake here in Oregon, and it got quieter and quieter, and this Indian legend began to come to me. I think of something that relates to this—when we were traveling in Mexico, we wanted to get some authentic serapes, authentic design. We went into a place where a fellow was weaving, and asked, is this authentic Mexican design? Yes, he said, because—here, I get it right out of this pamphlet from the museum in Mexico City. Well, he's lost. It is authentic in the sense you first mentioned, but it is not authentic.

I am struck by the word stories *in the title of your collected poems,* Stories That Could Be True. *What is the role of narrative in your poetry? Do you think of your poems as stories?*

I often do. I remember thinking years ago that one of the admirable things about Robert Penn Warren's poems is that many of them have a kind of narrative spine. And I like that, coasting along to what comes next and next. I don't write poems with the intention of telling stories, exactly, but a number of them do turn out to have narrative homogenized into them, or implied narrative, or a narrative hovering in the background of what actually is on the page. To me, the narrative spine and things connected with narrative are very much a part of the potential for a poem. Things like suspense, gradual emergence of pattern or realization, are part of the literary experience; you can link them to prose or you can link them to poetry, but I always feel them lurking there when I'm writing. They are all part of the suspenseful emergence of satisfying realizations.

Do you feel that there is an evolution to your poetic style? Are you aware of such a thing?

This isn't the sort of thing that I spontaneously brood about, and I never had any intent to change the way I write. But I believe there are changes that have happened without my being aware, changes that I recognize just in terms of the way writing feels to me. There's a kind of confidence about certain patterns that I might have been hesitant to try earlier.

Are these patterns more complicated than the ones used earlier, or simpler?

In many ways they would seem simpler, at least to a reader looking at the poems. But for me as the writer, they might well seem more complicated. I'll try to make sense of that. I'd say that earlier, if I was doing something that had been done before, something that I had experienced in other people's writing, then I could feel fairly confident. Now I feel more as if I'm leaving the diving board to do a free-form dive of any kind—you know, all kinds of things can happen in a poem. When I go back and read some of the things I wrote very early, say in the forties or early fifties, I am sometimes surprised at how many of them now seem pretty closely linked to patterns that I had experienced in other people's writing—I'm thinking about rhymed quatrains, meter, that kind of thing. I know that most people would say I have never had much meter and rhyme, but I feel even easier about it now.

James Wright once spoke about the liberating influence of tight forms. That is, the limitations of the imposed form actually caused or allowed things to emerge from the imagination that otherwise would not have come forth. Is this idea foreign to you?

I understand it, but it is foregin to my most fervent and most natural feelings about writing. I have a lot of respect for James Wright and his insights, but I think his statement reflects a prevalent way of talking about poetry. The forms that he was talking about are easily identified and easy to talk about, but there are many other forms. They are just there, ready to emerge, as the images hidden in photographic paper emerge when you apply the developer. I look at the paper as the words appear, and they begin to have forms that no critic has ever identified. There is no name for them, but as the poem develops it becomes full of incipient patterns, little places you can pet and bring along. What really entices me along through a poem are these satisfying closures of alerted attention, suspended possibilities, satisfactory resultants, all kinds of indirect and unanticipated things. So I wouldn't say it Wright's way, partly because it would lead a reader to believe I'm talking about the need for writing poems out of other poems, and I don't feel that need. I feel that I do write in patterns, but they are not the patterns that were formed long ago by somebody else.

You once said that what really matters in a poem is, not really what it reveals or says, but its "effect," which you defined as a harmony between what is said and how it is said. Could you expand on that?

Yes—that's awfully precious sounding to me, so I would like to expand on it. When people talk about what poetry does, so often they only want to identify topics and linear development. It makes me want to ask, "How about my friends the syllables, how about the actual feel of the language while you're saying it?" Nobody refers to that, which is what I was trying to get at there. Those people who take up writing, or literature in general, in terms of its topics and its ordinarily identified ways of developing, are sort of doomed to a repetition in literature. The areas of experiment, of exploration, of discovery, are those areas that have to do with the language experience that forces you to make leaps that you ordinarily wouldn't make. All sorts of little enticements show up in the syllables and in the pace of the phrasing, with the way the sequences go in the sentence and the alternatives that begin to occur to you. I feel that the power a writer has—the extra leverage, the vaulting pole that you carry when you're really a writer—is that you begin to lend your attention and your feelings of satisfaction to those little bonuses scattered through the language—things so small there aren't names for them. That's what I was trying to get at.

Granted that individual lyric poems are, as you said, a kind of "piddling" and "crochet work," at least when set beside a Hardy novel—isn't there a sense in which your whole body of work comprises something both large and coherent?

This idea occurred to me earlier this summer when I was putting together a reading which I gave at a writer's conference in Port Townsend, Washington. I began to feel that I had been writing one big, long poem all along, and that only certain parts of it had been polished and sent off. I haven't even written some of the connectives, but it's really one poem. So I said to the audience, "I want you to grant me something—don't think of these as poems. These are not poems. These are messages, pieces of language, and they are parts of a long work or a long statement with some pieces missing." If circumstances were just a little different—if we didn't have to write in brief intervals and if we didn't always send off the little pieces, maybe we could keep them by us long enough to crochet them together with an invisible seam into a great big whopping poem. I do feel wistful about big, unitary constructions, but I also think the individual poems come together—we just don't always know the connectives. It is like you are planting individual trees for years and suddenly realize you've got a forest. And the trees are still growing and gradually linking together.

In many of your poems there is a questing attitude, a reaching or longing for something not present or unseen. Often the speaker will leave the city or town and venture where man has never been before, looking for something elemental. Could you comment on this pattern?

This might be just a character trait or a quirk in personality, but I do feel within myself an appetite for something not achieved, a feeling of lack in life, an unsatisfied need. At a party I might go look out the back window to see what's happening out there in the dark, sort of longing for something distant and unachieved. So I am quite comfortable viewing it this way, though there is another, more general way to get at it. I think when you are doing art, you are enticed to go beyond apparent limits, and one apparent limit is just from here to there. So it's part of the dimensioning there is in art. When I write a poem, I start off in whatever direction presents itself, and then just keep right on going. And since the only real direction is outwards, the dark keeps getting darker, the far keeps getting farther, the cold keeps getting colder. You have to try to go as far as you can go. A year or so ago, someone hitchhiked up from California to tell me about my poetry. "I have heard that you are a nice guy and that you write nice poems, but I have read many of your poems and I want to tell you I think some of your poems are mean." He mentioned one in particular called "Judgments," which says things like: "I accuse Ella of becoming forty years old." He said, "When I read that poem, I hear a voice that is really condemning the people in it." I thought for a minute, and then said, "Well I do feel the possibility that that's in a lot of those poems." The way I accommodated it then and the way I'd accommodate it now is that second principle I just voiced—if you're going to write something, one way to go is *all the way*. If you say "Judgments," go ahead and indict people no one else would ever have thought of indicting. I would be happy if a book of mine gave readers long rides in all directions.

I am also curious about the word true *in the title* Stories That Could Be True. *What do you feel is the relationship between truth and poetry?*

When we were talking earlier about the little poem and the big poem, the crochet work and the tapestry, I was going to say that I have become less and less impressed by human scale, in a way. What's a long poem? *Paradise Lost*? Well, maybe here, now, but it is a function of our littleness to say that. And so human scale is part of what I would begin to say about truth—truth is something that human beings feel about certain conditions. If we knew more would we feel differently? Yes, I think we would, as a matter of fact. All human truth is a partial thing. Truth is too big a word for human beings to use, except for convenience, and I only use it for convenience in talking to other human beings. But if someone were to ask, "Is this truth ultimate?" I'd say, "No, it's not ultimate, it's only provisional, because it's human."

In one of the essays in Writing the Australian Crawl, *you talk about the liberating effect of arbitrariness in language—a writer should use the word he thinks of next, even if it doesn't seem to make sense. This is similar to something John Ashbery has said; before he begins writing, he will often go for a walk on the streets of New York. The words and phrases he overhears, generally meaningless to him and completely out of context, he will often be able to use in his poems—a similar regard for arbitrary language. Of course, in most ways, Ashbery's work is very different from yours, but might there be a similarity at this level of technique?*

I feel a lot of harmony with this. In fact, I feel a lot more harmony with someone like Ashbery and his assumptions about poetry—what it is, what it does, how you get into it—than I do with many other poets: Warren and Berryman, for example. If someon were to ask me, "Do you take seriously the important statements in Warren's and Berryman's poetry?" I would have to say, "No, no, I don't." And I have the feeling that maybe they do or—in the case of Berryman—did, though maybe they would respond the same way I do when I am charged with too much seriousness; I say, "Oh, you took all that seriously?" So yes, I do think that Ashbery's assumption about what happens in language is a lot closer to mine than is that of those people who seem to feel that they are corraling ultimate truth or essential human values. I just can't believe it. To me, it is much too serious, even mistakenly serious. It's like putting too many decimals in your figuring for the accuracy of your instruments. Berryman and Warren have a lot of decimals, but nobody's instruments are that good. I think poetry is ultimately playful, no matter what anyone says. And Ashbery is explicit about this, he verbalizes what happens to everybody—we are constantly being nuzzled and nudged by the little opportunities in language, not by the great truths—it is the syllables that carry us along.

A final question. Do you have a favorite among your poems?

I have one called "The Little Girl by the Fence at School" that seems to me just about right. It's such an economical poem. I have a feeling that, in language, there are little bonuses that are almost imperceptible, but they make a difference. We don't count them when we discuss poetry, but the best poems may survive by having a high incidence of these little shrimp, just little imperceptible forwarding elements that are too slight to have names or even to be noticed when we teach poetry. I think this poem came to mind because it might have a lot of those without having any of the things we ordinarily identify.

**Louis
Simpson**

Louis Simpson:
In Search of the
American Self

●

The story American literature tells is so often that of a virtuous individual, who seeks complete freedom for self-expression, pitted against a community that is at best repressive and at worst unjust, perhaps even immoral. Consider Melville's White Jacket and Billy Budd, rebels against society's sanctioned injustices. Consider his Bartleby, who in response to every entreaty from his eminently reasonable, successful, middle-American boss, says "I would prefer not to." Consider Huck Finn, who follows the promptings of his own heart, his innate sense of virtue, over what society tells him is right; "All right, then, I'll go to hell!," he says, embracing the cause of his black friend, Jim. Consider Hester Prynne, whose devotion is to passion, human emotion—to natural virtue rather than civil virtue—against the moral repression of her Puritan society.

Consider too those writers who speak more or less for themselves rather than through a character, chiefly the American transcendentalists. There is Emerson, whose counsel was to follow always your own path, no matter if it has *never* been trod before. There is Thoreau, whose independence of mind exasperated even his friend and mentor Emerson—Thoreau, who was among the first to oppose the implicit support of slavery that he found in Massachusetts, and who opposed as well that proto-Vietnam adventure: the Mexican War of 1846–48. And there is Whitman, who sang of himself only as a means of encouraging others to be more themselves: "Not I—not any one else, can travel that road for you, / You must travel it for yourself." These lists could be extended almost indefinitely—one thinks of Emily Dickinson, Isabel Archer, Edna Pontiellier, so many more. The point is clear: one of the most pervasive concerns of American literature has always been to support, promote, and encourage the individual vision, no matter how solid the opposition of the majority.

It is precisely this concern that we find at the heart of the poetry of Louis Simpson.[1] In recent years he has taken to writing narrative verse that uses many of the techniques of prose fiction. Thus we find in his work third-person protagonists who bear slight spiritual similarities to Huck Finn, Edna Pontiellier, and the others. Even at its most narrative, however, Simpson's poetry remains lyrical in its basis—and this means that the position of the individual sensibility in his work is defined most centrally by the personality of the poet himself. In his autobiography, *North of Jamaica,* Simpson gives the most important of his many definitions of poetry: "Poetry is essentially mysterious. No one has ever been able to define it. Therefore we always find ourselves coming back to the poet. As Stevens said, 'Poetry is a process of the personality of the poet.' This personality is never finished. While he is writing the poet has in mind another self, more intelligent than he. The poet is reaching out to the person that he would be, and this is the poet's style—a sense of reaching, that can never be satisfied."[2]

This sense of reaching always for a better self, which makes Simpson's individual poems so dynamic, is also what caused the profound changes that have occurred in his poetry generally since the beginning of his career. We can, in fact, identify three distinct phases within this body of work. The poems in Simpson's first three books—*The Arrivistes* (1949), *Good News of Death* (1955), and *A Dream of Governors* (1959)—are written in tight, traditional English lyric forms, forms that have the effect of dissociating the poet's sensibility from the very material he is attempting to write about. In many of these early efforts, Simpson sounds rather like the new metaphysical poets, who had their vogue in the 1940s and 1950s. The lyric "As Birds Are Fitted to the Boughs" is typical:

> As birds are fitted to the boughs
> That blossom on the tree
> And whisper when the south wind blows—
> So was my love to me.
>
> And still she blossoms in my mind
> And whispers softly, though
> The clouds are fitted to the wind,
> The wind is to the snow.[3]

However successful this poem is, there is nothing about it that is unique to the vision or voice of Louis Simpson—the subject is as conventional as the form, and we may be excused the feeling that it could have been written by almost anyone, including a poet (perhaps especially a poet) living three-hundred years ago.

In fact, "As Birds Are Fitted to the Boughs" is a "poem nearly anonymous" (as John Crowe Ransom might have said of it)—its form and sentiment both seem predetermined—inherited, not from the personal experience of the author, but from literary history. In addition to poems about love, these early books also contain most of Simpson's war poems. After coming to this country from his native Jamaica in 1940, at the age of seventeen, Simpson enlisted in the United States Army, serving first in the tank corps, then in the infantry; he was among the first to go ashore at Normandy and was awarded the Bronze Star for distinguished service and the Purple Heart for his injuries. One might expect his war poems to blister with immediate, felt experience; such is not the case, however. Again, the author's personality is buried beneath the demands of a form imposed from without rather than generated from within. Thus, even in the best of these poems, we feel, not the force of the poet's experience, but the force of his mastery of traditional English lyricism. "Carentan O Carentan," for example, is a powerful war lyric; I quote stanzas from the beginning, the middle, and the end:

Trees in the old days used to stand
And shape a shady lane
Where lovers wandered hand in hand
Who came from Carentan.
. . . .
I must lie down at once, there is
A hammer at my knee.
And call it death or cowardice,
Don't count again on me.

Everything's all right, Mother,
Everyone gets the same
At one time or another.
It's all in the game.

I never strolled, nor ever shall,
Down such a leafy lane.
I never drank in a canal,
Nor ever shall again.
. . . .
Carentan O Carentan
Before we met with you
We never yet had lost a man
Or known what death could do.

(*PLH*, 37–38)

The lyricism is beautiful, the irony between that formal characteristic and the content of the poem profound, but again the personal voice of Louis Simpson is missing.

When Simpson agrees with Stevens that "Poetry is a process of the personality of the poet," he is, among other things, also agreeing with Buffon's definition, "The style is the man." As he himself has explained, it was because he wanted to express his own personality more directly that Simpson undertook, between the publication of his third and fourth books, to change his style: "I had been writing poetry that was quite formal. . . . Over the next few years, I tried to write impeccable poems, poems you couldn't find fault with. Then between 1959 and 1963 I broke all that up and tried to write poetry that would be more free, that would sound more like my own voice. . . . Ever since then I've written mostly a kind of informal poetry."[4] (See "Interview with Louis Simpson.") In the second and third phases of Simpson's career, then, we encounter an authentic poetry of personality. Moreover, once he had made this important transition, it appears that Simpson was able to look back and define more clearly the relationship between the missing sensibility of his early poems and the society in which that sensibility attempted to live; I will begin my larger discussion of Simpson's work with these more or less anachronistic poems, poems that, by virtue of their content, actually (though not chronologically) belong in the first phase of his career.

The middle phase of Simpson's work consists of all of the poems in his fourth book, *At the End of the Open Road* (1963), and many of those in *Adventures of the Letter I* (1971), a transitional volume. The individual portrayed in these poems feels himself seriously alienated from American society, which in his view had not only killed the American Indians but was also participating, indefensibly, in an unjust war in Vietnam. Then a curious thing happens, marking the transition from the second to the third phase of Simpson's work—through a dual interest in the work of Chekhov and in his own Jewish Russian ancestors, the sensibility of these poems recognizes his inherent kinship with the ordinary citizens of the society he had been hating. He realizes that it is not they but their leaders who are responsible for what is wrong and repressive in that society. Thus, the third phase of Simpson's work is the empathetic, even the spiritual phase—the phase in which he comes to do his most memorable and original work. It begins with the Russian poems in *Adventures of the Letter I* and continues with the poems of middle America in *Searching for the Ox* (1976), *Caviar at the Funeral* (1980), and *The Best Hour of the Night* (1983).

Before proceeding any farther, we must pause to make a crucial distinction. Although Louis Simpson writes a poetry of personality, and although the most important unifying feature of his work is the sensibility that lies at its heart, he is not a confessional poet. In fact, Simpson has been very hard on this type of poetry, which he sees as part of the "cult of sincerity" ("Interview with Louis Simpson"). Confessional poetry is personal because it takes for its subject matter the literal details of the poet's life and feelings, the truth of that life as lived in the real world; Simpson's poetry is personal because it emerges from and expresses a single, central, perceiving sensibility. Although the effect of this can be even more intimate than what the reader experiences in confessional poetry, it is achieved while the poet maintains a reticent posture with regard to the external details of his life. In fact, Simpson prefers to speak of the sensibility that inhabits his poems as a created character—based upon himself, to be sure, but made up nevertheless: "I have a very funny sense of myself in the poem—I'm not talking about me, I'm talking about how the poems make a self for me."[5] How that might come about is explained in greater detail in the Afterword to Simpson's book *A Revolution in Taste*, where he gives a summary definition of what he means by a poetry of personality: "In contrast to this, what I have called the personal voice is an expression of character. And character is something made. The self that appears in the novel or poem has been constructed according to certain aesthetic principles. This version of the self is not intended to direct attention upon the author but to serve the work of art. The purpose is to create a symbolic life, a portrait of the artist that will have meaning for others and so create a sense of community, if only among a few thousand."[6]

The sensibility that unifies the poems of Louis Simpson, then, is this created "symbolic life," this "portrait of the artist"; it is a sensibility intended to express not just the personal feelings of one person but those of at least a small minority community existing within society at large. It is not until the last phase of his work, however, that Simpson's poetry will truly begin to embody this sense of community. In the first two phases we see instead a sensibility largely alienated from the society that surrounds it. As I said earlier, our understanding of the position of the Simpson sensibility in the first phase will come not so much from the poems actually written then but from later poems that comment on that phase. These poems, in fact, mostly appear together in the first section of Simpson's recent book, *People Live Here: Selected Poems, 1949–1983*—a structuring that indicates that they do indeed belong, because of their content, with the first phase.

For example, the poem "The Cradle Trap" (*PLH*, 28), originally published in *At the End of the Open Road*, seems to define the alienation of the Simpson character at almost its first moment of consciousness. The experience and feelings of the poem are those of a baby and are presented in the first two stanzas:

A bell and rattle,
a smell of roses,
a leather Bible,
and angry voices . . .

They say, I love you.
They shout, You must!
The light is telling
terrible stories.

The forces of society are represented by the baby's parents, who are willing to use every means at their disposal, including both violence and love, to impose their will upon him. In Simpson's poems generally, as here, the depersonalizing forces of society are associated with an unforgiving light, while darkness represents individuality and self-ful-fillment. Thus, it is the darkness that offers support and advice to the baby in the concluding stanza of this poem:

But night at the window
whispers, Never mind.
Be true, be true
to your own strange kind.

What is presented here in embryonic form is the conflict between the individual and the community that will dominate so much of Simpson's poetry. Already this particular character is seen as different from most people, one of a "strange kind." As we will learn in later poems, this strangeness results from a commitment not just to poetry but to a life of the mind generally.

While "The Cradle Trap" seems to set the Simpson character against all of society and both of his parents, another poem, "Working Late" (*PLH*, 168), indicates a potential for harmony that we will see fully manifested in phase three. The title of the poem refers to the speaker's father, a lawyer of precise and methodical character—"A light is on in my father's study":

He is working late on cases.
No impassioned speech! He argues from evidence,
actually pacing out and measuring,
while the fans revolving on the ceiling
winnow the true from the false.

Within the context of the poem, the father represents society, as his association with the artificial light source indicates. That there is something of value even here, however, is implicit in the way the poem ends:

. . . the light that used to shine
at night in my father's study
now shines as late in mine.

However, the real sense of kinship in the poem is felt between the speaker and his mother, who is both associated with the darkness and seen in conflict with the father:

All the arguing in the world
will not stay the moon.
She has come all the way from Russia
to gaze for a while in a mango tree
and light the wall of a veranda,
before resuming her interrupted journey.

The poem is autobiographical. Simpson's father was a lawyer; his mother, a passionate and restless woman of Russian ancestry, who happened to come with a dance troup to Jamaica, was courted by and married the elder Simpson, and left him some years later, when the poet was nearly grown. She functions as a sort of muse within the poem, prefiguring those human qualities that will characterize Simpson's maturest work—chiefly, the feeling of love, a sense of independence, devotion to the freedom of the self and to the creative spirit; identifying her with the moon, Simpson says: "she is still the mother of us all." For fullest expression, most of this will have to wait for phase three; until then, the sensibility that rules these poems contends instead with the negative, antagonistic feelings of betrayal expressed in "The Cradle Trap."

At the end of the first section of his new selected poems, Simpson has placed three poems that also stand together at the end of *Adventures of the Letter I*—"Trasimeno," "The Peat-Bog Man," and "The Silent Piano." The poems have much in common—each associates the light of day with a society that is somehow oppressive to the individual; each identifies as well a fugitive sense of spirituality, creativity, which is associated with the night and the moon and opposed to the forces of society. Perhaps we may take the middle poem (*PLH*, 33) as representative. Seamus Heaney, that fine Ulster poet, tells many stories of the peat bogs of Ireland, which have a way of preserving anything (including human bodies) that happens to fall into them. Centuries later, peat cutters will come upon these things, perfectly preserved. The title character of Simpson's poem "was one of the consorts of the moon" who "went with the goddess in a cart": "Wherever he went there would be someone, / a few of the last of the old religion." Once this brief characterization has been given, "the moon passes behind a cloud"; we don't see the peat-bog man again until, "Fifteen centuries" later, he is dug up—

. . . with the rope
that ends in a noose at the throat—
a head squashed like a pumpkin.

Simpson implies that the man was executed; apparently his sensitive, religious, poetic nature came into conflict with a brutal and repressive society. At the end of the poem, Simpson associates him with the creative spirit of earth, allowing for an indirect triumph after all:

> Yet, there is delicacy in the features
> and a peaceful expression . . .
>
> that in Spring the flower comes forth
> with a music of pipes and dancing.

Because of its method, the poem seems to offer almost a blanket condemnation of how such individuals have been treated by societies throughout time. The poem is nearly allegorical, generalizing as it does from an incident that is both ancient and vague. "The Peat-Bog Man" thus reflects a quality common to most of the poems in Simpson's first three books: they do not often deal directly, personally, with the actual world inhabited at the time of composition by the poet himself. It was not until 1963, with the publication of his fourth book, *At the End of the Open Road*—significantly following the major change in style discussed above—that Simpson began to write specifically about America, where he had been living for better than twenty years.

If not a paradox, it is at least a curiosity that Louis Simpson—that native Jamaican—has become, since the beginning of the second phase of his career, the most consciously American of all contemporary American poets.[7] This is true, not just because he has come to write mostly about American life and people, but because the sensibility that informs his poems from their creative heart thinks of himself as an American—for better (phase three) or for worse (phase two). In an essay written as early as 1962, Simpson recognized that his work was moving in this direction: "I think a great deal about the country I live in; indeed, it seems an inexhaustible subject, one that has hardly been tapped. By America, I mean the infinitely complex life we have. Sometimes when I look at Main Street, I feel like a stranger looking at the via Aurelia, or the Pyramids."[8] It is interesting that James Wright commented on this aspect of Simpson's work in his own essay on Walt Whitman: "Louis Simpson's imagination is obsessed with the most painful details of current American life, which he reveals under a very powerfully developed sense of American history. . . . Mr. Simpson describes America and Americans in a vision totally free from advertising and propaganda."[9]

As mentioned earlier, the poems in phase two are the bitterest of Simpson's career. It is almost as though, rebounding from the horrors of World War II, his protagonist felt danger lurking behind every bush, a murderous stench at large in the very atmosphere. He became an idealist, venting his anger most vigorously upon the hypocrites of this world, those who profess noble, moral aims while wallowing in the mire of man's inhumanity to man. The poem "On the Lawn at the Villa" (*PLH*, 54) is set in Tuscany just after World War II, and seems to take for its theme the contrast between American innocence and European sophistication, implying that the latter is cunning, given to evil, the former a sweetness yielding only to virtue.

Though the theme of the poem seems to come from Henry James, its voice sounds more like Augie March or Studs Lonigan—a wise guy who has read Whitman. He begins the poem by commenting on his title:

> On the lawn at the villa—
> That's the way to start, eh, reader?
> We know where we stand—somewhere expensive—
> You and I *imperturbes*, as Walt would say,
> Before the diversions of wealth, you and I *engagés*.

The irony of the voice seems at this point to be directed against the hollowness, the falseness, of wealthy European society, an impression that is strengthened when the speaker introduces his companions—"a manufacturer of explosives," his wife, and "a young man named Bruno"—and goes on to justify his own presence at this little tea party. He is, he says:

> Willing to talk to these malefactors,
> The manufacturer of explosives, and so on,
> But somehow superior. By that I mean democratic.
> It's complicated, being an American,
> Having the money and the bad conscience, both at the same time.

On its surface level, the poem suggests that it is people like the manufacturer of explosives who make war possible, thus perpetuating the kind of thing that destroyed "The Peat-Bog Man." The American is supposedly superior, if only because he can see the immorality inherent in this situation. However, there is another level of irony in the poem; being American is more "complicated" than it at first seems. While the speaker pretends to believe the American line, in fact he is directing his most serious criticism against it. He suggests that it is the Americans who are the greatest hypocrites in such situations. The arms maker pretends nothing; the American pretends to approve of the arms maker (no doubt for the "money" involved), meanwhile believing that he can preserve his own moral superiority through a "bad conscience." That this is a delusion is made clear through an image Simpson uses in the poem's concluding stanza:

> We were all sitting there paralyzed
> In the hot Tuscan afternoon,
> And the bodies of the machine-gun crew were draped over the balcony.

Everyone in the scene, that is, ignores this very basic reality, and all are equally guilty.

Poems from this phase that are set in America are, if anything, even more bitter than "On the Lawn at the Villa." Basically, Simpson chooses to contrast the American Dream—of justice, equality, freedom, and peace—with the reality he was observing around him. Most of these poems were written during the early phase of America's involvement in the war in Vietnam, at a time when American opinion supported that involvement. In an essay first published—ironically—in William Heyen's bicentennial anthology, *American Poets in 1976*, Simpson comments on the reaction of American poets to Vietnam by speaking first of how William Wordsworth felt when his country sided with the government against the peasants during the French Revolution: "he was cut off in his affections from the people around him. It is hard to imagine a more desolate situation for a poet, and it is the situation American poets have found themselves in for some time. It would be bad enough if poets alone felt so, but what poets feel many other people are feeling too. The United States contains a large number of people who no longer like it."[10] The people who no longer like it, in fact, are those few of a "strange kind," first mentioned in "The Cradle Trap."

In a poem with the ironic title "American Dreams" (*PLH*, 79), Simpson defines the position occupied by such a person in this country at that time. The poem begins by contrasting the kind of dreams the Simpson protagonist would normally have with a redefined version of the American Dream:

> In dreams my life came toward me,
> my loves that were slender as gazelles.
> But America also dreams. . . .
> Dream, you are flying over Russia,
> dream, you are falling in Asia.

We are reminded that the American Dream has not been limited to the basic definition given above. The English Puritans came here originally in pursuit of religious freedom—and immediately proceeded to outlaw all religions but their own. They also saw the American Indians as the Devil's minions, and set about to eradicate them from the face of the earth. This particular aspect of the American Dream is celebrated by Simpson in yet another poem, "Indian Country," where he describes how "The white men burst in at sunrise, shooting and stabbing . . . ,/ the squaws running in every direction" (*PLH*, 68). Were we to view this as a kind of genocide, and were we to combine that with yet another aspect of the American Dream (the one that sees the open road leading ever westward to new horizons), then we might have found an explanation for the American bombs falling in Asia.

The second stanza of "American Dreams" expresses the feelings of the speaker through an image as violent and surreal as the one that concludes "On the Lawn at the Villa": "on a typical sunny day in California," he dreams:

> it is my house that is burning
> and my dear ones that lie in the gutter
> as the American army enters.

The feeling is one of intense alienation; the speaker is committed to the original American Dream of peace and freedom for all, while his fellow citizens seem bent on forcing the entire world to conform to their way of life. The poem concludes:

> Every day I wake far away
> from my life, in a foreign country.
> These people are speaking a strange language.
> It is strange to me
> and strange, I think, even to themselves.

The situation is strange to the speaker because he is of the minority, one of that "strange kind" that remembers the basic moral principles on which this country was founded. That the situation may have been strange as well "even to themselves"—that is, even to ordinary citizens—history has come to prove through the eventual turning of public opinion against the war in Vietnam. Thus at the time of the poem, their behavior was unnatural, an unaccustomed hypocrisy.

Another, somewhat earlier, poem on the American Dream is the famous "Walt Whitman at Bear Mountain" (*PLH*, 64–65), originally published in *At the End of the Open Road*. It begins with a challenge to the statue of Whitman, asking "Where is the nation you promised?" and complaining that "The Open Road goes to the used-car lot." Simpson refers to the degeneration of yet another aspect of the original Dream.

Our ancestors only hoped for sufficient material goods to get by on, a chicken in every pot; we have progressed to the point where our insatiable hunger for wealth is scarring the countryside, polluting the air, and dropping either a porn emporium or a pizza shack on every village corner. Whitman is blamed because of the boundless opportunity that he seemed to promise and because his writings have been used by publicists and polemicists to forward just these debased goals. Simpson goes on to imagine an answer from Whitman, who points out that it was not the future of the country he was prophesying, "it was Myself / I advertised"—"I gave no prescriptions"—"I am wholly disreputable." Suddenly, for the speaker, "All that grave weight of America" is "cancelled." All those who have "contracted / American dreams"—"the realtors, / Pickpockets, salesmen"—can go their own ways, performing their "Official scenarios"; the individual has been freed to pursue his vision:

> . . . the man who keeps a store on a lonely road,
> And the housewife who knows she's dumb,
> And the earth, are relieved.

The answer that the speaker has found for this stage of his life is to try to ignore what goes on around him, to cultivate his own "Myself" in a kind of protective isolation—to live, that is, what is described in the poem's epigraph (from Ortega y Gasset): a "life which does not give the preference to any other life, of any previous period, which therefore prefers its own existence."

It is in another poem, "Sacred Objects" (originally published in *Adventures of the Letter I*), that Simpson gives a capsule version of the general lesson learned from Whitman; he says: "The light that shines through the *Leaves* / is clear: 'to form individuals'" (*PLH*, 178). The attempt to be true to the singular, individual vision of the self is the quest that entered Simpson's work once he decided upon a personal theory of poetry. It is given eloquent testimony in yet another poem from this period, "Summer Morning." Thinking back over fifteen years, the speaker recalls a morning spent with a woman in a hotel room, from which they watched workers across the way. The separation between him and them was more than just physical, as he now recognizes:

> I'm fifteen years older myself—
> Bad years and good.
>
> So I have spoiled my chances.
> For what? Sheer laziness,

The thrill of an assignation,
My life that I hold in secret.

(PLH, 90)

The tone of the poem is not one of regret but of triumph. The speaker's chances for a commercial life have been spoiled, it is true, but that is no loss; it is far preferable to have lived a life devoted to fugitive emotions, devoted to an individual vision, no matter how unpopular—a life devoted to that least commercial of all serious pursuits, poetry.[11]

Perhaps the strongest general impression one takes away from the poems written during this second phase of Simpson's career is of the alienation from society that his protagonist feels. Sometimes his attitude is bitter and sarcastic about that society; at other times he is sullen and withdrawn, almost sulking; at still other times he is strong, proud, defiant. In all cases, however, the alienation persists. Moreover, his distrust is not just of those who are obviously misguided (political leaders, pickpockets) but of common people as well—his fellow citizens, the workers in the window across the way. *At the End of the Open Road*, source of most of these poems and Simpson's most negative book, was published in 1963. Between then and 1971, when the transitional volume *Adventures of the Letter I* was published, his work began to develop away from this attitude towards a stronger feeling of brotherly love. An indirect but telling comment on what was happening can be found in his essay "Dogface Poetics," first published in 1965: "In recent years the closemouthed, almost sullen, manner of my early poems has given way to qualities that are quite different. Like other men of the war generation, I began with middle age; youth came later. Nowadays in my poems I try to generate mystery and excitement; I have even dealt in general ideas. But I retain the dogface's suspicion of the officer class, with their abstract language and indifference to individual, human suffering. You might say that the war made me a footsoldier for the rest of my life."[12]

The difference as expressed here is slight but significant; Simpson is coming to empathize more emphatically with his fellow "footsoldiers" and their ordinary "human suffering." No longer will his protagonist feel so "cut off in his affections from the people around him"; he will not hold the citizenry at large responsible for such atrocities as the American participation in Vietnam—that rap will be pinned on those who earn it, the "officer class" generally. The most important change in Simpson's work as he moves into the third phase of his career, then, is the increased sense of empathy those poems express for other people.[13] The change in attitude—and in method of operation—on the part of the Simpson protagonist is made clear in a poem like "The

Mexican Woman" (*PLH*, 103), originally published in *Caviare at the Funeral*. In the first section of this poem, the speaker is panhandled by an old man who claims to have been "in Mexico with Black Jack Pershing":

> He lived with a Mexican woman.
> Then he followed her, and was wise.
>
> "Baby," he said, "you're a two-timer,
> I'm wise to you and the lieutenant."

The second section tells the reaction of the speaker to this chance encounter; "the old man's tale still haunts me," he begins:

> I know what it's like to serve
> in Mexico with Black Jack Pershing.
>
> And to walk in the dust and heat . . .
> for I can see her hurrying
>
> to the clay wall where they meet,
> and I shall be wise to her and the lieutenant.

Through the use of his imagination, the speaker is able to become the old man, able to experience a portion of his life. The poem is curiously both objective and subjective; objective because of the interest in the life and concerns of a character other than the speaker, but subjective in that it is also his story, the story of his imagination.

In its use of a narrative structure and reliance on significant details that illuminate action, character, and meaning, this poem resembles prose fiction.[14] Simpson is the author of one novel, *Riverside Drive*, published in 1962, and has recently talked about writing another. In fact—if such things can be judged by what the protagonist of his poems says—it would appear that as a young man Simpson may have aspired more to writing fiction than poetry. For example, the speaker in "Sway" remembers a summer spent courting the already engaged girl whose nickname gives the poem its title: "Sway was beautiful. My heart went out to her"; "I told her of my ambition: / to write novels conveying the excitement / of life" (*PLH*, 108). In another poem, "The Man She Loved," the speaker remembers how, as a young student at Columbia, he would visit his relatives in Brooklyn on Sundays and spend at least part of the afternoon indulging in youthful, charmingly egotistical fantasies:

> Little did they know as they spoke
> that one day they would be immortal

in a novel that commanded the sweep
of Tolstoy, a magnificent creation
that would bring within its compass
offices in Manhattan and jungles
of the Amazon. A grasp of psychology
and sense of the passing of time
that can only be compared to,
without exaggerating, Proust.

                                        (*PLH*, 105)

And yet, despite this ambition, despite his skill at manipulating narrative, detail, and imagery, Simpson did not become a good novelist. In
fact, it is in the poem "Sway" that he himself gives what is probably the
best critique of *Riverside Drive*, as of his talent as a fiction writer generally. During that summer long ago, the girl has asked:

    . . . "When you're a famous novelist
will you write about me?"

I promised . . . and tried to keep my promise.

Years later the speaker comes upon the resulting pages in an old box;
the images are touching, the buildup to action promising, but: "Then
the trouble begins. I can never think of anything / to make the characters do" (*PLH*, 110). The failure occurs in the area of plot—the individual scenes of *Riverside Drive* are pointed and affecting, excellent at
conveying mood, but they never add up to a cohesive overall statement.
In short, Simpson's fiction embodies all the qualities that would be
needed should one wish to write a narrative kind of lyric poetry—
which is precisely the choice he ultimately made. In an essay published in 1976, he explains in hypothetical terms the use to which such
a poetry would put narrative: "As it deals with life, this poetry will
frequently be in the form of a narrative. Not a mere relation of external
events, but a narrative of significant actions. The poet will aim to con-
vey states of feeling. In our time poets have stayed away from narrative
because it has often been merely descriptive—there has been too much
dead tissue. But this can be avoided if the poet reveals a situation with
no more than a few words, and concentrates on the feeling."[15]
    Narrative is used in Simpson's best poems, then, not to channel ac-
tion towards an exciting climax but to organize images and relatively
minor incidents towards some revelation of personality and feeling.
Because this poetry is more or less static in terms of external action,
imagery is of considerable importance in the achievement of its effects.
Simpson, in fact, considers himself a kind of latter-day imagist poet,

which makes his definition of the goal of imagist writing important here: "There is a time lag, therefore a separation, between thought and experience. The more elaborate the comparison, as in Milton's epic similes, the harder it is to 'feel' the thought. An imagist poem, on the other hand, concentrates on giving you the experience—handing over sensations bodily, as Hulme said. Imagist writing aims to make you feel, rather than to tell you what feeling is like."[16] In Simpson's use of imagery there is something of the idea behind Eliot's objective correlative: if the image is properly prepared for and invested with appropriate suggestions, it should call up in the reader the same emotions it evokes in the author or in the character he is writing about.

Most often, the feelings that are expressed in the poems of phase three are again those of the Simpson protagonist, the sensibility that has always been at the heart of his work. However, because of the greater degree of empathy that informs this phase, we find poems as well that are spoken by characters who are obviously different from this one; also, there are poems written from the third-person point of view, in which Simpson imagines from the outside and sympathetically presents the feelings of another. Simpson is, in short, actively following advice he gave indirectly to Robert Lowell in a review written in 1977: "He ought to try getting inside the skin of a few people who aren't like himself."[17] Perhaps the most astonishing thing about Simpson's recent work is just how different the people he writes about are—not just from the sensibility that inhabits his work, but from the characters who appear in contemporary American poetry generally. In fact, without the example of Simpson, we might not be able to tell just how special, how atypical, that cast of characters generally is.

Most contemporary poets, of course, write primarily about their own personalities; Simpson is no exception to this rule. When we get beyond this level, what we generally find is characters who are very much like the poets—sensitive, intelligent, well-educated, of refined taste in food, music, literature, what have you. When we go beyond the poet as character in the poems of Simpson's phase three, by contrast, what we find are the *ordinary* citizens of America—not college professors and orchestra conductors, not manual laborers and nuclear protestors, but middle-class burghers; people who shop in shopping centers rather than in boutiques; people who watch *Love Boat* rather than *Masterpiece Theatre*; people who worry about their mortgages, their false teeth, their teenage children when they don't come home on time. Simpson's goal is to write, not about an unusual and privileged way of life, but about the life most real people are living in this country today. As he said in his address to the Jewish Book Council in 1981: "At the present time American poetry has very little to say about the world we live in. The American poet is content to have a style that sets him apart, to produce a unique sound, to create unusual images. But in my poems I have been attempting to explore ordinary, everyday life with the aim of showing that it can be deep, that though the life itself may not be poetic and, in fact, can be banal and sordid, yet it is the stuff of poetry, and the kind of poetry I believe to be most important—that which shows our common humanity."[18]

"Quiet Desperation" (*BHN*, 15–17), which appears in Simpson's most recent individual book of poems, *The Best Hour of the Night* (1983), is written from the third-person point of view and concerns a single day in the life of an unnamed citizen of suburbia. The poem begins while this man is doing errands, probably on a Saturday afternoon:

> At the post office he sees Joe McInnes.
> Joe says, "We're having some people over.
> It'll be informal. Come as you are."

When our hero arrives home, he finds his wife preparing dinner, "an experiment":

> He relays Joe's invitation.
> "No," she says, "not on your life.
> Muriel McInnes is no friend of mine."
>
> It appears that she told Muriel
> that the Goldins live above their means,
> and Muriel told Mary Goldin.
>
> He listens carefully, to get things right.
> The feud between the Andersons and the Kellys
> began with Ruth Anderson calling Mike Kelly
> a reckless driver. Finally
> the Andersons had to sell their house and move.
>
> Social life is no joke.
> It can be the only life there is.

At first reading, a passage like this sounds very much like prose. One thing that makes it poetry is the understatement, the restraint and precision, of the writing. The lines are mostly end-stopped, and many of them consist of single sentences; there is nothing here of the easy flow prose normally has. There is also no extravagance in the images and incidents; again, everything is kept to a careful and pointed minimum. Finally, as is characteristic of lyric poetry to a far greater degree than of prose, the passage depends for its coherence less on its details than on the sensibility that perceives and reflects on these details. The plainness of language is typical of Simpson in this phase; like Wordsworth (and others) before him, he wishes to write his poems essentially out of the mouths of his ordinary characters; as he has said in an essay: "In my attempts to write narrative poetry I have used the rhythms of speech. I bear in mind what it would be like to say the poem aloud to someone else. This helps me to form the lines. At the same time it eliminates confusion—I have to make my ideas clear. I eliminate words out of books, affected language, jargon of any kind."[19]

In the second section of the poem, the protagonist goes into the living room where his son is watching a movie on television: "the battle of Iwo Jima / is in progress." He watches for a moment; the Americans are pinned down by machine-gun fire; a man falls; "Sergeant Stryker / picks up the charge and starts running." He watches until the pillbox is destroyed by Stryker, then gets up and goes out: "He's seen the movie. Stryker gets killed / just as they're raising the flag." This man is restless and dissatisfied, and as the third section of the poem begins, we learn what he is feeling:

> A feeling of pressure . . .
> There is something that needs to be done
> immediately.
>
>   But there is nothing,
> only himself. His life is passing,
> and afterwards there will be eternity,
> silence, and infinite space.
>
> He thinks, "Firewood!"—
> and goes to the basement.

After cutting several logs into the proper size, arranging them carefully by the fireplace—but still restless, still feeling the pressure—he thinks of "The dog! / He will take the dog for a walk."

It is autumn and the trees are turning yellow; approaching "the cove," he admires the blue water and the swans. The poem ends:

> But when you come closer
> the rocks above the shore are littered
> with daggers of broken glass
> where the boys sat on summer nights
> and broke beer bottles afterwards.
>
> And the beach is littered, with cans,
> containers, heaps of garbage,
> newspaper wadded against the sea-wall.
> Someone has even dumped a mattress . . .

a definite success!
Some daring guy, some Stryker
in the pickup speeding away.

He cannot bear the sun
going over and going down . . .
the trees and houses vanishing
in quiet every day.

The story of an ordinary mid-life crisis perhaps, but told with sympathy and from the inside of the man who is suffering through it. He feels his age when he looks at his son, when he remembers how long ago it was that he first saw the movie; he feels the futility of his life in the encounters with his wife and Joe McInnes, the emptiness of human contact. All around him are images of mortality—the death of Stryker, the firewood, the yellow leaves on the trees—culminating in the image of the setting sun, how everything is "vanishing" into "eternity / silence, and infinite space."

"Quiet Desperation" establishes a common ground of ordinary human feelings where the guiding sensibility of Simpson's poems and his middle-class protagonist can meet to share what they have in common. There are many poems like this in the third phase of Simpson's work, poems that express, on the part of that sensibility, an authentic degree of empathy for humankind generally. However, there are also many poems in this phase that express something that may seem contrary to this—the continuing recognition by the Simpson sensibility of a difference between himself and most other people. It is not the feelings themselves that make him different, nor their quality and depth; rather, it is the degree to which these feelings are speculated upon and understood. This realization does not lessen the empathy felt by the protagonist, but it does reinforce his sense of isolation, of an ultimate and irremediable aloneness.

"Encounter on the 7:07," also from *The Best Hour of the Night* (8–12), is spoken from the first-person point of view and puts the Simpson speaker in contact with a man something like the central character of "Quiet Desperation." Again, the poem is long, in this case organized into six sections. The speaker is riding a commuter train when "a man of about forty, with a suntan" gets on and sits next to him. The man's doctor had advised a vacation, so he had gone to Florida. Meanwhile, on the train itself there is a "car card advertising / 'Virginia Slims'":

The man sitting next to me,
whose name is Jerry—Jerry DiBello—
observes that he doesn't smoke cigarettes,
he smokes cigars. "Look at Winston Churchill.

He smoked cigars every day of his life,
and he lived to be over eighty."

An ordinary guy who likes to talk—the advertisement provides
enough of an excuse for this personal comment.

Later he says that "His family used to own a restaurant," that his
father had come "from Genoa / as a seaman, and jumped ship," got a
job washing dishes, and "Ten years later / he owned the restaurant."
Jerry goes on to say that he sells cars, etc.,

But I'm not listening—I'm on deck,
looking at the lights of the harbor.
A sea wind fans my cheek.
I hear the waves chuckling
against the side of the ship.

The passage illustrates that same empathy, that same imaginative absorption into the skin of another character, that we saw in "The Mexican Woman."[20]

The thematic heart of this poem comes in its fifth section; the
speaker says that he had brought along a copy of *Ulysses* to read on the
train and begins by giving D. H. Lawrence's opinion of the book:

"An *olla putrida* . . .
old fags and cabbage-stumps of quotations,"
said Lawrence. Drawing a circle about himself
and Frieda . . . building an ark,
envisioning the Flood.

But the Flood may be long coming.
In the meantime there is life
every day, and Ennui.

Ever since the middle class
and money have ruled our world
we have been desolate.
. . . .
A feeling of being alone
and separate from the world . . .
"alienation" psychiatrists call it.
Religion would say, this turning away
from life is the life of the soul.

This is why Joyce is such a great writer:
he shows a life of fried bread
and dripping "like a boghole,"

an art that rises out of life
and flies toward the sun,

transfiguring as it flies
the reality.

The problem that the sensibility of Simpson's poems faces is that the society of which he is a part is so much more superficial in its interests than he is; it is committed to money, to the everyday problems of work, but ignores the depths of human emotion, the life of the soul. Lawrence provides no answer, because he went to the opposite extreme; he wrote of the depths but ignored the superficial realities of life. Thus, it is left to James Joyce to be the literary hero of this poem, the one who could write about both things at the same time, transfiguring reality while flying it toward the sun. This is precisely the goal that the speaker of "The Man She Loved" had wanted to express to his relatives:

. . . how could he explain what it meant to be a writer . . .
a world that was entirely different,
and yet it would include the sofa
and the smell of chicken cooking.

(*PLH*, 105)

The alienation of Simpson's protagonist results precisely from his devotion to the things that are unseen by the middle class generally—a full range of genuine emotions, the life of the soul. In the final section of "Encounter on the 7:07," we are returned to Jerry DiBello, who had encountered a hurricane during his stay in Florida; "For days afterwards they were still finding bodies":

When he went for a walk
the shore looked as though it had been swept
with a broom. The sky was clear,
the sun was shining, and the sea was calm.

He felt that he was alone with the universe.
He, Jerry DiBello, was at one with God.

Although a casual reader might not at first think so, these lines are neither satirical nor sarcastic; they give a straightforward, even sympathetic, rendering of the feelings this automobile salesman had when confronted with a vision of the ultimate. We must remember that he only went on this trip because of a doctor's orders, thus bringing with him a newly discovered awareness of his own mortality. As the poem ends, the speaker recognizes both his difference from DiBello and the human bond that they share.

Reactions to poems like these vary, but a common one is the assumption that Simpson is being satirical.[21] In the interview that follows, Simpson described both the original response to his poem "The Beaded Pear" and his motivation:

> The poem is meant to be absolutely descriptive of the kind of domestic life we actually live in this country today. When the poem first came out—in the Long Island newspaper *Newsday*—it upset a lot of people. I got hate mail from people who thought I was being devastatingly sarcastic. But I don't see it that way. There is an element of ridicule in the poem, but it is directed at the culture which fosters these kinds of values, not at the people themselves. No—mostly it is a purely descriptive poem, an attempt at absolutely dead-on, accurate truth. There is even a touch of pathos at the end.

This attitude is given further amplication in yet another comment in the same interview: "Now this may be romantic, but I feel that the ordinary people are pretty decent, even though their attitudes may not be mine. I don't feel that they're at all contemptible. I mean the people you meet in a shoestore or pub or shopping mall. I have always felt that there is a lot of poetry in those people."

And yet those crucial differences between the Simpson protagonist and the average middle-class citizen remain. It is the expression of these differences that makes some readers think such poems are satirical. The tone of these poems is an extremely delicate one and results from the understatement and restraint that is built into their form. Simpson is attempting to balance very different opinions of two nearly identical things—his empathy for the people and his contempt for the values by which they sometimes live their lives. How delicate this tone is, how hard for some readers to understand, is indicated by the following, rather remarkably misguided, judgment: "Louis Simpson's work now suggests too much comfort: emotional, physical, intellectual. He has stopped struggling, it seems, for words, for rhythms, for his own deepest self. His is a middle-class, middle-brow poetry, the major value of which is to steer other poets from the same course, and to raise some questions about poets joining an Establishment, whether it be one of social class, national or literary identification."[22]

How far Louis Simpson is from joining the middle-class "Establishment" is apparent in another new poem, the longest of his career. "The Previous Tenant" (*BHN*, 21–36) consists of ten sections and deals once again with the conflict between society and the individual. It is spoken from the first-person point of view by the Simpson sensibility and is primarily concerned with the story of his alienation from the suburban community in which he lives—ironically named Point Mercy. The speaker's awareness of his own alienation is brought to the surface through the story of Dr. Hugh McNeil, whose illicit love affair makes him the enemy of the forces of decency in the town. The speaker is renting a cottage—

> Thoreau, who recommends sleeping in the box
> railroad workers keep their tools in,
> would have found this house commodious.

—that contains several cartons of goods left behind by the previous tenant, McNeil; he learns McNeil's story from his landlord, from some letters he finds, and from community gossip.

Probably the most important "character" in the poem is the collective force that acts as antagonist to both these men—the society itself. At first McNeil and his family are welcomed with open arms to the community; he is an ideal citizen,

> . . . one of the fathers on Saturday
> dashing about. He drove a green Land Rover
> as though he were always on safari
> with the children and an Irish setter.

An early and very mild conflict involving him helps to define the community. He speaks at a village meeting in favor of "retaining / the Latin teacher at the high school"; despite his arguments, the community votes instead to

> . . . remodel the gymnasium.
> McNeil accepted defeat gracefully.
> That was one of the things they liked about him.

In a summary comment, Simpson speaks ironically for the community, which is able to find a silver lining in this incident:

> Contrary to what people say
> about the suburbs, they appreciate culture.
> Hugh McNeil was an example . . .
> doing the shopping, going to the club,
> a man in no way different from themselves,
> husband and family man
> and good neighbor, who nevertheless spoke Latin.

The passage reflects the "thinking" of Helen Knox, president of the Garden Club and the character whom Simpson uses as spokesperson for Point Mercy. She has a rare ability:

> She knew how to put what they were feeling
> into words. This was why
> she was president—elected not once
> or twice . . . this was her third term in office.

Like her highly cultured community, Helen Knox is anti-Semitic and a racist. Thus, when McNeil begins his adulterous affair with Irene Davis, whose maiden name was the Italian Cristiano, Helen says:

> "I met her once". . .
> "Harry introduced her to me
> at the bank. A dark woman. . . .
> I think, a touch of the tar brush."

Things start to get out of hand—McNeil appears one day with "broken ribs, black eyes, / and a missing tooth," claiming that he was mugged. A service-station attendant comments:

> "He was never mugged.
> It was Irene Davis's brothers,
> the Cristianos. They had him beat up."
>
> He knew about gansters. They would beat up a guy
> to warn him. The next time it was curtains.

Helen Knox leads a delegation that calls on the chief of staff at the hospital to demand McNeil's dismissal. Dr. Abrahams replies that "McNeil's private life / . . . / had nothing to do with his work"; "they were fortunate / to have a surgeon of Hugh McNeil's caliber." Helen Knox sums up the feelings of the entire Garden Club:

> "What can you expect?" . . .
> "It was bad enough letting them in,
> but to make one chief of staff!"

Eventually, McNeil is divorced and moves into the cottage now occupied by the speaker; he breaks up with Irene, begins seeing her again, breaks up again. Finally he comes back to pick up his things, "accompanied by a young woman / wearing jeans and a sweater":

> It appeared he was back on the track
> once more, after his derailment.

With a woman of the right kind at his side
to give him a nudge. "Say thanks!"

It is at this point in the poem that the story of the speaker's own conflict with the society of Point Mercy comes to the fore. He is eating
lunch with his friend Maggie at the Colony Inn when he sees Irene
Davis for the first time:

They said she was dark. What they hadn't said
was that the darkness, jet-black hair,
was set off by a skin like snow,
like moonlight in a dark field glimmering.

In the final section of the poem, a minor incident causes an argument
between the speaker and Maggie. A gazebo has been vandalized, and
Maggie defends the youth of Point Mercy: "I'm sure . . . it wasn't anyone / from around here." The speaker replies that "You don't have to go
into New York City" to find "vandals," "thieves," and "illiterates." His
attack on the community convinces Maggie that the speaker is "cynical," a disease that infects his whole "attitude":

"Like what you said in the restaurant
about Hugh McNeil and the Davis woman
being better than the rest of us."

Then she becomes "really angry":

"I know, you prefer vulgar people.
Anyone who tries to be decent and respectable
is either a hypocrite or a fool."

Certainly the speaker does hate hypocrisy, but the real basis for this
disagreement is his admiration for people who are true to their emotions, whatever the cost in social respectability or status. This is the
same attitude that made the speaker of "Summer Morning" "spoil his
chances," for "The thrill of an assignation, / My life that I hold in
secret." In the eyes of society, conformity is more important than self-
fulfillment, complimentary fictions more comfortable than the truth
about themselves. Thus, despite the affection that he has learned to
feel for individuals, the Simpson protagonist still can never have more
than an uneasy alliance with American society at large. His sensibility
is that of the young poet "Peter," as defined in the poem of that title
originally published in *Caviare at the Funeral:*

Stupidity reassures you; you do not belong
in a bourgeois establishment, it can never be your home.
Restlessness is a sign of intelligence;
revulsion, the flight of a soul.

(*PLH*, 169)

At the end of *The Best Hour of the Night*, Simpson has placed an ars poetica devoted to the plight of the poet who chooses to live and work in suburbia. Entitled "The Unwritten Poem" (*BHN*, 69), it begins by asking where poetry is to be found; "Not in beautiful faces and distant scenery," he answers, but:

In your life here, on this street
where the houses from the outside
are all alike, and so are the people.
Inside, the furniture is dreadful—
floc on the walls, and huge color television.

However much he may dislike the details of this way of life, its taste-lessness, the absence of emotion, the poet still must also love the people he writes about; as Pound said fifty years ago, unless poetry is based upon affectionate feelings, it will inevitably corrode and die from the inside out. Simpson knows, however, that his feelings will never be reciprocated by the community: "To love and write unrequited / is the poet's fate." The poem ends with a vision of the soullessness of American life, as the poet watches the morning commuters, "grasping brief-cases," as they "pass beyond your gaze / and hurl themselves into the flames." They are like the dead souls of Eliot's "Waste Land," seen crossing London Bridge every morning. It is, then, finally the soul-lessness of American life that places the individual in Simpson's poems at odds with this society.

The fugitive-agrarian poets—John Crowe Ransom, Robert Penn War-ren, Allen Tate—used to say that, because the South lost the Civil War, southerners were more in touch with the humble realities of life, with its tragic potentialities, than northerners. It is when he looks at Ameri-can life as a whole that Simpson finds the emptiness that the earlier poets found in the North. Americans have been too successful, too insulated from want and deprivation.

"The Inner Part," for example—a one-sentence poem first published in *At the End of the Open Road*—makes this point in a striking fashion:

When they had won the war
And for the first time in history
Americans were the most important people—

When the leading citizens no longer lived in their shirt sleeves,
And their wives did not scratch in public;
Just when they'd stopped saying "Gosh!"—

When their daughters seemed as sensitive
As the tip of a fly rod,
And their sons were as smooth as a V-8 engine—

Priests, examining the entrails of birds,
Found the heart misplaced, and seeds
As black as death, emitting a strange odor.

(*PLH,* 72)

It is because of this moral emptiness, this lack of tragic experience, this absence of failure, in America that Simpson turned for the subject matter of many of his poems to Russia, home of his and his mother's ancestors. There he found a people who had suffered, a people who knew the full range of indignities life has to offer those who haven't won every battle.

The poem "Why Do You Write About Russia?" (*PLH,* 137–40) draws essentially this contrast between the two nations. It begins with the speaker sitting in his suburban American home, remembering how his mother used to tell him, a child in Jamaica, stories about the old country, "of freezing cold," wolves, and cossacks. The poem is meditative; as he looks out of his window, the speaker contrasts the dreamlike stories he remembers with the life that now surrounds him:

This too is like a dream, the way we live
with our cars and power-mowers . . .
a life that shuns emotion
and the violence that goes with it,
the object being to live quietly
and bring up children to be happy.

Because it exists in the absence of all other emotions, the speaker feels that such happiness can only be a delusion; this is a crazy way to bring up children. Thus dissatisfied with the life that surrounds him, he asks himself, "What then do I want?":

A life in which there are depths
beyond happiness. As one of my friends,

Grigoryev, says, "Two things
constantly cry out in creation,
the sea and man's soul."

Grigoryev is an imaginary friend, whom the speaker has created to tell
him stories about the old country, identified later as "the same far
place the soul comes from."

The poem ends with an indirect definition of Russia that indicates
what the speaker feels he has inherited from his ancestry:

When I think about Russia
it's not that area of the earth's surface . . .
. . . .
It's a sound, such as you hear
in a sea breaking along a shore.

My people came from Russia,
bringing with them nothing
but that sound.

It is that crying out, that longing, that loneliness, that hunger of the
unfulfilled soul, that defines the sensibility of the poet and makes poetry what it is.

When pushed to an ultimate extreme, such an intense loneliness of
the soul reflects a religious or a spiritual longing, and in the poems of
Louis Simpson there is indeed posited a relationship between the poetic sensibility and the religious sensibility. "Baruch" (*PLH*, 134–36) is
one of his best and most characteristic poems; through the stories of
two other characters, Russian ancestors of the nineteenth century, it
leads up to a central revelation about its speaker, the Simpson character we have been following throughout this chapter. The first section
of the poem deals with the title character:

There is an old folk saying:
"He wishes to study the Torah
but he has a wife and family."
Baruch had a sincere love of learning
but he owned a dress-hat factory.

When the factory burns down one night, Baruch takes this as a sign
from God to "give myself to the Word." He has only begun his studies,
however, when death takes him: "For in Israel it is also written, /
'Prophecy is too great a thing for Baruch.' "

The second section tells of

> Cousin Deborah
> who, they said, had read everything . . .
> The question was, which would she marry,
> Tolstoy or Lermontov or Pushkin?

Her family makes the choice and marries her off to a timber merchant from Kiev; when they are locked in the bedroom after the ceremony, she cries and screams all night long:

> As soon as it was daylight, Brodsky—
> that was his name—drove back to Kiev
> like a man pursued.

The third section is reflective and personal; the Simpson protagonist is traveling late at night:

> The love of literature goes with us.
>
> On a train approaching midnight
> everyone else has climbed into his sarcophagus
> except four men playing cards.
> There is nothing better than poker—
> not for the stakes but the companionship,
> trying to outsmart one another.
> Taking just one card . . .
>
> I am sitting next to the window,
> looking at the lights on the prairie
> clicking by. From time to time
> two or three will come together
> then go wandering off again.
>
> Then I see a face, pale and unearthly,
> that is flitting along with the train,
> passing over the fields and rooftops,
> and I hear a voice out of the past:
> "He wishes to study the Torah."

All three characters feel the tension that exists between the world of physical reality and the world of the spirit or the imagination. Though he at first thinks otherwise, Baruch belongs in the shadowless world of everyday reality. Cousin Deborah suffers from no such delusion; she exists entirely at the opposite pole. It is left for the Simpson protagonist to live in both worlds at once, to love the physical and to venerate something spiritual at one and the same time.

Louis Simpson is by no means an overtly religious poet; and yet among the poems in the third phase of his career, the phase that locates the poet so firmly in the American suburbs, are several that quest for something spiritual: "I feel that I have two directions I must follow—one leads to this straightforward kind of poem about ordinary life as it really looks and smells, and the other leads to a poetry which is altogether more imagistic and more mysterious" ("Interview with Louis Simpson").[23] Insofar as this thinking is based upon traditional religious ideas, it grows out of Simpson's studies of Zen Buddhism, about which he has said:

> Buddhism teaches that your physical existence and your mental existence are one thing; in the West, we tend automatically to split them apart, as in the Christian idea of the body and the soul. I prefer the medieval idea—they had a term for the body which recognized it as the form for the soul, which I take to mean that the body is the outward garment of the soul. Whitman says that too, that there is no split between the body and the soul. And this is what the Buddhists say also. This way of thinking leads to a poetry that is very physical in its orientation, a poetry that concentrates on ordinary life. ("Interview with Louis Simpson")[24]

Simpson's most ambitious poem of a more "mysterious" sort—based very loosely on the ox-herding cartoon series by the Zen master—is "Searching for the Ox" (*PLH*, 183–87). The poem consists of a "free-floating series of associations," all of which help express one idea. Section two speaks of those who wish to manipulate the world through an abstract understanding of it—"engineers from IBM," for example. Their success at sending a rocket towards the moon is very impressive, the speaker says, but

> . . . still, I must confess,
> I fear those *messieurs*, like a peasant
> listening to the priests talk Latin.
> They will send me off to Heaven
> when all I want is to live in the world.

Similarly, when he learns the practice of Zen meditation in section five and tries to follow "in the Way / that 'regards sensory experience as relatively unimportant,' " the speaker finds instead that "I am far more aware / of the present, sensory life." The poem ends with a central understanding that sends the Simpson protagonist back to where he started:

> There is only earth:
> in winter laden with snow,
> in summer covered with leaves.

Simpson can, at times, sound almost like a mystic when discussing this aspect of his work; the poem "Adam Yankev," for example, asserts: "Around us / things want to be understood" (*PLH*, 124)—and in the Afterword to *People Live Here*, he says: "I have always felt that there is a power and intelligence in things. I felt it as a boy when I watched the sun setting from the top of a mountain and rode a bicycle in the lanes on Kingston and walked along the shore, listening to the sea. I felt that power when I first saw Manhattan rise out of the Atlantic, the towers a poet describes as 'moody water-loving giants.' "[25]

However, just as he is probably the most consciously American of the poets treated in this book, Simpson is also the most pragmatic of them. Simpson's orientation, even at its most religious, is not other-worldly; for him, the ultimate meaning of the world, of the earth, is to be found in "the things of this world" themselves and not in abstract ideas about them. In the poem "The Foggy Lane" (*PLH*, 182), Simpson's speaker encounters in succession three abstractionists: the first extols poets who deal only in a world of dreams; the second is a radical who wants "to live in a pure world"; the third is a salesman who thinks an insurance policy can protect one from harm. In the final stanza, the speaker replies to them all:

> Walking in the foggy lane
> I try to keep my attention fixed
> on the uneven, muddy surface . . .
> the pools made by the rain,
> and wheel-ruts, and wet leaves,
> and the rustling of small animals.

What we see here is not just a theory of poetry but a philosophy of how the world should be understood and dealt with; it is real, it is uncertain, it is beautiful, and it deserves our complete attention.

Interview with
Louis Simpson

●

The interview was originally conducted at Mr. Simpson's home in Port Jefferson, New York, in March of 1977. *Searching for the Ox* had been published in 1976 and Mr. Simpson was working on his third volume of criticism, *A Revolution in Taste: Studies of Dylan Thomas, Allen Ginsberg, Sylvia Plath, and Robert Lowell* (1978). The interview was updated in Mr. Simpson's hotel room on the campus of the University of Houston in the spring of 1980, just before the publication of *Caviare at the Funeral*.

When did you begin writing poetry?

My first published poems came out in a school magazine when I was thirteen or fourteen. But in those days I mostly wanted to write prose. The first thing I published outside of school was not a poem, it was an essay on the coronation of King George V, which won first prize in a competition and was published in the *Daily Gleaner.* That was the big newspaper on Jamaica, and they gave me five pounds. The next year I won a second prize for a short story, which was also published in the *Daily Gleaner.* After that I began writing with a group that published in a newspaper-magazine called *Public Opinion.* That was a great deal of fun—we were all trying to win Jamaican independence. I published short stories there, and also some poems, when I was about sixteen. I was reading Faulkner and Saroyan and wanted to write like them.

What finally turned you to poetry?

Well, that was after the war. When I was seventeen. I went from Jamaica to New York and attended Columbia University. I wrote poems that were published in the *Columbia Review,* and also some prose. Then the war came, and I didn't write anything for three years. When I came back to Columbia, I wrote a short story that *Esquire* took. That was the first thing I ever published in an American magazine. Then I began working on the *Review* as an editor, and published some short stories there. I finally turned to poetry because I found that I could get out of my system certain things in a short space that I couldn't get in prose. And actually, the kinds of things I could do were much better suited to poems. I didn't have much knowledge of the world, the way things are done and run. Outside of my knowledge of the army, I didn't have any experience. What I did have was a great deal of emotional intensity, which was wrapped up with certain things I'd seen—and that shaped the poems, it made me write poems. That was about 1947. Some of my first poems were taken by *Wake*, the magazine edited by Seymour Lawrence up in Cambridge; *Harper's* took one, and *Partisan Review* took one or two.

By the end of 1949 I had enough poems for a book. I was living in Paris, where I stayed for a year, and found a very good publisher, a man who put out fine editions. He did a beautiful printing of *The Arrivistes*. He printed 500 copies, of which about 200 were distributed from New York by a man named Gustav Davidson. I tried to find out where the rest were, but all he said was that they'd been lost. I never did learn how you can lose 300 copies of a book. I paid for that book myself—$500 for 500 copies, which is an incredible price. But I still didn't want to lose 300 copies. Recently they've been turning up, selling for $300 a copy. Anyhow, I returned to the states and took a job as an editor for Bobbs-Merrill, where I lasted five years.

I had another bad experience with my second book. I sent it in to a competition called the Borestone Mountain Award. I was delighted when, months later, they called to say I had won. But then a few days later they told me that there had been a recount of the votes and they had made a mistake, I had not won. The prize was going instead to someone called Leah Bodine Drake. The judge was Robert Lowell—I suppose he changed his mind for some reason. And what was the funniest thing, they asked me not to say anything about this because it would hurt the reputation of the Borestone Mountain Award. And would you believe it, I didn't say anything, not for four years. That was a blow. But finally John Hall Wheelock at Scribner's took the book and they published it in their Poets of Today series. They would put three manuscripts by three different writers into a single volume, and that is how *Good News of Death* finally appeared. It got some good reviews, but the critics insisted on treating it as one of three, as though we poets were in competition and the only point was to say which was best.

My third book, *A Dream of Governors*, was published in 1959. Between then and 1963, when I published *At the End of the Open Road*, I underwent a big change. I had been writing poetry that was quite formal; one reason for that, I think, was Randall Jarrell's review of *The*

Arrivistes. He said very nice things—that I was a very good poet, a very promising poet, but that there wasn't a single really good poem in the book, nothing was quite finished. So I decided I'd better learn how to finish poems. I had a lot of fun in *The Arrivistes* kicking things around in all sorts of shapes and forms. Now I decided I should learn how to write the perfect poem. So over the next few years, I tried to write impeccable poems, poems you couldn't find fault with.

Then between 1959 and 1963 I broke all that up and tried to write poetry that would be more free, that would sound more like my real voice. *At the End of the Open Road* does have a few poems in traditional forms, but it also has a considerable amount of free verse. Ever since then I've written mostly a kind of informal poetry. I work very hard to get the shape and sound of a poem just right, to get the lines breaking right, but I'm not working in regular stanzas and meters. So that was a big upheaval and a big change for me. And of course you never please people. Someone will always say, "Oh, that early stuff was the best; we wish you'd never changed." Then there are the others who say that everything before *At the End of the Open Road* was a terrible mistake. Neither point of view is true, of course. Some of the early poems, I think, hold up very well, especially those about World War II. But, you do what you feel you have to do, and sometimes that means changing very strongly. I know some poets don't. They keep writing the same kind of poem forever. But I've always been changing, and this has made problems for me as far as the public goes. They can't typecast me as easily as they'd like to.

How do you compose your poems? Do you work in longhand or at the typewriter? Do you work in bursts or long stretches?

I work in bursts and I work at the typewriter. When I've done a draft of a poem, I take the sheet out of the typewriter and work on it in longhand. Then I type up a clean sheet and start the process all over again. My pages end up completely filled with corrections. There are periods, sometimes for months, when I don't really feel like writing poetry. I haven't written a poem now for about two months because I've been writing prose. Writing poetry for me demands a kind of preoccupation, a slow process of being bothered by something, thinking about it and trying to pull it together. The last poem I wrote took only one day, but that was because I had been thinking about the subject for a long time.

Do you ever have a poem, the way some people say happens, just burst into your head so that the composition takes only as long as it takes to write the words?

I've had that happen two or three times in my life, but no more. Once was in Paris in 1949 when I wrote the poem called "Carentan O Carentan." That was a dream—I dreamed the poem, then I sat down and wrote it. It came practically complete at the first writing. The same thing happened with another war poem, "I Dreamed That in a City Dark as Paris." One or two others have come very fast, but in general, no. Usually I get a few lines easily, maybe half the poem, and the rest comes only through very hard work. Right now I have about five different clusters of things in my head that could be poems, but I haven't seen the way yet to make them poems. When I say cluster, I mean material that's new—scenes, sequences of ideas, or images. The poems themselves will probably take me a long time to get. I work very hard on poems. That's why I can't do prose and poetry at the same time, they both take a lot of rewriting and continuous effort.

So when you are about to start a poem, it's a cluster of images in your mind rather than some abstract idea that gets you going.

It's not an abstract idea. I don't think abstract ideas are a good beginning for poems, not for me anyhow. I wouldn't know what to do next— illustrate the idea with images, I guess. No, I start with a scene or with something that I don't think has been written about; there are always an incredible number of things that haven't been written about. I'll give you an example. I have an idea for a poem now that I don't know if I can write, but it would be a very good poem. It would be a new kind of story in which there are no characters, just things seen on a highway, a succession of signs and objects. It would be a love story, actually, but the two people might not even meet. It would just be the things that they pass through in order to meet each other. The point of the poem would be that our real experience in situations today has more to do with things like driving a car than with human relations. This is the general framework of the poem, the idea that would make a poem. I've already ridden the highway with a notebook on my knee taking down signs. I have three pages of notes, but making it come alive as a poem would depend on the movement of the lines, the feeling you'd get into the lines themselves, and I don't know if that'll ever come. These are things that have to sit and wait until I am, I suppose the word is "inspired."

Would you say that your service in World War II had an important effect on your work as a poet?

Very important. First of all, surviving the war made me realize that, in a sense, my life was mine to do with as I pleased. I could be a poet or anything I liked. Also, the war created a big difference between me and some of my contemporaries, who were only slightly younger. For example, my attitudes are very different from those of someone like Allen Ginsberg, because he was not in the war and I was. Our attitudes toward America are completely different. I have a certain innate respect and love for the United States and its government that some younger people, for whom the war was an imposition, don't have. My feeling of affection for the country has been badly damaged at times, but I have never had that hostile attitude toward it which has been common among younger people. I felt the war was something that had to be done by my generation, and we did it.

This has some bearing, I'm sure, on my attitude toward some of the rioting of the sixties and seventies. I took part in the Berkeley protests against the war in Vietnam because I thought it was a very bad thing. On the other hand, the absolute sweeping denigration of the United States which was fashionable in the sixties, when they were looking for the *meanest* possible motive in ordinary people's attitudes, seemed to me to be equally disgusting—just as the attitude of the people who were making the war in Vietnam. The radicals seemed just as fascistic to me as the war makers, and it was the ordinary people, the citizens, who were suffering. Now this may be romantic, but I feel that the ordinary people are pretty decent, even though their attitudes may not be mine. I don't feel that they're at all contemptible. I mean the people you meet in a shoestore or pub or shopping mall. I have always felt that there is a lot of poetry in those people.

As a matter of fact, the poetry I'm trying to write these days—with *great* difficulty—is an attempt to talk about the ordinary life around us, not the rarified life of a thief or an intellectual. Maybe this cannot be done. It may be that a commercial, industrial civilization puts so many layers over things that there's no reality left. I'm not sure, but I would like to write a poetry of ordinary things. I began doing this in earnest in *Searching for the Ox,* and I got the impression from some of the reviews, especially the English reviews, that some readers didn't quite understand what it was all about. They couldn't see the poetry in lines that look so prosaic and ordinary. But I feel that I have two directions I must follow—one leads to this straightforward kind of poem about ordinary life as it really looks and smells, and the other leads to a poetry which is altogether more imagistic and more mysterious. I don't see why I can't do both.

You spent five years in publishing after World War II. Did you learn anything as a poet from that experience?

The only thing I learned as a poet was that sitting in that office was a complete waste of time. The books were not worthy of attention, and I discovered that you could spend entire days of your life doing nothing of any real satisfaction. I have never felt that way about teaching. The university is a much better place for a writer—at least you can read good books, and the people you meet, the students, are alive. Being a teacher also makes you work harder at ideas than you might otherwise, and this is valuable. Of course, any job that you might have is going to use up some of your valuable time, but for a writer, being a teacher is better than most other jobs. Your time is freer and that means you can write more.

You don't seem to be a regular participant in the creative-writing industry that is so prominent a part of so many universities. Why is that? Do you just prefer teaching more customary academic courses?

I think it is better to be writing your own stuff than telling other people how to write; it takes away from your own writing to be vicariously writing. It is also much more difficult to teach writing than it is to teach literature. You're more involved with the students' personalities, and when their feelings get hurt, you have problems on your hands. Then there's the old question of whether writing can even be taught. You cannot teach a nonwriter or a mediocre writer to be a good writer. About the best you can do is show good writers where they're making mistakes, where something can be improved. But at least half of the students in creative-writing classes have no real talent. All you can do is pat them on the head and try not to hurt their feelings.

Even for the potentially good writers, the creative-writing programs present certain dangers. In my experience, these programs tend to make the students rather self-conscious in the wrong way. They learn too much about what is "going" at the moment, who's in and who's out, and this destroys their innocence. I think a real poet has to find out certain things for himself, grope his own way a lot of the time. That's what makes his poetry different and original. But these people are taught poetry as a career. They become very competitive, and this is the last thing a poet should be. A poet should stick to his writing and not worry about his competition or whether he's getting published or not. I'm a terrible romantic about poetry. I believe it is something that you do for your own pleasure, and if it pleases you then maybe someone else will get pleasure out of it. But I'm against the competitiveness and the self-consciousness; I don't like that atmosphere at all.

You have written two volumes of literary criticism—Three on the Tower *and* A Revolution in Taste. *What made you want to invest that much time and energy in an activity peripheral to your central task of writing poetry?*

Well, I don't write poetry all the time, I can't write poetry all the time, but I do have a lot of things going on in my head *about* poetry, and I want to be able to express them. And I like writing prose—it is hard as hell, but it also has a pleasure to it. Also, if I possibly can, I would like to affect the climate in which poetry is read today. I think that there is a need for clear speaking about poetry, that there is a lot of obfuscation taking place. There is a whole group of academic critics, men such as Harold Bloom, who seem to me to be completely mistaken or self-serving when they write about poetry. They have a theory which they insist on applying to all writers, even when it doesn't fit at all. I wouldn't mind if a man like Bloom limited himself to writing about Shelley, but he undertakes to talk about contemporary poetry, and it's quite clear to me that he knows very little about it. His values are completely cockeyed; he has a theory which he is trying to impose like a dead brick on contemporary poetry. The trouble is that people who are intimidated by the appearance of learning are likely to believe what he says. I remember meeting a woman who told me that she didn't understand him, but that he was very important. A lot of people feel that way. The reason she couldn't understand him is that he doesn't make *sense*. So, one reason I write criticism is to cut through the nonsense and say something intelligible. I think we need good critics very badly—people who will talk about what is really there on the page and who will do so out of an emotional commitment to the poetry.

At one time Whitman was an important influence on your work. What was the source of that importance?

He was important to me in this opening up of the form, the line, which allows you to think of the poem, not as a structure of stanza and meter, but as a structure of cadences determined, really, by the content and the feeling of the poem. His freedom of form and his belief that the job of the American poet was to name things, to say things for the first time. I like to think, when I write a poem, that I'm saying something for the first time or creating a new situation or telling a kind of story that no one else would tell. I've been working lately on a kind of narrative of ordinary situations, and I don't know that many other people are doing that.

You are often referred to as an intensely American poet, perhaps the most consciously American of all current poets, and yet the first many years of your life were spent in Jamaica. Do you have any explanation for this seemingly paradoxical situation?

When I was growing up in Jamaica, I learned about America from my mother, who was American, and from movies we saw. I developed a somewhat romantic attitude about America—it was an exciting place to me, very different from the restrained English life we had in Jamaica in the thirties. I thought of America as a place where people had a very exciting life and the freedom to behave as they pleased. Then too, when I came to America, I knew I was going to stay here and that I was going to be a writer. So I tried to find out about the country as hard as I could. This was my material as a writer, and I wanted to understand it. My attitude as a writer has always been to be concerned with the material, not with my own salvation. I think that many poets are concerned with working out their own personal salvation through their work, projecting an emotional outcry of their soul. This has never been part of my intention—my own personal identity seems very unimportant to me. In fact, some Englishman pointed out in a review of *Searching for the Ox* that the ego had disappeared almost totally from my work, and I hope that's true.

I try to see myself as a transmitter and the poem as a transmission—I stand between the material, which is out there, separate from myself, and the created work. My job is to select from the material what I think will make a poem, shape it, and pass it through. So I have tried to absorb America as hard as I could, because that is the material I've been given. I've tried hard to understand it, but I never had to try to like it—I always did like it. Even the horrible, ugly things to me were stuff that could make poetry. I have just tried to find and state the essential truth of things. I think this is why I am so fond of writers like Dreiser and Whitman. A few years ago I did quite a long review of a book on Dreiser for the London *Times*. What I like about such writers is *not* their philosophy—that is very awkward and naive. In fact, most writers are not very good philosophers. The excitement in Dreiser is that he's saying something for the first time; he's taking this absolutely rough and raw material, showing it to you, and paying careful attention to it.

And that's how *I* feel about America, and that's what I have been trying to do. But there are problems, undeniable problems. For one thing, I am an outsider—I grew up in Jamaica. And then, not long after I arrived in America, I left it to fight in the war—and that was a European experience. So I had to find my bearings all over again. Another problem is the material itself—can it be turned into poetry? Maybe it's just too flat, too dead. And the language which this material demands is not exciting either. I don't use colorful or fancy language because that would be an interruption of the truth I want to get across; I'm trying to get across the poem as a *whole*. The whole poem—one page, three pages—is a single word almost, one whole expression. It is as though the event were speaking to the reader. I want to write an almost transparent poem in which you can't find the writer and in which the language draws no attention to itself. I know this attitude toward the language of poetry is completely different from that held by a poet like Dylan Thomas, back then, or today by a poet like Charles Wright, where the words are so important, or John Ashbery, where the individual sentences call so much attention to themselves.

So—to get back to your original question—I just saw this as my material, my American material. In the beginning, I wrote about it in big generalizations—I wanted to eat the country up all at once. Now I'm doing a different kind of thing: I'm trying to get at it by writing about individual scenes and people. Of course, the irony of it is that the great American poem may well be written by a poet who doesn't think of himself as American at all, who writes American poems because he happens to live in America. He would be surprised to be called an American poet—just as Thomas Hardy would have been surprised to be called an English poet. He wrote that way because he lived there.

You've been quoted as having said: "The main fact about the American artist is his feeling of isolation." Do you still have this feeling of isolation as a poet in America?

Oh, very much. American poets tend to find themselves separated from each other by geographical space—we don't meet in cafés; we rarely talk to each other; we see very little of each other. You may as a person have a life with other people, but as a poet you are isolated, you don't see the people you really have a lot in common with for a year or two at a time.

I also think the poets are isolated, spiritually and intellectually, from society at large. American society does not need its poets—and I'm not being cynical; I'm just stating facts. This observation is certainly not original with me. The American economy can go through a day completely oblivious of poetry without the slightest jar. And the people—there are very few readers of poetry in America. I figure that, at the most, there are ten thousand people in the United States capable of reading a book of modern poetry. I said "capable" of reading it, which doesn't mean that they will actually read it. A new book of poetry, by a good poet and with good reviews, is very lucky if it sells three thousand copies. The only way for a poet to bridge this gap is to cease being a poet and become something else—a novelist, a scriptwriter for television, something like that. As Randall Jarrell said, a poet can become famous in America if he writes a novel or does some other popular thing, but not by writing poetry.

I take it, then, that you don't expect your poetry of ordinary American life to gain a large audience of ordinary American readers?

Oh, the people I write about will never read it, even though they could. And this can make you angry. Let me give you an example. I recently talked to a woman who complained about some modern art that she found incomprehensible. So I said to her: "This is all very well and good, but when some of us do write or paint stuff that is comprehensible, you don't support that either." Every now and then you will see a newspaper or magazine article about modern poetry in which it's claimed that the poets don't make enough effort to get to the common man or to write about common things. This is complete nonsense. There are many contemporary American poets who write perfectly understandable poems about things that interest everyone—about the most domestic subjects, if that's what the American public wants—about mothers and children and fathers and gardening and the day's work and the ordinary feelings people have. And the public doesn't *care.* They still complain that all this modern poetry is obscure. It's just nonsense; they don't care about it because there are other things that interest them more. I don't want to sound cynical, but I do feel that any serious American poet who keeps on writing past the age of forty has got to have an awful lot of motivation within himself because he's not going to get it from the public. No—you have to do it for yourself.

If there is a literary center in America, a community of writers, it is probably in New York. You live close to New York, but apparently don't find that community supportive.

There are writers in New York who support one another. Certain publishing firms and magazines that wouldn't flourish anywhere else flourish in New York. But for me as a poet, the city is a physically impossible place to live. The atmosphere is depressing, the enclosure by walls has almost a physical impact on my mind. In my view, the poet needs to have a sense of space, sense of innocence. In New York, you are constantly being bombarded by horror—in a single walk down the street you can see more horrors than you want to see for the rest of your life. And the so-called literary life in New York—people stand around and talk about what everyone is doing. Some people are working, of course, but many don't *do* anything, they *talk about* doing it. When I write about New York, I always present it in the grimmest, most forbidding terms: it appears in my poems as a sinister place.

Robert Bly has a reputation for having had a radical influence on certain poets, yourself included. Did he influence you to change your style back in the late fifties?

There's been a lot of talk about this sort of thing. One man who wrote a book on modern poetry—I've forgotten his name—said that my change of style was influenced by Robert Kelly and Robert Bly. Now I have scarcely even read Robert Kelly, much less been influenced by him. This astonishing remark was made in a book that was sold in stores and was no doubt read by students. Now Robert Bly *did* have an influence on me between about 1959 and 1963. But it is also quite possible that I had an influence on Robert Bly. Nobody ever thinks about this possibility, but I think the influence was mutual. When I was breaking out of traditional English forms, Robert helped me—he is an excellent critic of the individual poem. Later, I found that there are certain areas in which I did not want his criticism; he did not understand the ways of making a poem that I was becoming interested in. I also found what I consider a serious defect in him as a reader: he is unable to detach the writer from the subject. He is so eager to find the thought behind a poem that he cannot conceive that the writer is detaching himself from what he's writing about. Iago does not speak for Shakespeare any more than Othello does. They are independent creations of the poet. Bly seems to want to see every poem as a subjective outpouring, a revelation of the writer's secret and hidden wishes, which is nonsense. Quite often, a man will sit down and write a poem in which he himself is dramatized; he is looking at himself quite objectively. This Robert cannot understand. So I don't lean on his criticism of my poems anymore. In fact, I think he's a much better poet than critic. He has been very useful in bringing in foreign poetry, and this gave him a reputation as a critic. But I do think that he is one of the few poets in America that really can do something memorable. But we have gone, he and I, in very different directions in our writing, so we don't agree on things much anymore. I believe I am being accurate when I say that Robert is very strongly influenced by the ideas of Carl Jung, and I certainly am not. The belief I have in a poetry of ordinary events would not interest Robert, and Robert's ideas about the supernatural don't interest me at all. They have no connection with any life I've ever seen or believe to be true. So we have gone in two very different directions—I am very much tied to things of this world, and Robert is looking for some sort of supernatural answer to existence.

You have spoken of a cult of sincerity in contemporary poetry. What do you mean by that?

This is an assumption which I think has dominated American poetry at least since the late 1950s. It says that if you tell the truth about your life and your feelings, if you will directly express your emotions, then by virtue of the sheer honesty of your expression, you will have written poetry. This reflects a very American preoccupation—what was it Whitman said in his "Preface?"—"I will not have anything to come between me and the reader," he says. "I will not have any hanging of curtains." You can find this sort of thing in writers like Henry Miller and William Carlos Williams, but where it really took over poetry was in Allen Ginsberg's *Howl*, back in the fifties. That book was quickly followed by Snodgrass's *Heart's Needle* and Lowell's *Life Studies.* Of course you have several subdivisions in American poetry over the last twenty years—there is the school of the "deep image," there is the Black Mountain school, there is the confessional school—but if you look at all of them, what they have in common is a belief in sincerity of utterance.

This is true, I think, even of poets who pretend to objectivity. Charles Olson, for example, was hung up on science and geography and typography, and he had all these theories about poetry. What Williams said about place in a man's life and poetry—Olson took this literally, and he made all these maps of Gloucester, and he really believed that there was a relationship between all that and his life and his writing. But when you look into the poetry, you discover that this worked-up objectivity is just a mask for an underlying sincerity—it's all about Charles Olson.

Now this cult of sincerity seems to be a very liberating thing, and that is why it became so popular—half of the poems still being written today are by young people who think that, if you just say who you are, what you do, who your friends are, then you've got a poem. Now it may be very liberating, but there are a couple of things missing, things like drama and narrative and even imagination. Imagination is a big thing to eliminate from poetry; you are left with only the actual circumstances of your life, and that is extremely limiting. People who write this kind of poetry really seem to believe that any making up of anything—any form of artificial making up, any creation of story—is cheating somehow, and dishonest. And of course any form of irony is completely anathema, any double view of the subject is suspect, some-how evil. Without full use of the imagination, you are left with only the facts of your own life, and this can cause a serious confusion be-tween art and life. You end up having to justify your art by your way of life, and vice versa.

The tragic thing about the confessional poets is that they took all this the most seriously. Poets like Berryman and Sexton and Plath sim-ply were unable to draw a separation between poetry and life—they could not find any relief, they had to be "on" all the time. They could not write a poem and then knock off and go into life. To them, poetry was life and life was poetry, so they were always on stage. They thought that they could—they thought they *had* to—find their salvation through poetry. If there is one thing we can be sure of about poetry, it is that poetry is nobody's salvation. It is not a substitute for religion. It is *poetry*. As playing the violin is playing the violin, writing poetry is only writing poetry, an activity—it is not a way of life. These people became trapped by this view of poetry, and it ended up destroying them.

In the case of writers like Berryman and Plath and Sexton, you have a degree of psychological disturbance, a negative and depressive view of life. So they wrote about their lives as tragic and terrible, and this poet-ry fed back into their lives, and it created a trap. Way back in about 1900, Joseph Conrad wrote about this kind of writing. He said that, once you have told the terrible truth and made a sensation, what are you going to do next? You have to turn up the volume, write an even more terrible truth. And all the time the poetry and the life are feeding on each other, until pretty soon you cross a line and pass from emotion to hysteria. Ultimately there is only one way left to prove your sin-cerity, and that is to kill yourself. They had the wrong theory of art; their sincerity created a confusion between life and art. They were looking for salvation, but that is not what they found. It is time to go forward, to get away from this absorption in the individual life and find a more objective and healthy theory of art.

Doesn't the title Adventures of the Letter I *take us in that personal direction? What distinctions would you make between your own voice and the voice that you adopt in that book?*

Well, you see, the letter *I* is not me. The letter *I* is something that appears in a poem and says, "I do this and I do that," but it is not me—it's the letter *I*. Of course, a lot of the stuff that I have written in the last few years has been autobiographical, but there is an enormous dif-ference between what I'm doing and confessional poetry. I am merely an observer in my poems. I'm not trying to solve the problems of my own life through poetry. Nor am I asking the reader to think that I'm a wonderful, interesting person. The *I* appears in these poems as an observer, like Marlowe in the Conrad stories—a commentator, an observer, a small actor, but not someone who is engaged in a struggle for his soul.

You see, I am really pretty different from most poets today. I am not involved in the cult of sincerity. I think of myself as an objective observer—a transmitter of things that I am seeing. I think that what we need now in poetry is imagination, pleasure. I'm sick of the puritans and the moralists, who have held sway for twenty years. It is like the Victorian age all over, except that now they're preaching sincerity, drugs, self-indulgence, an absolute cultivation of the egocentric soul. I would like to see a return to what Rimbaud said—he said, "I is another." Well, that's what I was trying to say with the letter *I*—"I is another"; it's not me, it's the letter *I*. These are essentially narrative poems, and narrative is something I would definitely like to see more of in poetry. It is the antithesis of the kind of subjective writing I've been talking against, which I see as so limiting. Narrative poetry means imagination, creation of character, creation of scene, creation of action, creation of objective ideas about life. I would like to see that very much.

Your recent poems emphasize narrative and use a plain kind of free verse. What is it that makes these poems poetry, specifically, rather than a brief form of short story, something like that?

The difference is that they are written in lines—the rhythmic part of the poem enfranchises it from prose completely. You could argue other things—for example, that there is a greater concentration in the poems than you get in prose, or that there are more images—but these arguments are fallacious because they can't be held logically to the ultimate. You could have a short story which is just as concentrated or intense as a poem, and you could have an example of prose which has more images. No, it's the old difference between verse and prose—it is the line. And I work very strongly in lines. It may not be evident on the page, but I think that when these poems are heard aloud, it is clear that they have a strong rhythm. I'm very insistent on this point, that the line of verse is the absolutely essential thing.

How do you feel about the concept of the prose poem then?

I'm one of the few public enemies of the prose poem. I think it is a mistake because it abandons the strong points of both prose and verse.

The strong point of prose fiction for me is that it develops a narrative that goes somewhere. And it is a vehicle for information—even the most beautiful prose is a vehicle for information of some kind. Now the prose poem does not carry information, it does not usually develop a narrative, and it lacks the line of verse, obviously—it breaks down into sentences. The unit of attention in poetry is the line, and to do without it is to leave out the musical elements entirely. I think some of Baudelaire's prose pieces are magnificent—but they are called prose poems only out of whim. There are no rules governing the prose poem—it can be anything you like. Verse is like a dance that is occurring in front of you—the poet's words move in measure. Verse imposes certain laws upon the writer from outside. In a way it makes writing more difficult, but in another way it gives verse an objective reality that prose does not have. The prose writer has nothing to sustain him but appetite and reason—apart from the laws of grammar and syntax, usage and punctuation, there are no rules that the prose writer has to follow. Everything else can be determined by his will at the moment of composition.

You have said that you try to adhere to an organic notion of form in your poetry. Could you say a little more about that?

Yes, I believe that it is the cooperation between the writer and his material that should determine the form of the poem. You don't start with the idea that you are going to fill up two-hundred lines of blank verse, and then put anything in just to fill up the lines. You can write only as long as you have something to say, and then you stop. If what you are going to talk about is brief, simple, a momentary thing perceived, then the poem will be short. If your idea is complicated, then the poem will be longer and may break into separate blocks and developments. Emerson has a beautiful description of it, about the growth of a poem being like the growth of a plant, with different branches and blossoms and so on. The opposite of this idea would be something like the sonnet, which always has fourteen lines, no matter how large or how small the subject you're dealing with.

Ultimately, I suppose a poem is an emotion which uses certain facts and images in order to generate itself. But the emotion is what forms the poem, and when the emotion is dead, then the poem must stop. It is the emotion formed by the material that makes the form of the poem. When I am writing, I immerse myself in the subject and try to remove from my vision of it anything distracting at all, including language, anything that distracts from the experience. My object is to get the original vision across to the reader, and when I have done that, I'm through. I think this makes me very different from a writer like James Merrill, for whom the language is always a distraction; it is always calling attention to itself, pulling the poet away from the original experience. That is the polar opposite of what I'm talking about.

You've also suggested that, by using free verse rather than some more rigid, restrictive form, a poet will be more likely to express the truth of his experience or vision. Could you say something more about that?

Well, in free verse you are much more likely to follow the cadences of your thinking voice. I'd rather use that term than the word *speech*, because we don't speak aloud in our heads. Now the voice in which you think is the voice in which you are most likely to tell the truth. We don't think in iambic pentameter or trochaic tetrameter. So by writing free verse, you are more likely to bring over into poetry the cadence of your real feelings as expressed in words.

Is your book Searching for the Ox *based on ideas grounded in Zen Buddhism?*

Yes. The title poem in fact had its origin in a Zen cartoon series, the Ox-herding Series. This herd boy is searching for the lost ox; he finds a footprint, then he finds the ox; he starts leading it home, then he rides on it; in the next panel you see a little cottage and the moon and a branch, and then the cottage and the moon and the branch vanish; everything is gone except a big circle in the sky, which is ultimate reality. It is a parable of the search for mastery of the self. The ox is the self, which is found, then mastered, then eliminated, so that the Zen objective can be reached. The Buddhist goal is to merge with the universe in Nirvana and to cease searching. That's what I had in the back of my mind while writing that poem, though it appears only obliquely. Mostly, the poem is a free-floating series of associations which somehow hold together.

Some time before I came to write that book, I spent two years in London, studying Zen Buddhism, among other things. I read many books on the subject, and I would go to the Buddhist Institute, where I learned meditation. The process of Buddhist meditation is an attempt to eliminate distractions and to attain objectivity by escaping a narrow vision of the self. You try to feel the life which is around you, throughout the universe, by concentrating on the process of your own breathing. In the poems, this shows up as a concentration on the object, not distracted by any intrusion of my own personality—it is a clear view of the thing.

This is true even in the poems that begin with *I*—it's an attempt to be objective about myself as well as everything else. I am trying to get past the limitations of the personal ego and link up with an impersonal reality somewhere outside myself.

For example, in the book there is a poem called "The Middle-Aged Man." It is an attempt to look at the man exactly as he is, in all of the triviality of his life. I keep staring at him, until finally, at the end of the poem, his eyeglasses become burned into my consciousness. Buddhism teaches that your physical existence and your mental existence are one thing; in the West, we tend automatically to split them apart, as in the Christian idea of the body and the soul. I prefer the medieval idea— they had a term for the body which recognized it as the form for the soul, which I take to mean that the body is the outward garment of the soul. Whitman says that too, that there is no split between the body and the soul. And this is what the Buddhists say also. This way of thinking leads to a poetry that is very physical in its orientation, a poetry that concentrates on ordinary life. The Buddhist says: "Your ordinary life, that is the way." To believe that—*really* to believe it—is to have it made. Then you really could live life fully and be an intellectual at the same time. Otherwise, one tends to live an unsatisfactory daily life, and compensate for it by creating in dreams the life one would prefer to live.

To write poetry of ordinary life, especially of ordinary American life, seems to be the goal of your recent poetry.

I came to the United States when I was seventeen, almost forty years ago. I'd had a very rough time in Jamaica—my brother and I had just been swindled out of our inheritance from my father. I had a wonderful time at Columbia before the war—I was sort of born again. My intellectual allegiance since that time has been very strongly American—I have been constantly thinking about this country, even when I have been away from it for prolonged periods. I feel absolutely no affinity for Jamaica at all, because the culture is still so English—they are still under the shadow of the English, and I'm not. The English culture, which I've also seen recently in Australia, is lagging very far behind us in poetry. American poetry is really much, much more alive than English.

My latest book, *Caviare at the Funeral,* tries again to capture some of this. The poems in the first section attempt to recreate an atmosphere—they cover things I have seen and lived through since about 1940. The second section turns to contemporary American life, which I present mostly in domestic terms. In the third section, I have written about my Russian family background. This is a contrast to the first two sections, but it also shows our American ethnic diversity. The fourth section is more wide-ranging—there's something in there about what modern technological life is doing to man and his world. I use a lot of Australian material also.

The book as a whole I think has less of a unity of content than it has a unity of tone. I have tried very hard to eliminate insincerities of language and form in order to write narrative poems that bring out a quality of feeling in myself, in others, or in the scenes themselves. It is this feeling or tone that determines the detail and the unity of a given poem. There is a kind of poetry in America today in which we see the words playing with themselves. The language is looking at itself—it's a game within the poem itself. In the kind of poem I am writing, the language points outward from the poem to the things and people and scenes that are being described. I am trying to bring out the feelings inherent in that material.

There is a poem in the book which does not at first glance seem to belong—the one on Magritte.

That poem is quite a departure for me, but it is based on a feeling I have of kinship with Magritte. The more I look at his paintings the more I think we are trying to do something very similar. He takes images of very common objects and juxtaposes them in odd ways. What you end up with is something both very common and surrealistic, and it shows how weird the ordinary can actually be.

Would that impulse or desire have anything to do with the poem "The Beaded Pear"?

Yes. The poem is meant to be absolutely descriptive of the kind of domestic life we actually live in this country today. When the poem first came out—in the Long Island newspaper *Newsday*—it upset a lot of people. I got hate mail from people who thought I was being devastatingly sarcastic. But I don't see it that way. There is an element of ridicule in the poem, but it is directed at the culture which fosters these kinds of values, not at the people themselves. No—mostly it is a purely descriptive poem, an attempt at absolutely dead-on, accurate truth. There is even a touch of pathos at the end.

What really pleases me about that poem is the way it incorporates things like *TV Guide*—the real stuff of our everyday lives. There are too many poems today in which sophisticated, contemporary Americans—who watch TV and drive cars on freeways—pretend that they are Indians. Well, we are the tribe that chews gum and wears polyester and blow-dries our hair, and these things belong in our poems. You can do this in narrative or dramatic poems, work it naturally into the situation without giving sermons. The comparison may sound somewhat farfetched, but isn't this what Chaucer did for his own time? By incorporating the actual details of people's lives, he managed to portray the texture, the feel of life in his time. I mean, it is our life, it is what we use and do everyday. Shouldn't there be some connection between that and the poems we write?

**James
Wright**

James Wright:
The Quest for Home

●

James Wright is perhaps the most "questing" of all contemporary poets; there is in his poems a general feeling of dissatisfaction with where he is at the present time and a corresponding desire to be somewhere else. We would expect such restlessness in the author's unhappy books; what is more interesting is that we find it as well, and to a rather surprising degree, in his happiest books—*The Branch Will Not Break*, for example. In the pages that follow, I will examine the individual quests undertaken in various books; at the same time, I will attempt to show how these smaller quests function as parts of a larger, more encompassing quest—one that operates from the beginning of the career until its very end.[1] To make the pattern of this larger quest clear, I will refer occasionally to various essays written by James Wright. Most of this material, interestingly, comes from the early 1960s, a time of great change in Wright's life and work. Although he is generally writing about other authors in these pieces, it is apparent that Wright is also defining his own situation and seeking solutions to his artistic and personal troubles.

The most important such document is the introduction to *Breathing of First Things*, a book of poems by Hy Sobiloff published in 1963. Wright begins by noticing that Sobiloff's primary theme is a quest nearly identical to that pursued earlier by William Wordsworth: "the search for the child within the self."[2] Having generalized thus far, Wright soon goes even farther by characterizing this quest as that of "the new poet"; it seems clear that he is now speaking—however indirectly, however unconsciously—of himself and his own work.

> The new poet . . . tells us . . . what . . . he is struggling to learn: how to be true to his own self. . . . the struggle . . . involves a good deal more than the rediscovery of a childlike radiance and joy, though that rediscovery may lie at the end of the journey. The journey itself is a dark one. It is neither more nor less than the attempt to locate and reclaim those healing powers within

one's self that are able to provide sufficient courage and literal physical strength for one to confront and overcome the agonies of the world which exists beyond the womb and which, for better or worse, does not happen to be shaped and arranged in a pattern identical with the orchards and rivers and meadows of that earliest garden, sunken now almost below memory and, whether wasted or redeemed, lost somewhere between the morning of dancing animals and the tousled dusk of sorrowing human faces. Beyond that garden we live a good deal of our death. . . . But there really seems to be a true path back to the lost paradise, back home to the true child in one's self, back to the source of healing strength—back to the Kingdom of God which, we have been told, is within us. If there really is a true path home-ward, then it appears that certain heroic men found it dark, sometimes yawning with dreadful pits of fire, sometimes winding and confusing and heavy with the whispers of murderers, backbiters, and the unseemly con-torted apparitions of our own vanity. In short, there have been heroes on the earth, whose heroism consisted in their willingness to face the facts of pain; and their motive, as far as I can grasp it, was the motive of Thoreau: to front life openly and to live it fully, and, if it proved to be mean, then to get the true and genuine meanness out of it. . . . the heroes open their arms to the world as it happens to have been arranged when they were flung down into it without their suspicion or desire.[3]

Generally speaking, a quest is linear in pattern and depends for its significance on the establishment of a polar opposition between two places or states of being—the quester attempts to progress from one of these poles (the place or state of being he occupies at the beginning) to the other (the place or state of being he wishes to occupy when his search is done). In the specific case encountered in James Wright's poems, the quest pattern seems to be more clearly circular than linear. The positive "pole" is located both at the beginning (as a "childlike radiance and joy") and at the end (as "the Kingdom of God") of man's life. As the quester—the generalized speaker of Wright's poems— moves from an idealized beginning to a gardenlike end, he must pass through the vale of tears, the valley of the shadow of death, which he finds such a prominent component of everyday reality. The *deepest* goal of the quest undertaken in Wright's work is to regain nothing less than that paradise dimly remembered from before the speaker's birth.

On the surface of his work, however, it often appears that what Wright is questing for is a time-bound, explicitly human, heroism— the heroism, that is, of the man who is strong enough to take all of "the genuine meanness" that life has to offer and to triumph over it, triumph simply by surviving. Although these two desires seem contra-dictory to one another, in fact they are complementary, as Wright him-self recognized by speaking of the world of time, not as a place of per-manent residence, but as a path: "If there really is a true path homeward, then it appears that certain men found it dark." James Wright's thinking is both idealistic and realistic; though the hero of his poems desires an escape into a paradisal existence, he knows he is stuck in the fallen world for the time being, and that he might as well deal with it courageously.

Wright's thinking resembles, in certain important ways, that of Wordsworth, as expressed in his "Ode: Intimations of Immortality from Recollections of Early Childhood." The relevant lines are well-known; having asked "Whither is fled the visionary gleam," Wordsworth goes on to explain:

> Our birth is but a sleep and a forgetting:
> The Soul that rises with us, our life's Star,
>   Hath had elsewhere its setting,
>   And cometh from afar:
>   Not in entire forgetfulness,
>   And not in utter nakedness,
> But trailing clouds of glory do we come
>   From God, who is our home:
> Heaven lies about us in our infancy!
> Shades of the prison-house begin to close
>   Upon the growing Boy,
> But He beholds the light, and whence it flows,
>   He sees it in his joy;
> The Youth, who daily farther from the east
>   Must travel, still is Nature's Priest,
>   And by the vision splendid
>   Is on his way attended;
> At length the Man perceives it die away,
> And fade into the light of common day.[4]

The soul enters human life directly from a realm of paradise, perhaps after having crossed over the river of forgetfulness, Lethe. The memory of paradise has not been completely erased, however; some remnants of it linger into childhood, gradually fading as man matures. Although Wordsworth does not explicitly say so in his poem, his title does seem to hint at the hope that, at death, man will return to paradise, perhaps by being ferried across the river Styx. Finally, both poets recognize that man has to live his life, not within paradise, but within the fallen and tragic world of reality. While Wordsworth's unhappiness over this fact is at worst rueful, Wright's unhappiness is often very intense.[5] Thus, his overall quest to escape from the burdens of reality into something at least resembling paradise is powerful, poignant, and multiform. It should also be noted that, while the pattern of Wright's quest, when stated conceptually, is circular, our experience of it as readers of his poems is linear. That is, although Wright implicitly recognizes the paradise of preexistence, he also knows he must live within time. Thus, his search is not backward, toward something that might have existed in the past, but forward, toward something he hopes will exist in the future.

In his first two books—*The Green Wall* (1957) and *Saint Judas* (1959) (which I will treat here as one unit)—we can see Wright taking leave of the dimly remembered paradise and entering "the agonies of the world which exists beyond the womb," the world in which we must live "a good deal of our death." The interrupted Wordsworthian search for the lost paradise is begun in a poem called "Father," which was published in *The Green Wall* and which describes the birth voyage of its speaker:

> In paradise I poised my foot above the boat and said:
> Who prayed for me?
> But only the dip of an oar
> In water sounded; slowly fog from some cold shore
> Circled in wreaths around my head.
>
> . . . And the wind began,
> Transfiguring my face from nothingness
> To tiny weeping eyes.⁶

The mythic system alluded to in this poem is, of course, classical and pagan; that alluded to elsewhere in the book (as in its title) is Christian, referring to the myth of man's fortunate fall from the Garden of Eden.

Robert Bly, in the first full-length essay written on Wright's work (1966), comments on the latter pattern. He begins by contrasting Wright to "almost all Americans"—people who "imagined the writing of poetry as a climb" *into* the walled garden: "leaving the vicious, chaotic world behind, the poet finds himself abruptly in a walled enclosure with fairly tame animals as decoration. When people praised order in a poem, as they did much in those days, they were praising the ordered world possible to them only in a poem."⁷ The direction taken in James Wright's early poetry, according to Bly, is the opposite of this:

> In the first poem of *The Green Wall*, "A Fit Against the Country," Mr. Wright declares his intention to go to some other world:
>
> . . . .
> Be glad of the green wall
> You climbed across one day,

When winter stung with ice
That vacant paradise.

He immediately begins to introduce into poems the scarred and hated.[8]

When he commented some years later on what he was trying to achieve in *The Green Wall*, Wright seemed to echo Bly's view: "I tried to begin with the fall of man, and acknowledge that the fall of man was a good thing, the *felix culpa*, the happy guilt. And then I tried to weave my way in and out through nature poems and people suffering in nature because they were conscious" (see "Interview with James Wright"). The two halves of this statement contradict one another in an interesting way; we have to wonder just how "happy" was the fall of man in Wright's view if he also was convinced that it brought about such a wealth of conscious "suffering." The aspect of man's journey away from paradise that seems to cause the most unhappiness in Wright's first two books is the sense of separation that is an inevitable result of it. In the poems, Wright speaks of this separation, not directly (in connection with the loss of paradise), but indirectly: he ties it to the sense of disjunction man experiences when confronted with death and to the sense of alienation that an individual (either the speaker or a character who interests him) may feel from society.[9] In fact, separation in these books marks the negative pole for a smaller version of the larger quest that we have been tracing. Separation is seen as a fact of life; the solution to it is love. But because the logic of Wright's scheme inevitably associates love with the ideal world, the "lost garden," it follows that love is more a dreamed-of solution to the problem of disjunction than a real solution. The protagonists in most of these early poems are loveless, either because they are outcasts from society or because death has severed them from the ones they love. It is for this reason that these poems are so relentlessly unhappy.

In his foreword to *The Green Wall*, W. H. Auden noted that "Two of Mr. Wright's poems, 'The Assignation' and 'My Grandmother's Ghost,' are about the dead coming back to haunt the living."[10] Auden understates the case—many more poems could be added—and doesn't comment at all on the significance of the motif. Such poems might well be seen as attempts to overcome the separation caused by the fact of death, attempts inevitably doomed to failure. "The Accusation," for example, is addressed to a girl who is now dead, whose face was disfigured, and with whom the speaker had been in love. When they were together, the girl had tried to hide her face from her lover; now that she is gone, he complains:

How can I ever love another?
You had no right to banish me

From that scarred truth of wretchedness,
Your face, that I shall never see
Again, though I search every place.

(CP, 72)

The separation that provides the theme of this poem came about when
the girl escaped back into paradise, leaving her lover stranded alone in
an empty and hostile world.

"The Assignation" (*CP*, 40–41) views the problem from the other
side, being spoken by a dead woman to her now faithless lover, who had
promised as she lay dying "to love me after I was dead, / To meet me in
a grove and love me still." She rises from her grave to meet him, but he
does not appear:

O then it was you I waited for, to hold
The soft leaves of my bones between your hands
And warm them back to life, to fashion wands
Out of my shining arms.

In a similar vein are these lines from "But Only Mine":

I dreamed that I was dead, as all men do,
And feared the dream, though hardly for the sake
Of any thrust of pain my flesh might take
Below the softening shales. Bereft of you,
I lay for days and days alone.

(CP, 76)

Again, the primary emphasis of this poem is not upon the sting of
death itself, but upon the loneliness of separation, the fear of being
completely alone.

The other form that separation takes in Wright's early work—alienation from society—is reflected in the many poems in these books that
are concerned with social outcasts: criminals, murderers, betrayers,
lesbians, skid-row characters, poets. In fact, the two poems that conclude *Saint Judas*—"At the Executed Murderer's Grave" and "Saint
Judas"—give ample illustration to both sides of this concern with social pariahs: separation and love. In *The Green Wall* there is "A Poem
About George Doty in the Death House"; Doty, now dead, is also the
subject of "At the Executed Murderer's Grave" (*CP*, 82–84). The complex tone of the poem somewhat frustrates the reader's expectations,
for it is not the pious platitude about capital punishment one might at
first expect. It begins:

My name is James A. Wright, and I was born
Twenty-five miles from this infected grave,
In Martins Ferry, Ohio.

The true protagonist of the poem is not George Doty but the poet, who is searching for a way to get beyond platitudes to an elemental level of truth:

Now sick of lies, I turn to face the past.
I add my easy grievance to the rest:

Doty, if I confess I do not love you,
Will you let me alone?

Being sick of lies, he is also sick of himself for what he does: "I croon my tears at fifty cents per line." The reference is to poems like "A Poem about George Doty in the Death House," in which the killer is idealized (he bears "What no man ever bore"; the poet mourns "no soul but his"—*CP*, 26). Here Wright clearly expresses the theme he was writing around in the earlier poem: "I do not pity the dead, I pity the dying."

This strong and bitter protestation out of the way, the tone begins to modify as Wright concedes: "And yet, nobody had to kill him either." The poem builds to a vision of the day of judgment, when men will be viewed by "God's unpitying stars":

Staring politely, they will not mark my face
From any murderer's, buried in this place.
Why should they? We are nothing but a man.

The poet identifies himself here with the worst of society's outcasts, with an executed rapist and murderer, and the point is clear: all men are imperfect, no one is any better than another. The point is re-emphasized in the last line of the poem, where Doty is called "Dirt of my flesh, defeated, underground." The poem is, finally, not so much about either Doty or the poet as it is about death:

Order be damned, I do not want to die,
Even to keep Belaire, Ohio, safe.
The hackles on my neck are fear, not grief.

—the fact that all men must die—and this is the basis of the brotherhood it advocates. Advocates, but doesn't realize. Doty is an executed murderer, and although the poet sympathizes with him, the group they form has but two members, and one of them is dead.

In its style, the poem attempts to be rigorously truthful, to cut through the dishonesty Wright found all too often in conventional poetry. Thus, he chooses to speak unmasked, in his own voice, in an attempt to make the poem more clear and direct. The dissatisfaction he expresses for the sometimes empty rhetoric of his own early poems, for what he calls his "widely printed sighing," is in part a reaction to a correspondence Wright was engaged in with James Dickey at the time he was writing this poem. In a review of the anthology *New Poets of England and America*, Dickey had seemed to refer to Wright's contribution as "ploddingly 'sincere' "; he continued: "There are many poets here who may eventually emerge as significant, but at present . . . most of them are exemplars of the thing they must overthrow in order to do so."[11] In response to this review, Wright wrote Dickey a letter, and the two entered into a vigorous correspondence that ultimately led Wright to question his commitment to the traditional forms of English poetry. In fact, the most stylistically radical poem in *Saint Judas* is "At the Executed Murderer's Grave," and significantly, it is dedicated to Dickey ("J. L. D.") as a tribute to the way he had inspired Wright towards a greater directness in his work. Thus the method of the poem looks forward to the method of the later poems, in which Wright wears far fewer masks.

"Saint Judas" (*CP*, 84–85) is one of Wright's most remarkable poems, a sonnet as tight and yet as rich as any by Robinson. It is a poem of great compassion for man in general and for the outcast in particular. Although the title has occasionally puzzled readers of a theological frame of mind, the poem seems to explain it adequately. It would be hard to imagine a more universally reviled man in the Western world than Judas, Christ's betrayer—he is the archetypal moral outcast. Wright takes him up after he had both "Bargained the proper coins" and turned against himself, deciding to commit suicide. The poet creates a situation that will test Judas's humanity: "When I went out to kill myself, I caught / A pack of hoodlums beating up a man." His instinctive reaction is to aid the man, and in the process he forgets his own troubles: "Running to spare his suffering, I forgot / My name, my number, how my day began." The poem concludes:

Banished from heaven, I found this victim beaten,
Stripped, kneed, and left to cry. Dropping my rope
Aside, I ran, ignored the uniforms:
Then I remembered bread my flesh had eaten,

The kiss that ate my flesh. Flayed without hope,
I held the man for nothing in my arms.

Judas is the down-and-outer par excellence and has nothing to look
forward to either in life or in death. With absolutely no possibility of
gain for himself, in this world or the other, he makes the instinctively
humane gesture and tries to protect the suffering man. That is why
Wright has chosen to canonize him—not because he has lived a pure
life away from the harsh demands and temptations of reality, but because, a man like all men, he has redeemed his unspeakable act of
betrayal through an act of love. In the vale of tears to which man is
mostly condemned in Wright's poems, it is love that matters above all
else, for it is only through love that men can overcome the separation
that is their natural lot in life. As Wright has said in an interview: "We
do get a few people who understand the intensity and the true beauty
of life in the face of death and pain. And what else have we got except
love? We've got to have it because the only other thing there is is death
and pain. That, I take it, is the meaning of that shocking statement
'God is love' " ("Interview with James Wright").[12]
Judas, who overcomes his sinfulness through love, is thus a kind of
hero for Wright, representing the most that man can achieve (endurance and love) within the fallen world. However, we must not over-
look the fact that the tone of this poem (like most others in the first
two books) is one of despair. No matter how hard a man may labor to
make the most of the fallen world, he remains, by virtue of his residence there, separated from that paradise where he seems to have
known an ideal kind of love. In his third book of poems, *The Branch
Will Not Break* (1963), Wright does manage briefly to reenter the paradisal garden lost at birth. The volume presents the most complete of
the miniquests enacted in his work; in fact, it could be said to contain,
not one quest, but two. The first, in the area of style, basically continues the movement away from the garden and into reality that was
begun in the first two books; ironically, the second, in the area of content, proceeds in the opposite direction—the speaker's goal is, not to
emerge from, but to get back into the "lost garden." As Robert Bly
recognized in 1966, Wright's escape from paradise in *The Green Wall*
and *Saint Judas* is only partial. The forms that are favored there—the
carefully patterned iambic structures of traditional English poetry—
express an implicit desire for the harmony that can only be found in an
idealized world. By changing his style so significantly after *Saint Judas*,
Wright was trying to make the form of his poems mirror more closely
the disorderliness of reality already reflected in his subject matter.

I do not intend to discuss in any detail Wright's use of free verse; what is of more interest to the present argument is the effect of his change in style and the motivation behind it. An important clue to the latter can be found in Wright's review of Robert Penn Warren's book *Promises*, written for the *Kenyon Review* in 1958. Wright praises Warren for loosening his own style:

> One of the innumerable ironies which hound writers, I suppose, is the fact that the very competence which a man may struggle for years to master can suddenly and treacherously stiffen into a mere *armor against experience* instead of an instrument for contending with that experience. No wonder so many poets quit while they're still behind. What makes Mr. Warren excitingly important is his refusal to quit even while he's ahead. In *Promises*, it seems to me, he has deliberately shed the armor of competence—a finely meshed and expensive armor, forged at heaven knows how many bitter intellectual fires—and has gone out to fight with the ungovernable tide.[13]

That he is implicitly questioning his own practice, and indicating the direction of his own development, Wright makes clear later in the review by commenting on "the ten thousand safe and competent versifyings produced by our current crop of punks in America. . . . we know who we are . . . us safe boys."[14] It is the "armor of competence" at the old forms that keeps a poet toiling on safe ground, in the garden, Wright says; in order to write within the real world, to front the "ungovernable tide," it is necessary to drop the traditional defenses and begin to deal directly and openly with "experience."

For an indirect description of the effect of Wright's new way of writing, we might turn to a contrast drawn by D. H. Lawrence in the introduction to his *New Poems*. Lawrence suggests that there are two types of poetry. One of them, the poetry of the ideal—which seeks perfection in both form and content—generally turns to either the past or the future for its setting: "The poetry of the beginning and the poetry of the end must have that exquisite finality, perfection which belongs to all that is far off. It is in the realm of the perfect." In contrast to this is the type of poetry to which Lawrence himself aspired, the poetry of today's real world: "But there is another kind of poetry: the poetry of that which is at hand: the immediate present. In the immediate present there is no perfection, no consummation, nothing finished. The strands are all flying, quivering, intermingling into the web, the waters are shaking the moon." Such poetry exhibits, "not fixity," but "inconclusiveness, immediacy" and "the rapid momentaneous association of things"; it has "no rhythm which returns upon itself, no serpent of eternity with its tail in its mouth. There is no static perfection, none of that finality which we find so satisfying because we are so frightened."[15]

Although the spiritual quest undertaken in *The Branch Will Not Break* carries Wright towards the perfection of "the beginning" and "the end"—and thus would seem logically to demand an "exquisite . . . perfection" of form—there is an important sense in which the content of these poems demands "the poetry of . . . the immediate present." As we read the early parts of this book, we are not aware of the sense of fulfillment that lies at its end. Instead, we overhear the speaker's thoughts as he lives through the quest, uncertain of the future. Thus, his conclusions are sometimes tentative rather than firm, the stages of his progress sometimes vague and inconclusive rather than clear and final. It is appropriate that the form of these poems should reflect the uncertainty of his progress by assuming more nearly the structural pattern found in life than that found in well-made works of art.[16]

The form of the quest in the content of this book is specifically pastoral; in his search for comfort, sustenance, and consolation, the poet whom we had seen so distraught by his engagement with reality in *The Green Wall* and *Saint Judas* turns from the city to the country, from society to nature, from human beings to animals, and from a fear of the finality of death to a trust in immortality. He wishes to rediscover the "dancing animals," "the orchards and rivers and meadows of that earliest garden," mentioned in his introduction to Sobiloff's book. *The Branch Will Not Break* has for its epigraph eight lines by the German poet Heinrich Heine. Apparently Wright chose these stanzas (which I give in translation) because of the way they express both his speaker's sense of entrapment and his desire to escape:

Oh, if I could go there,
And there gladden my heart,
And be free of all torture,
And be free and blissful.

Oh, that land of bliss!
I often see it in my dreams.
But with the coming of the morning sun,
It melts like sea foam.

(*CP*, 109)

After this opening, the book settles into a more or less chronological account of the speaker's quest. The negative pole of his existence, from which he wishes to escape, has two general aspects. First, his separation from nature, a result both of being human and of living in the city, has made him conscious of death, fearful of death, and self-absorbed. Second, the society of which he is a part—America—is seen as sterile, soulless, and destructive.

Wright explained his general view of man's separation from nature (a view that will be modified toward the end of *The Branch Will Not Break*) in an interview: "Human beings are unhappily part of nature, perhaps nature become conscious of itself. . . . I love the natural world, and I'm conscious of the pain in it. So I'm a nature poet who writes about human beings in nature. I love Nietzsche, who called man 'the sick animal'" ("Interview with James Wright"). This statement gives an accurate description of the position man occupies with respect to nature in the early poems in the book. Wright generally sees American society as out of phase with nature, but here even the speaker functions as a "sick animal." A striking example of this discordance occurs in the poem "A Message Hidden in an Empty Wine Bottle That I Threw into a Gully of Maple Trees One Night at an Indecent Hour" (*CP*, 115–16). The poem begins with an image in which no two elements are harmonized:

Women are dancing around a fire
By a pond of creosote and waste water from the river
In the dank fog of Ohio.

The phrase "waste water from the river" pits even nature against nature, as the river expels part of itself.

The speaker is in no better shape than the women: "I am alone here," he says, "And I reach for the moon that dangles / Cold on a dark vine." The image is not a comfortable one, romanticism turned on its head. The poem ends with a fearful prayer:

Come out, come out, I am dying.
I am growing old.
An owl rises
From the cutter bar
Of a hayrake.

The first two lines are addressed to whoever is intended to pick up the wine bottle mentioned in the title. And who is that? An imagined lover perhaps, or, as seems more appropriate, a nymph, a nature goddess. The last three lines reemphasize the feeling of mortality—owls are predators, and the cutter bar on a hayrake could be seen as akin to the scythe carried by the figure of Death. Finally, as the owl lifts off, it is as if nature were deserting man, as well it should in a poem like this. Similar poems from this part of the book are "In Fear of Harvests" and "In Face of Hatred," both based on natural mortality.

Wright communicates his speaker's sense of egotistical self-absorption—characteristic of the man cut off from nature—in his adaptation,

"Three Stanzas from Goethe" (*CP*, 112–13). Here the speaker views himself from the outside, as a man "lost in the thicket," "whose balm" has "turned poison," who

> . . . kills his own life,
> The precious secret.
> The self-seeker finds nothing.

The concluding stanza is again a prayer; it reiterates the quest motif that underlies this book:

> Oh Father of Love,
> If your psaltery holds one tone
> That his ear still might echo,
> Then quicken his heart!
> Open his eyes, shut off by clouds
> From the thousand fountains
> So near him, dying of thirst
> In his own desert.

In most of his poems, Wright attaches to water the same connotations we are familiar with from much of English and American poetry—that is, he generally uses water to represent the possibility of rebirth, a creative fertility, and also suggests, however vaguely here, the final river that man must cross to regain the ultimate paradise.

A poem with nearly the same message as "Three Stanzas from Goethe"—but specifically written by James Wright rather than translated by him from the German—is "Lying in a Hammock at William Duffy's Farm in Pine Island, Minnesota" (*CP*, 114). The poem is thirteen lines long and, though it exhibits neither rhyme nor regular meter, has the effect of a sonnet. It is divided into four groups of lines, each of which presents a different scene. The first, second, and fourth are three lines long, the third is four lines long. Each of the first three groups consists of a single, flowing sentence, while the fourth consists of three separate sentences—a change that announces that the end of the poem is coming, thus preparing its readers for the dramatic close. The entire poem is subjectively presented—we are always conscious of the speaker's interpreting eye—though it is not until the final line that he comments explicitly on himself.

Each of the first three groups of lines presents an image of nature that emphasizes its beauty, its balance, its magic, its happy rightness. The third group is typical:

> To my right,
> In a field of sunlight between two pines,

The droppings of last year's horses
Blaze up into golden stones.

The imagery associates nature, in striking fashion, with paradise—
surely nature's harmony and healing power must be very great if its
beauty can transform horse droppings into sacred objects. In the final
group of lines, the imagery becomes less paradisal in order that the
feeling of loneliness and the sense of searching that are so much a part
of this speaker's sensibility may be emphasized. The poem ends:

I lean back, as the evening darkens and comes on.
A chicken hawk floats over, looking for home.
I have wasted my life.

Several critics have expressed dislike for this poem; the complaint usually made against it is that the last line has not been prepared for, that
the speaker's moral self-condemnation represents an unwarranted intrusion of the ego into what should be an entirely objective poem.[17] Of
course, the poem is subjective from beginning to end—the images are
carefully selected to reveal the orientation of the speaker, who feels so
strongly throughout this part of the book his own separation from the
glories of nature. He is not condemning himself in the last line, and
certainly not morally; instead, the line should be read as expressing
desire, a vow taken for the future. Like the chicken hawk, the speaker
longs for home—for the paradisal, pastoral "lost garden" he is beginning to recognize in the natural beauty that surrounds him.[18]

Unfortunately, however, he is not yet ready to join nature; first he
must escape from what he sees as the dominant factors in American
society, one of which is presented in conjunction with nature and with
the speaker's beloved animals in the poem "Fear Is What Quickens
Me" (*CP*, 115). The first three lines embody a contrast between the
gentleness of nature and the rapaciousness of society:

Many animals that our fathers killed in America
Had quick eyes.
They stared about wildly.

In the concluding line of the poem, the speaker identifies himself with
the fear felt by the animals: "*I* look about wildly" (emphasis added). It
may be that this identification is with the animals themselves (rather
than just with their fear), but this still would not be health-giving for
the speaker. What he is searching for is a sense of *positive* harmony
with the natural world—but in much of this book, even the animals
themselves are out of phase with that world.

Opinions expressed about America in *The Branch Will Not Break* reveal with great clarity the speaker's feeling of alienation from American society. He associates America primarily with two qualities: hopelessness and political repression. The book contains five explicitly political poems, grouped together beginning with "Two Poems about President Harding" and ending with "The Undermining of the Defense Economy." "Eisenhower's Visit to Franco, 1959" succinctly states the theme of these poems in its first two lines: "The American hero must triumph over / The forces of darkness" (*CP*, 121). Light and whiteness are here (though not everywhere in the book) associated with a military-industrial mentality that wishes to suppress the "darker," more natural, earthy, and humanistic way of thought and life exhibited by peasants—"Wine darkens in stone jars in villages. / Wine sleeps in the mouths of old men, it is a dark red color"—and poets (*CP*, 122). Surely by design, the poem immediately following this one is "In Memory of a Spanish Poet," which contains this positive evocation of "the forces of darkness":

> I dream of your slow voice, flying,
> Planting the dark waters of the spirit
> With lutes and seeds.
>
>   (*CP*, 122)

In the earlier poem, when Eisenhower arrives in Spain he is greeted by Franco, who, significantly, "stands in a shining circle of police" and "promises all dark things / Will be hunted down" (*CP*, 122).

Whereas ordinary citizens in a country like Spain (when it was ruled by Franco) are presented as living fulfilling lives despite oppression by their government, the lives of ordinary Americans in this book are almost always seen as hopeless. A desperate coal miner in Ohio, for example, "Stumbles upon the outside locks of a grave, whispering / *Oh let me in*" (*CP*, 118). For the American woman especially, life is a series of broken dreams, as in "American Wedding" (*CP*, 132):

> She dreamed long of waters.
> Inland today, she wakens
> On scraped knees, lost
> Among locust thorns.

Again we see the desire for self-fulfillment associated with water imagery. Real life is not felt to be rewarding by this representative American wife, and she responds by sinking into hibernation:

> Now she is going to learn
> How it is that animals

Can save time:
They sleep a whole season
Of lamentation and snow,
Without bothering to weep.

American society represents a dead-end road in these poems, and must be escaped. Some of Wright's characters move, as does this American wife, from one form of hopelessness to another. The speaker of these poems is luckier; his journey away from society will return him to nature and will provide, in the process, a more balanced, fulfilling, even beatifying life.

When he learns to recognize in nature, not fear, but those positive, sustaining features so absent from society, and when he learns to recognize in his own intimate kinship with animals a release from self-consciousness and death-consciousness—that is when Wright's speaker begins to succeed in his quest. The first instance of a positive identification with an animal comes in the second of the "Two Hangovers," where the speaker watches a blue jay

> . . . springing up and down, up and down,
> On a branch.
> I laugh, as I see him abandon himself
> To entire delight, for he knows as well as I do
> That the branch will not break.
>
> (*CP*, 125)

However, a strong break *is* made with society, as in "Depressed by a Book of Bad Poetry, I Walk Toward an Unused Pasture and Invite the Insects to Join Me," where the speaker ends up preferring the "clear sounds" of grasshoppers and crickets to the cluttered sounds of the bad poet (*CP*, 125). A similar renunciation is made in "A Prayer to Escape the Marketplace"; and "Snowstorm in the Midwest" contains this clear rejection of society in favor of nature:

> Escaping in silence
> From locomotive and smoke,
> I hunt the huge feathers of gulls
> And the fountains of hills,
> I hunt the sea, to walk on the waters.
>
> (*CP*, 130–31)

Early in this book, as we have noticed, most of the images drawn from nature had, despite their beauty, threatening undertones, as in the owl rising from the hayrake. Now nature functions only positively, and gives reassurance of immortality. This theme strikingly enters the book in "Today I Was So Happy, So I Made This Poem":

> As the plump squirrel scampers
> Across the roof of the corncrib,
> The moon suddenly stands up in the darkness,
> And I see that it is impossible to die.
> Each moment of time is a mountain.
> An eagle rejoices in the oak trees of heaven,
> Crying
> *This is what I wanted.*
>
>   (*CP*, 133)

It is "impossible to die" because of the existence of the gardenlike paradise portrayed in the final four lines of this poem. It is the "Peaceable Kingdom" we see in paintings by Edward Hicks and others, a place where the lion and the lamb can lie down in harmony, where strife no longer exists between man and nature, man and society. In an interview ("Interview with James Wright"), Wright claimed to have experienced such a place personally at the time he was writing these poems. Living in Minneapolis, he would escape on weekends to visit Robert Bly on his farm in western Minnesota. Bly had a dog named Simon and a horse named David who would sit together, "looking over the corn fields that lead onto the prairies of South Dakota." Occasionally, the poet would join them: "They liked me. . . . One afternoon, a gopher came up out of a hole and looked at us. Simon didn't leap for him, David didn't kick him, and I didn't shoot him. There we were, all four of us together"—together in the Peaceable Kingdom.

Once Wright's protagonist has achieved this degree of unity with nature in *The Branch Will Not Break*, he is able to speak poems of great descriptive beauty about the natural world and its creatures. "Milkweed" (*CP*, 135–36), which evokes both sides of the quest enacted in this book, is also a kind of ars poetica that explains what the speaker does in many other poems here. It begins with him "lost in myself"; then, suddenly, "It is all changed," and he gains magical powers, the ability to create:

>   At a touch of my hand,
> The air fills with delicate creatures
> From the other world.

The result of this process is a series of beautifully descriptive, clear and imagistic, poems describing delicate creatures drawn from nature. Georg Trakl has often been named as an influence on Wright at the time he was writing this book, and in his short essay, "A Note on Trakl," Wright gives one reason why this is so; speaking of the German poet's "small animals, his trees, his human names," Wright says: "Each one contains an interior universe of shapes and sounds that have never been touched or heard before, and before a reader can explore these universes he must do as this courageous and happy poet did: he must learn to open his eyes, to listen, to be silent, and to wait patiently for the inward bodies of things to emerge, for the inward voices to whisper."[19]

The poems that result from such a feeling are so simple as not to require analysis, but it is important to point out that, without a successful conclusion to the speaker's quest, none of them would have been possible. "March," which describes the end of a season of hibernation for a mother bear, is typical:

> A bear under the snow
> Turns over to yawn.
> It's been a long, hard rest.
> . . . .
> When the wind opens its doors
> In its own good time,
> The cubs follow that relaxed and beautiful woman
> Outside to the unfamiliar cities
> Of moss.
>
> (*CP,* 128)

From this sense of union with nature achieved within the Peaceable Kingdom of pastoralism to the sense of a spiritual union such as might take place beyond the final river is but a short step—a step Wright takes in what is probably the most famous poem in this book.

"A Blessing" (*CP,* 135) begins when the speaker and a friend stop their car in order to greet two horses grazing in a pasture. The horses feel neither fear nor hostility: "they can hardly contain their happiness / That we have come." They are as affectionate towards the humans— "she has walked over to me / And nuzzled my left hand"—as the humans are towards the horses— "the light breeze moves me to caress her long ear / That is as delicate as the skin over a girl's wrist." In the last three lines of the poem—

> Suddenly I realize
> That if I stepped out of my body I would break
> Into blossom.

—Wright's speaker achieves the sense of apotheosis he has been seeking since he awoke from the dream described in the book's epigraph, an ultimate spiritual union beyond the bounds of physical limitation.[20] It is unfortunate that, within the larger pattern of Wright's total career, this fulfillment should be so short-lived. But at least for now, we see his protagonist happy and at peace with the world. The speaker's quest has taken him from solipsistic self-absorption to identification with the animals, from an end-stopped despair at death to an inherent faith in natural immortality, from man to nature and beyond.

Wright's fourth book, *Shall We Gather at the River* (1968), is also structured as a quest, but has a much different pattern from that in *The Branch Will Not Break*. The search it undertakes is best understood if we divide the book into three parts, the quest into three stages. In the first part, we see Wright's speaker-protagonist once again trapped in a hostile urban environment, the poet down and out in Minneapolis and St. Paul. In the middle part of the book, he attempts to escape (also again) to the western edge of Minnesota; this time, however, the pastoral world offers no solution. While he is composing a poem entitled "Outside Fargo, North Dakota," the speaker seems to realize what he must do: "I nod as I write good evening, lonely / And sick for home" (*CP*, 150). The third part of his quest, then, takes him back to what he thinks of as home, to the river from which he started, the Ohio:

> Murdered, I went, risen,
> Where the murderers are,
> That black ditch
> Of river.
>
> (*CP*, 155)

Throughout the book, the speaker orients himself to various rivers: in the first poem, we see him gazing into the Mississippi in Minneapolis, imagining "old men" who are "dreaming / Of suicide in the river" (*CP*, 140); in the middle of the book, he looks down into the Minnesota River:

> This is the firmest
> Net I ever saw, and yet something
> Is gone lonely
> Into the headwaters of the Minnesota.
>
> (*CP*, 163)

The river of the title, however, is not one of these, but the Ohio, goal of the speaker's quest and the river that he identifies with the Styx, the river of death.

In fact, the impulse that motivates the speaker of this volume is a powerful death wish, always associated with the Ohio River. The poem that Wright has placed as a prologue to the body of the book, "A Christmas Greeting" (*CP,* 139), addresses a character named Charlie, who many years earlier had committed suicide in the Ohio: "You died because you could not bear to live, / Pitched off the bridge in Brookside." The poem speaks, not to the Charlie who is in his grave, but to a Charlie who has risen from the dead:

> . . . lip by lip,
> Affectionate, the snub-nosed demons kiss
> And sting us back to such a world as this.

The poem is important because the position that Charlie occupies in it is very like the position that Wright's speaker sees himself occupying throughout his quest; he is one of the living dead, a man so torturously unhappy that all he can do is fumble at the locks of graves, his own and those of others. The cause of his misery is the absence of love in his life. Then in an important poem in the middle of the volume, a prayer entitled "Speak," he remembers Jenny, someone whom he had loved when he was young, but who had drowned in the river. Thus, the speaker's quest finally takes him to the banks of the Ohio, river of death, across which he wishes to be ferried into paradise, or out of which he wishes to resurrect the only person who could save him, Jenny.

Although the poem "Willy Lyons" (*CP,* 158–59) is atypical of this volume—its tone is too placidly happy—it does express the mythological framework of which I have been speaking. In fact, because it features a character who is ferried across the river Styx, the poem could be viewed as a companion piece to the much earlier "Father," in which a character was ferried across Lethe. "Willy Lyons" presents an image of what the speaker hopes for when he desires his own death. The poem begins:

> My uncle, a craftsman of hammers and wood,
> Is dead in Ohio.
> And my mother cries she is angry.

In the speaker's attempt to calm his mother's sorrow and anger, we find a definition of the world that lies beyond death, on the other side of the river. Willy, it turns out, has floated over in his coffin:

> It is nothing to mourn for.
> It is the other world.
> She does not know how the roan horses, there,
> Dead for a century,

Plod slowly.
Maybe they believe Willy's brown coffin, tangled heavily in moss,
Is a horse trough drifted to shore
Along that river under the willows and grass.
. . . .
The long box is empty.
The horses turn back toward the river.
Willy planes limber trees by the waters,
Fitting his boat together.
We may as well let him go.
Nothing is left of Willy on this side.

It is a world of peace and contentment with none of the agony experienced by those whom Willy has left behind, for example the speaker's mother, "Weeping with anger, afraid of winter."

It is indicative that the most positive poem in this book deals, not with the world of reality within which the speaker must live his life, but with the mythological world of paradise to which he wishes to escape through death. The depth of his unhappiness is defined in the first several poems of the volume, where he is portrayed as an impoverished outcast who encounters only coldness and hostility in the city. In "The Minneapolis Poem," he complains that "There are men in this city who labor dawn after dawn / To sell me my death" (*CP*, 141); and in "Before a Cashier's Window in a Department Store," we see just how deep is the alienation he feels:

The beautiful cashier's white face has risen once more
Behind a young manager's shoulder.
They whisper together, and stare
Straight into my face.
I feel like grabbing a stray child
Or a skinny old woman
And driving into a cellar, crouching
Under a stone bridge, praying myself sick,
Till the troops pass.

(*CP*, 148)

The speaker does pray often in this book, but never feels that he is listened to, much less answered. The world he inhabits is godless, a fact that adds powerfully to his sense of loneliness.

Knowing the pattern of *The Branch Will Not Break*, we would expect that the pastoral world of western Minnesota and North Dakota would provide some relief in the middle poems of *Shall We Gather at the River*. Unfortunately, the speaker's mood has changed significantly, rendering even nature empty of consolation for him. "Late November in a Field" (*CP*, 152), for example, begins: "Today I am walking alone in a bare place, / And winter is here." Animals do appear in this world, but the idea of apotheosis does not. Instead, Wright creates images of animals in danger, images that mirror externally the inner state of the speaker. When he sees two squirrels dragging a branch towards a hiding place, his reaction is based on the fact that winter is coming: "they ought to save acorns / Against the cold." The poem ends with an image of the speaker's coldness, loneliness, and unhappiness:

> The earth is hard now,
> The soles of my shoes need repairs.
> I have nothing to ask a blessing for,
> Except these words.
> I wish they were
> Grass.

A refugee from the city, the speaker finds that he is also unable to function in the country.

And so, in order to complete his quest, the speaker turns towards home, towards the river, and to thoughts of Jenny. But Jenny is dead, and the Ohio River is the river of death; we must therefore recognize that what the speaker is enacting in the process of this quest is his own powerful death wish. It is in a poem called "The Life" that the speaker reveals this truth by asking:

> And if I come back to my only country
> With a white rose on my shoulder,
> What is that to you?
> It is the grave
> In blossom.

> (*CP*, 155)

The placement of the rose upon his shoulder is not accidental; in many of these poems, Wright alludes to man's fallen state by mentioning his missing wings, his empty shoulder blades, his inability to fly. Because they have the power of flight, birds serve a positive, almost an angelic, role within the cosmology of James Wright. In this book, their primary function is to act as guides to the dead, leading them across the waters of death to the other world. In "Old Age Compensation," the speaker imagines what will happen after the old people die:

> They'll be safe enough.
> Their boats are moored there, among the cattails
> And the night-herons' nests.

All they have to do now
Is to get one of those lazy birds awake long enough
To guide them across the river.

(CP, 147)

It is this pattern that explains the speaker's strange desire, expressed in
"The Small Blue Heron": "He is not the last one. / I wish he were" (*CP*,
158). For the speaker, the last heron will be the one come to guide *him*
across the waters.

The most poignant of the many poems about birds in this volume is
"Three Sentences for a Dead Swan," which seems to kill, along with
the bird, the possibility of resurrection for the speaker. It is in the
poem's last stanza that he consigns the swan back to its tomb:

Here, carry his splintered bones
Slowly, slowly
Back into the
Tar and chemical strangled tomb,
The strange water, the
Ohio river, that is no tomb to
Rise from the dead
From.

(CP, 156)

It may even be that this bird represents Jenny, the lost love, whom it
would be entirely appropriate for Wright to call "My black Ohioan
swan." The name *Jenny* appears alone on the dedication page of *Shall
We Gather at the River*; she is the persistent ghost of the entire book,
but makes her grandest and most heart-wrenching appearance only in
the final poem, significantly titled "To the Muse" (*CP*, 168–69).[21]

The poem is another of those spoken by a person who is living to
someone who is dead. This one is no idle complaint of abandonment,
however; the speaker's position by now has become almost unbearable.
In his loneliness, he has concocted a scheme whereby Jenny can be
brought back from the dead to resume their courtship. The poem
begins:

It is all right. All they do
Is go in by dividing
One rib from another. I wouldn't
Lie to you. It hurts
Like nothing I know. All they do
Is burn their way in with a wire.
It forks in and out a little like the tongue

> Of that frightened garter snake we caught
> At Cloverfield, you and me, Jenny
> So long ago.

The speaker seems to understand this process, especially its pain-fulness, from the inside, and we recall earlier poems in which he re-ferred to himself as already dead, risen to return to the river. Mention of the snake reminds us as well of the "lost garden" of childhood, which Jenny and the speaker inhabited together so many years ago, and which is analogous in Wright's thinking to the mythological Garden.

As the poem continues, the speaker presses his suit by telling Jenny what he hopes to accomplish:

> I would lie to you
> If I could.
> But the only way I can get you to come up
> Out of the suckhole, the south face
> Of the Powhatan pit, is to tell you
> What you know:
>
> You come up after dark, you poise alone
> With me on the shore.
> I lead you back to this world.

In the next two stanzas, the speaker goes into greater detail about the medical procedure he is fantasizing; it will be performed by "Three lady doctors in Wheeling" who "open / Their offices at night." The images become increasingly bizarre, until finally the speaker comes to recognize that his desperation is verging upon insanity. It is at that moment that he unleashes, in an apostrophe addressed to Jenny, a cry of anguish from the depths of his soul:

> Oh Jenny,
> I wish to God I had made this world, this scurvy
> And disastrous place. I
> Didn't, I can't bear it
> Either, I don't blame you, sleeping down there
> Face down in the unbelievable silk of spring,
> Muse of black sand,
> Alone.
>
> I don't blame you, I know
> The place where you lie.
> I admit everything. But look at me.
> How can I live without you?
> Come up to me, love,

Out of the river, or I will
Come down to you.

Love and death are intermingled in this book, as the speaker quests
first for one, then for the other, and finally for both; the muse he loves
and longs to please is dead, unreachable. It is ironic that these same
two goals are the ones Wright will continue to quest for, successfully
this time, throughout the rest of his work. The book that he published
after *Shall We Gather at the River* is his *Collected Poems*, which was
awarded the Pulitzer Prize in 1972. At the beginning of that volume,
again as a prologue, Wright placed a poem entitled "The Quest" (*CP*, 3).
In this poem's four eight-line stanzas, the speaker is seen searching for
something—love, a meaning to life—in four separate places. His first
of three failures occurs in a grove of trees, where he comes upon a "gray
nest" held in the tree "As in the arm of a dead girl / Crippled and torn
and laid out bare." In the second stanza, the speaker's search takes him
to a "bare house," where he finds only "gray hollows." Outside once
more, he reaches in the third stanza for "a nest / Of stars," but comes
away empty-handed. Finally, in the fourth stanza he turns to the bed of
a sleeping woman, his newly found beloved, and there finds happiness.

> So, as you sleep, I seek your bed
> And lay my careful, quiet ear
> Among the nestings of your hair,
> Against your tenuous, fragile head,
> And hear the birds beneath your eyes
> Stirring for birth, and know the world
> Immeasurably alive and good,
> Though bare as rifted paradise.

The love that he finds here will sustain Wright's speaker throughout
the rest of his work.

Perhaps the most moving testimony made to this woman comes at
the end of "To the Creature of the Creation," the poem that concludes
the volume *Two Citizens*:

> You are the earth's body.
> I will die on the wing.
> To me, you are everything
> That matters, chickadee.
> You live so much in me.
> Chickadees sing in the snow.
> I will die on the wing,
> I love you so.[22]

Even here, in a transcendently happy love poem, we see again the mingling of death and love so characteristic of Wright's work in general.
However, the feeling of a successful resolution to the love quest is
everywhere to be found in his last three books, *Two Citizens* (1973), *To
a Blossoming Pear Tree* (1977), and *This Journey* (1982). At this point in
the overall span of his work, Wright seems to have found as much as he
is going to within the fallen world of everyday human reality. His
speaker has reached—to return to the geometrical figure introduced at
the start of this essay—the bottom of the circle of his overall quest and
is now on his way back to the original source of "childlike radiance and
joy," lost in earliest life but still waiting at the end of time.

Because the state of Ohio was literally James Wright's boyhood
home, he thought of it as the goal of his quest for "home"—at least
until the end of *Shall We Gather at the River*, when a new sense of its
reality apparently began to emerge. The importance of the idea of
home in Wright's thinking is indicated in comments he made when
writing about two other writers; in 1964, before *Shall We Gather at the
River*, he said of Theodor Storm that he "understood that the main
thing . . . is not to get on in the world but to get home."[23] Six years
later, after the publication of *Shall We Gather at the River*, Wright
compiled a selection of poems by Herman Hesse; in his introduction
he explained:

> All I wish to do is to offer a selection of Hesse's poems which deal with the
> single theme of homesickness.
>
> That is what I think Hesse's poetry is about. He is homesick. But what is
> home?

Wright answers this question indirectly by quoting from *Steppenwolf* a
passage in which the girl Hermine explains what it is that the sensitive
man searches for in his life: "It is what I call eternity. The pious call it
the kingdom of God. I say to myself: all we who ask too much and have
a dimension too many could not contrive to live at all if there were not
another air to breathe outside the air of this world, if there were not
eternity at the back of time; and this is the kingdom of truth. The
music of Mozart belongs there and the poetry of your great poets."[24]

Having plumbed the depths of reality, having achieved the greatest
degree of heroism available to him within the fallen world—a heroism
based both on love and on a sense of stoic endurance of what hurts—
Wright's speaker now begins to turn his attention back to the realm of
eternity, to the "lost paradise" of childhood that is the "Kingdom of
God," as it is described in his introduction to Sobiloff's book. Of the
final three volumes, it is *This Journey* that gives the most rounded,

most fully realized expression of both sides of this inherently pastoral quest, and it is to that book that I will now devote my attention. There is an undeniable pastoral dimension to the poetry of James Wright. Among his earliest poems, those written when he was in high school and college, are dozens that are explicitly and traditionally pastoral, idylls and eclogues and country elegies. And yet many years later Wright said: "I'm antipastoral. I've worked on farms and I would never work on another one. I've got up at four o'clock in the morning and shovelled the cow manure out of the barn and bailed away the horse urine. The hell with it."[25]

The criticism of pastoral poetry that Shakespeare (for example) made in *As You Like It* was of its idealized, unrealistic portrayal of nature; such poetry was based upon the premise that one could live in the country without suffering discomfort, inconvenience, or devastation from rodents, insects, hailstorms, manure, and aching backs. Wright's view of pastoralism—when it concerns the actual countryside—is as realistic as Shakespeare's; his goal is to resurrect, not a "naturalistic" pastoralism, but a mythological, truly "idealistic" pastoralism. To accomplish this aim, he had first to reject the fake pastoralism surrounding the Ohio of his boyhood. Much of Ohio is indeed a land of great rural beauty—gently rolling hills give way to verdant valleys with quietly gurgling streams; cows may be heard lowing in the fields, while horses scamper among the trees; farms peopled by swains and maidens give way to nineteenth-century villages with their plump housewives, prosperous burghers, and hayseed children riding bicycles. "Isn't it pretty to think so?," James Wright apparently came to ask ironically late in his life, echoing Jake Barnes. It was Wright's misfortune to have been raised in the Ohio River Valley, which can offer the appearance of country beauty but is actually a suppurating wound on the face of the earth, a wound kept open by industry, strip mines, pollution of water and air. It is this contrast between appearance and reality that comes to animate Wright's view of Ohio in his final three books. "Ohioan Pastoral," from *This Journey*, embodies Wright's fullest definition of the deceptiveness of this landscape:

> On the other side
> Of Salt Creek, along the road, the barns topple
> And snag among the orange rinds,
> Oil cans, cold balloons of lovers.
> One barn there
> Sags, sags and oozes
> Down one side of the copperous gulley.
> The limp whip of a sumac dangles
> Gently against the body of a lost

Bathtub, while high in the flint-cracks
And the wild grimed trees, on the hill,
A buried gas main
Long ago tore a black gutter into the mines.
And now it hisses among the green rings
On fingers in coffins.

(*TJ*, 46)

Because the poem reproduces in the mind of the reader the same disillusionment originally experienced by the speaker, it is as misleading as the landscape it describes. Wright begins by noting one of those gurgling streams, a road, and several barns. Then the barns in general begin to fall into a random collection of garbage, while one barn enters a toxic trench. The imagery at the end is almost apocalyptic, as the industrial poisoning is doubled (hissing gas invades an abandoned mine), attacking even the bodies of the dead.

The landscape of Ohio as presented in this book is not just blighted, wasted by industrial pollution, it is also distinctly murderous. Another general definition appears at the end of the poem "Chilblain," where we are told that "Ohio is":

Where violets last only a little.
Mill-smoke kills them halfway through spring,
And chilblain still stings
In June when earth smokes like slag.

(*TJ*, 25)

Poisons carried by the air are especially prominent in such poems; another speaks of "The mill smoke that gets everything in the end" (*TJ*, 17). As bad as this landscape, this airscape, is, it is not the only treacherous thing in Ohio. Increasingly in Wright's poetry, the people of the state appear murderous as well. In *Two Citizens* it is the "Ohio Valley Swains" who rape a young girl, friend of the speaker:

You thought that was funny, didn't you, to mock a girl?

. . . if I ever see you again, so help me in the sight of God,
I'll kill you.[26]

And in *This Journey*, Wright speaks of his favorite season, which somehow is able to survive even in Ohio:

The still totally unbelievable spring beauty
That for some hidden reason nobody raped
To death in Ohio.

(*TJ*, 57)

Ohio is finally recognized as a false home in the mind of this speaker—and so his search for a real "home" goes on.[27] Because death is so pervasive a presence in *This Journey*, a hidden and not-so-hidden topic, it would appear that Wright is turning his eyes toward the lost garden— the "Kingdom of God"—he had written of so many years earlier. Indeed, the reader of these poems cannot help but feel that the poet is anticipating his *own* death. Even the gardenlike landscape of Europe is filled with intimations of mortality. Of the many statues Wright speaks of here, nearly all are wasting away; either they are pockmarked and rotted by polluted air (as in Venice, where "North of the city . . . factories / Murder the sun and what is left of the city"—*TJ*, 48), or they are crumbling under the decadent weight of the flowers that climb upon them.

In the poem "Wherever Home Is" (*TJ*, 12), Wright effects the transition from the world of decay and death into the world of paradise that his work has been flirting with since the beginning of his career. At the start of the poem, a statue of Leonardo is presented as dying thanks to the combined efforts of both the pollution and the flowers mentioned above:

> Leonardo da Vinci, haggard in basalt stone,
> Will soon be gone,
> A frivolous face lost in wisteria flowers.
> They are turning gray and dying
> All over his body.
> Subtlest of all wanderers
> Who live beautifully by living on other lives,
> They cannot find a warm vein
> In Leonardo, and Leonardo
> Himself will soon
> be gone.

Even the flowers in this passage are dying. Later, the poem will present the possibility of a renewal of life, though in a realm different from this one:

> One brief lizard
> Lavishes on Leonardo and on me
> The whole spring.

Before we can deal with the issue of rebirth as presented in this poem and elsewhere, however, we must take account of Wright's final attitude towards the fallen world of time as it is expressed in one of the best poems he ever wrote.

In "The Journey" (*TJ*, 30–31), Wright creates a landscape wholly of earth, a landscape littered with intimations, not of Wordsworthian immortality, but of an inevitable and even predatory mortality. His purpose is obviously to indicate how those "heroes on the earth" mentioned in his introduction to Sobiloff's volume must ultimately deal with the harshest facts of life. In the opening stanza of the poem, the speaker tells how he and a companion "were swept out . . . by the wind," "far up the mountain, behind the town" of Anghiari. The landscape is extremely dry:

> Wind had been blowing across the hills
> For days, and everything now was graying gold
> With dust, everything we saw.

The omnipresent dust in this poem carries with it familiar connotations of mortality, though within this frame of reference the dust also becomes a source of santification. We see this when the speaker bends down in this completely arid landscape, no water anywhere, to wash *with* the dust "the dust from my face." We also see it in the middle stanza, where he meets the spider that will embody the message of the poem:

> I found the spider web there, whose hinges
> Reeled heavily and crazily with the dust,
> Whole mounds and cemeteries of it, sagging
> And scattering shadows among shells and wings.
> And then she stepped into the center of air
> Slender and fastidious, the golden hair
> Of daylight along her shoulders, she poised there,
> While ruins crumbled on every side of her.
> Free of the dust, as though a moment before
> She had stepped inside the earth, to bathe herself.

Like the speaker, the spider—in order to bathe herself "free of the dust" by stepping "inside the earth"—would have to have washed *with* dust. The landscape that surrounds this remarkable creature is of her own making; the web is a trap that she uses to capture the insects whose remains litter the ground below.

What Wright's speaker learns from gazing upon this scene of blight and execution is the answer, finally, to the question of how one can live within the fallen world, how a sensitive person can come to terms with the physical fact of death. It is the spider who illustrates this lesson as she is generalized and redescribed in the poem's concluding stanza:

Many men
Have searched all over Tuscany and never found
What I found there, the heart of the light
Itself shelled and leaved, balancing
On filaments themselves falling. The secret
Of this journey is to let the wind
Blow its dust all over your body,
To let it go on blowing, to step lightly, lightly
All the way through your ruins, and not to lose
Any sleep over the dead, who surely
Will bury their own, don't worry.

We have indeed traveled a long way from *The Green Wall*, where the speaker was so terrified of death, so paralyzed by the effect of losing a few of his friends. Now Wright's emblem for the figure of death is described as occupying "the heart of the light."

It is in the image of the light that Wright indicates how this contradiction is to be resolved. Like Whitman so many years before him, Wright has learned to treat death as a positive force, and we must know how this can be so. In fact, when Wright envisions someone stepping "lightly, lightly / All the way through your ruins," he is not just advising the reader on how to deal with the fact of mortality—he is also envisioning how a man might step *through* death itself, through his own death, into another realm altogether. In his article " 'The Heart of Light,' " Hank Lazer suggests that the image of light has always represented something like salvation, something like paradise, something like God, in the poetry of James Wright: "God's presence is implied or inferred, never directly stated in Wright's poetry. His 'the heart of light,' 'impossibly hovering in the air over everything,' and 'black as the inmost secret of light,' translates traditional, mystical illumination into his own uncertain natural theophany."[28]

I want now to resume my interrupted discussion of "Wherever Home Is," the physical setting of which is a landscape of decay and disintegration that is gradually destroying the statue of Leonardo da Vinci. When we left the poem, Wright had just noticed the possibility of some kind of rebirth within this context:

One brief lizard
Lavishes on Leonardo and on me
The whole spring.

In the concluding stanza, Wright's speaker defines what he means by the word *home:*

I am going home with the lizard,
Wherever home is,
And lie beside him unguarded
In the clear sunlight.
We will lift our faces even if it rains.
We will both turn green.

The lines clearly describe a garden within which an apotheosis is possible for the speaker—his desire to "turn green" is very similar to his earlier desire to "break into blossom."[29] That the agency for the change is here a lizard rather than a horse is of no real importance—the function of such creatures throughout Wright's work is remarkably consistent.[30] What does matter is that the background to the desire for apotheosis has changed.

At the beginning of *The Branch Will Not Break*, Wright's speaker found himself alienated from his physical environment, the city and its citizens, and wished to remove himself to the pastoral peace of the country. In *This Journey*, the negative pole of the speaker's quest is not defined in terms of the city—most of the poems are set in the Italian countryside—but by instances of decay and disintegration, instances that the speaker is psychologically unable to ignore because they so forcibly suggest his own impending death. That Wright so often ties these images of mortality to poisons in the air is especially significant. It is an unfortunate fact that, shortly after writing many of these poems, James Wright died of cancer of the tongue and throat—a cancer caused in large part by the poisoned air of cigarette smoke. It is altogether possible that many of the poems in *This Journey* are based upon a subconscious awareness of this disease, and that this is why they are so suffused by images of death, decay, disintegration, and poisoned air. Thus, the desire to escape in this volume takes a more extreme form than that found in *The Branch Will Not Break*. Instead of simply wishing to escape from the city into the country, James Wright now longs to escape from the fallen world of disease and physical suffering into the unchanging health of paradise.

How that paradise is imagined in *This Journey* is best illustrated by "Yes, But," another poem in which Wright speaks of his own death—envisioning an afterlife for himself, creating the garden he would like to rest in, and populating it with the creatures he would like to rest with:

Even if it were true,
Even if I were dead and buried in Verona,
I believe I would come out and wash my face
In the chill spring.

I believe I would appear
Between noon and four, when nearly
Everybody else is asleep or making love,
And all the Germans turned down, the motorcycles
Muffled, chained, still.

Then the plump lizards along the Adige by San Giorgio
Come out and gaze,
Unpestered by temptation, across the water.
I would sit among them and join them in leaving
The golden mosquitoes alone.
Why should we sit by the Adige and destroy
Anything, even our enemies, even the prey
God caused to glitter for us
Defenseless in the sun?
We are not exhausted. We are not angry, or lonely,
Or sick at heart.
We are in love lightly, lightly. We know we are shining,
Though we cannot see one another.
The wind doesn't scatter us,
Because our very lungs have fallen and drifted
Away like leaves down the Adige,
Long ago.

We breathe light.

(*TJ,* 79)

By beginning the poem with a vision of his own death, Wright immediately leaves behind the fallen world of physical reality—with its motorcycles, its Germans, its predators—and enters a gardenlike realm characterized by light and love. The poisoned air of reality is no longer a danger: "The wind doesn't scatter us, / Because our very lungs have fallen and drifted / Away. . . ." This is, in fact, the garden lost in childhood, "the Kingdom of God," the Peaceable Kingdom in which the lamb can lie down with the lion.

James Wright comes full circle in this poem, reoccupying the paradise left behind when he climbed over the green wall in his first book. I would like to conclude by quoting one last passage from Wright's introduction to Hy Sobiloff's book; in a final imagining of what will happen in that glorious moment at the end of the poet's Wordsworthian quest, the moment when he will regain his childhood home, Wright says: "the poet extends his hands to the child in the darkness; and, as poet and child embrace, they look about them to see that all has grown light again, it is the first dawn, the passing of time was only an evil dream, and the poet has come home to himself at last."[31]

Interview with
James Wright

●

The interview was conducted at Wright's apartment in New York City over a span of two days in April of 1972. *Collected Poems* had been published in 1971, and Wright had been awarded the Pulitzer Prize earlier in 1972. His next book, *Two Citizens* (1973), had been written but not published.

Mr. Wright, you taught at the University of Minnesota with John Berryman. What is your feeling about him as a poet?

John Berryman was a very great poet and I think his work is going to endure. And not just because he was a good craftsman, but because he was demonstrating in his poetry, I think without realizing it completely, the fact that a poem is not only a single thing that can be made and very beautifully constructed, but that poetry is also something that can go on being made and it can almost reach a point where it re-creates itself. By the growth of his work, and he never stopped growing, he was showing that there is something about poetry in the human imagination which is like the spring. Dr. Williams is a great poet for the same reason.

Tolstoy worried about this question. He was asked in a letter by a pacifist group if he could give them a definition of religion and, if he could do that, to explain to them the relation between religion, that is, what a person believes, and morality, that is, the way he acts in accord with some notion of how he ought to act. Tolstoy worried about this letter, and then, as I recall it, he said: "I can only go back to myself. I look around myself and I see every year that, no matter what people do to themselves and to one another, the spring constantly renews itself. This is a physical fact, not a metaphysical theory. I look at every spring and I respond to it very strongly. But I also notice that every year the spring is the same new spring and every year I am one year older. I have to ask the question: what is the relation between my brief and tragic life and this force in the universe that perpetually renews itself? I further believe that every human being asks this question. He cannot avoid asking it—it is forced upon him. And his answer to that question is his religion. If he says the relation between me and this thing is nothing, then his religion is nihilism. As for morality, what ought I to do? I wish I knew." That was a great letter.

Berryman's greatness included, of course, his utter mastery of the craft of the language. But he also was demonstrating that poetry is not simply an ornament, that poetry has some deep-rooted relation to life itself, the way we go on living.

What is it to be a poet?

I can only tell you what it is to me. I regard myself primarily as a craftsman, as a Horatian. My favorite poet is Edward Thomas, and the person whom I would like to be my master is Horace—Horace, who was able to write humorously and kindly in flawless verse. I've achieved that maybe twice in my life, but that is what I would like to be.

Of course there are many other kinds of poets. There is Jack Finnegan, for example. Jack Finnegan is a friend of mine, a learned gentleman whom I sometimes meet at Jack Loftus's Bar. There is a tradition in Irish poetry in which the poem itself is an answer to a question which someone has posed. Somebody says to a guy who is standing in a bar: What are you doing with those dice? The guy turns and says:

God rest that Jewy woman,
Queen Jezebel, the bitch
Who peeled the clothes from her shoulder-bones
Down to her spent teats
As she stretched out of the window
Among the geraniums, where
She chaffed and laughed like one half daft
Titivating her painted hair—

King Jehu he drove to her,
She tipped him a fancy beck;
But he from his knacky side-car spoke,
'Who'll break that dewlapped neck?'
And so she was thrown from the window;
Like Lucifer she fell
Beneath the feet of the horses and they beat
The light out of Jezebel.

That corpse wasn't planted in clover;
Ah, nothing of her was found
Save those grey bones that Hare-foot Mike

Gave me for their lovely sound;
And as once her dancing body
Made star-lit princes sweat,
So I'll just clack: though her ghost lacks a back
There's music in the old bones yet.

Which is a way of saying, "You sing your business and I'll sing mine."
The poem, by the way, is "Song for the Clatter-Bones" by the Irish poet
F. R. Higgins.

Well, I thought it was only a literary convention, and you're not
going to believe this, but I swear in the sight of God that it is the truth.
I went over to Loftus's the other day, and I saw Jack Finnegan. I said,
"Jack, how are you?" "OK, Professor," he said, "how are you?" Then I
asked him a question—and by God it turned out to be a living thing.
He could not have known what question I was going to ask him. I said,
"Jack, what do you think about Nixon's visit to China?" And he turned
to me and very beautifully sang:

In Peking's fair city
    Where the girls are so slitty
'Twas there I met witty
    Miss Molly Wong Wong.

She drove a wheel barrow
    Through streets broad and narrow
Singing Szechuan, Peking,
    Alive a long dong.

Alive a long dong,
    Alive a long dong,
Crying Szechuan, Peking,
    Alive a long dong.

He sang it on the spot. What was I going to say to him? Jack, you made
it up? Of course he made it up, he made it up on the spot. I was present
at the creation.

There is another Irish tradition I'd like to mention. It is based on
sheer arrogance, the determination to live. Poetry can keep life itself
alive. You can endure almost anything as long as you can sing about it.
Do you know Raftery? Anthony Raftery, from the eighteenth century,
blind and illiterate, who carried a hand harp. He was standing in a bar
and someone asked, Who is that poor, frail old man leaning there in the
corner with a harp in his hand? Raftery turned around and said: "I am
Raftery, the poet, full of hope and love, with no light in my eyes, and
with gentleness that has no misery, going west upon my pilgrimage by

the light of my heart, though feeble and tired to the end of my road, and behold me now, with my back to the wall, playing music unto empty pockets."

Do you find being a poet painful, like playing music to empty pockets with your back to the wall?

Well, as you know, I'm also a professor. I've written books of verse, but I'm a professor. And to me personally, teaching is the art that gives me the more pleasure. I'm not trying to put myself down as poet, but I mean what I say. That is, the contact with my students, and my reading of books and trying to share my thoughts and feelings with my students, gives me more pleasure, and I honor this as a high art. Remember that the teachers include, Jesus, Socrates, Siddhartha, Meister Eckhardt. In short, yes.

Poetry is something that you can't escape from yourself?

I'm afraid I have to admit that I cannot escape it, and to that extent I regard it as a kind of curse. I've thought that many a time. Why the hell couldn't I have been a carpenter or a handyman?

Is there behind that the feeling that to be a poet is to be too conscious of too many things?

Well, no, it doesn't mean that to me so much. I'm conscious of many things, only strange things happen, strange things happen to me. And although I say that my ideal would be Horatian, I suspect this happened to beautiful Horace too. Sometimes there is a force of life like the spring which mysteriously takes shape without your even having asked it to take shape, and this is frightening, it is terribly frightening. It has happened maybe a few times to me—times when I've been able to get the poem finished in almost nothing flat.

What poems are they? Do you remember which ones finished themselves in nothing flat?

A poem called "Father," a poem called "A Blessing." Where did they come from? If you were to ask me that question, I would have to say, How should I know? Being a poet sometimes puts you at the mercy of life, and life is not always merciful.

Have you ever taught creative writing?

I tried it once and failed at it completely because all I could do was sit and talk to the class. And someone would ask me a question, how I worked on something, and all I could do was grunt. This is not to say it can't be done, it can be done very brilliantly, as we know from the work of Theodore Roethke, who was a very great teacher.

Was he your teacher?

Yes, and he was my good friend for four years.

Oh father dear,
Do ships at sea
Have legs way down below?

Of course they do,
You goosey you,
Or else how could they go?

Roethke used to toss up a lot of them like that.

What did he teach you?

He taught mainly the craft, and he, like Berryman and like Lowell, was an entirely conscious craftsman. He understood that the relation between the craft and the mysterious imagination is not what we conventionally think it to be. There are some people who think that a very careful, conscious craftsmanship will repress your feelings. And Roethke understood that it is careful, conscious craft which liberates your feelings and liberates your imagination.

I know you took a master's in creative writing. I'm not aware of how many poets actually study creative writing in a formal situation. Is there any real value in that, or does one still have to learn the essential things by himself?

I took the master's in creative writing to get it the hell out of the way. Don't you have to learn every essential thing by yourself? Stanley Kunitz said to me once: "You've got to get down into the pit of the self, the real pit, and then you have to find your own way to climb up out of it. And it can't be anybody else's way. It has to be yours."
May I tell you why I took the M.A. by writing a book of verse? I wanted to be a serious teacher and I wanted to get the M.A. out of the way so I could get down to the serious work of the doctorate, which I

did. And I wrote it on Dickens. My subject as a teacher, my main subject, is the history of the English novel.

For a poet?

Oh, there is a plenty of poetry in it. "And it's old and old it's sad and old it's sad and wary I go back to you, my cold father, my cold mad father, my cold mad feary father, till the near sight of the mere size of him, the moyles and moyles of it, moananoaning, makes me seasilt saltsick and I rush my only into your arms"—*Finnegans Wake.* Do you want to hear another one? This is from *Tristram Shandy.* Tristram, the narrator, has been trying to get to the place where he is born. At the end of chapter 8 of volume 9 he thinks he can finally tell what happened the night he was conceived, but then he suddenly remembers from what his Uncle Toby told him, that the night he was conceived his father, Walter Shandy, and his mother got into a quarrel. It had something to do with who was to put the cat out and who was to wind the clock or something like that. And suddenly Laurence Sterne breaks through his own narrator, in the middle of the argument, and he says this. This is prose in a novel:

> I will not argue the matter: Time wastes too fast: every letter I trace tells me with what rapidity Life follows my pen; the days and hours of it, more precious, my dear Jenny! than the rubies about thy neck, are flying over our heads like light clouds of a windy day never to return more—every thing presses on—whilst thou are twisting that lock—see, it goes grey; and every time I kiss thy hand to bid adieu, and every absence which follows it, are preludes to that eternal separation which we are shortly to make—Heaven have mercy upon us both!

And the whole of Chapter 9 is: "Now for what the world thinks of that ejaculation, I would not give a groat." And then a little later in the novel he interrupts himself again and says: "You wonder who Jenny is, don't you? Well, you pay attention to your own business and get back to the story."

I want to ask what poets influenced your early work and what did you learn from them?

> All suddenly the wind comes soft,
>   And Spring is here again;
> And the hawthorn quickens with buds of green,
>   And my heart with buds of pain.

My heart all Winter lay so numb,
  The earth so dead and frore,
That I never thought the Spring would come,
  Or my heart wake any more.

But Winter's broken and earth has woken
  And the small birds cry again;
And the hawthorn hedge puts forth its buds,
  And my heart puts forth its pain.

Can you guess who wrote that?

Robinson?

You would never guess, would you? Rupert Brooke. And he was a
very good writer for a sixteen-year-old to read. "Down the blue night
the unending columns press." People never give him a tumble anymore, but he was pretty good. He's dead.

In the note attached to The Green Wall, *you mentioned Robinson
and Frost as influences.*

Well, I was somewhat older then. When I wrote that book I was twen-
ty-seven years old. I could tell you the kind of thing I had in mind. I
wrote a sonnet called "Saint Judas," and in that sonnet I was trying to
do two things technically: to write a sonnet that would be a genuine
Petrarchan sonnet and at the same time be a dramatic monologue. I got
that idea from Robinson, who has a sonnet called "How Annandale
Went Out." Do you know what *went out* means? Well, this is conventional hospital parlance for dying. So and so went out last night. Annandale is a character Robinson had written about before, but in this
particular sonnet the doctor is speaking. And, as usual in a dramatic
monologue, he is speaking to another person, so that what you are
doing is overhearing a conversation in which one person speaks and the
other is listening. The doctor was a friend of George Annandale.
George Annandale was an alcoholic who was suffering terribly with his
death, and so the doctor gave him an injection. That's what the word
engine means in this poem. He gave him an injection which killed
him; that is, he administered euthanasia. Then he gets drunk, and in
the poem he is talking to another friend of George Annandale's. What
is he trying to do? And Robinson—great Robinson!—leaves you hanging there saying, yes, what was he trying to do? Here is the sonnet:

"They called it Annandale—and I was there
To flourish, to find words, and to attend:

Liar, physician, hypocrite, and friend,
I watched him; and the sight was not so fair
As one or two that I have seen elsewhere:
An apparatus not for me to mend—
A wreck, with hell between him and the end,
Remained of Annandale; and I was there.

"I know the ruin as I knew the man;
So put the two together, if you can,
Remembering the worst you know of me.
Now view yourself as I was, on the spot—
With a slight kind of engine. Do you see?
Like this . . . You wouldn't hang me? I thought not."

Then we have my poem on Judas, who is, I suppose, the ultimate lost
betrayer. It is a—well, I wouldn't call it a literal imitation of Robinson,
but if I hadn't read Robinson's sonnets I know that I wouldn't have
tried to write that poem.

What did you learn from Frost?

Well, first of all I think that there is his profound, terrifying, and very
tragic view of the universe, which seems to me true. I've never said life
is meaningless, I've said it is tragic. I think it is intensely precious.
God, sometimes I think I'm so happy I don't know what to do with me.
But it hurts like hell. There is that, but also technically there is something in Frost. He knows how to keep the adjectives out. An example is
his poem "Lodged." A very short poem, it has one adverb in it—"actually"—and that one adverb, it seems to me, strikes like a bullet.

*Frost—America's great nature poet. Would you call yourself a
nature poet?*

In part, yes.

*The reason I ask this is that your early poems seem partly nature
poems, but also there are a lot of poems about people. The Branch Will
Not Break is almost entirely a nature book. Shall We Gather at the
River is something else, more personal. And the new poems, probably
growing out of your life here in New York, are almost urban poems. I
mean, there is an urban landscape as opposed to the earlier Minnesota
and Ohio landscapes.*

Human beings are unhappily part of nature, perhaps nature become
conscious of itself. Oh, how I would love to be a chickadee! But I can't

be a chickadee, all I can be is what I am. I love the natural world, and I'm conscious of the pain in it. So I'm a nature poet who writes about human beings in nature. I love Nietzsche, who called man "the sick animal."

Is it fair to ask you which of your own books is your favorite, which one you like best?

Yes, that's fair enough. My own favorite is *Saint Judas.* I tried to come to terms in that book with what I felt to be the truth of my own life, which is that of a man who wants very much to be happy, but who is not happy. I do not have the talent for happiness. There are some people who do. I have a friend, a student, and you heard me tell her yesterday on the telephone that one of the high-rise buildings in New York is a cathouse. And she roared and roared with laughter and said it will set her up for the whole day. I do not have that gift; I wish I had. And in *Saint Judas* I tried to face the fact that I am not a happy man by talent. Sometimes I have been very happy, but characteristically I'm a miserable son of a bitch. I tried to come to terms with that in the clearest and most ferociously perfect form that I could find and in all the traditional ways. That was partly a defensive action, because I hurt so much then. After I finished that book I had finished with poetry forever. I truly believed that I had said what I had to say as clearly and directly as I could, and that I had no more to do with this art.

You've told me that before. What was wrong, and how did you get going again?

At that time I had come, for personal reasons but also for artistic reasons, to something like a dead end. I was in despair at that time, and what usually has consoled me is words—I've always been able to turn to them. But suddenly, it seemed to me that the words themselves had gone dead, I mean dead in me, and I didn't know what to do. It was at that time that Robert Bly's magazine, which was then called *The Fifties,* appeared. I wrote him a long letter because his magazine contained a translation of a poem by Georg Trakl. Some years earlier, at the University of Vienna, I had read in German the poetry of Trakl, and I didn't know what to do with it, though I recognized that somehow it had a depth of life in it that I needed. Trakl is a poet who writes in parallelisms, only he leaves out the intermediary, rationalistic explanations of the relation between one image and another. I would suppose that Trakl has had as much influence on me as anybody else has had. But the interesting thing is that when I read Robert Bly's magazine, I wrote him a letter. It was sixteen pages long and single-spaced, and all he said in reply was, "Come on out to the farm." I made my way out to that farm, and almost as soon as we met each other we started to work on our translation of Trakl.

You should see us working together on something. We get up in the morning and won't even look at each other. We pace back and forth. He'll turn without looking at me and say to his wife, Carol, "Yeah, he likes J. V. Cunningham." Then I get one up on him by quoting him a Cunningham poem. And we sit and stare at each other. We would say things that I would not repeat even for the *Paris Review*. And yet I'm a member of his family too. I'm Mary's godfather. They loved me and they saved my life. I don't mean just the life of my poetry, either. To think of Carol Bly is to defeat despair. Never mind my small experience of human beings. Carol is one of the noblest persons who ever lived, as far as I'm concerned.

Did he have the strong influence on your work of that time that is sometimes ascribed to him?

Yes. He made it clear to me that the tradition of poetry which I had tried to master, and in which I'd come to a dead end, was not the only one. He reminded me that poetry is a possibility, that, although all poetry is formal, there are many forms, just as there are many forms of feeling.

The book that followed, of course, is The Branch Will Not Break. *How do these things show up there?*

At the center of that book is my rediscovery of the abounding delight of the body that I had forgotten about. Every Friday afternoon I used to go out to Bly's farm, and there were so many animals out there. There was Simon, who was an Airedale, but about the size of a Great Dane. There was David, the horse, my beautiful, beloved David, the swaybacked palomino. Simon and David used to go out by Bly's barn. David would stand there looking out over the corn fields that lead onto the prairies of South Dakota, and Simon would sit down beside him, and they would stay there for hours. And sometimes, after I sat on the front porch and watched them, sometimes I went and sat down beside Simon. Neither Simon nor David looked at me, and I felt blessed. They allowed me to join them. They liked me. I can't get over it—they liked me. Simon didn't bite me; David didn't kick me; they just stayed there as they were. And I sat down on my fat ass and looked over the corn fields and the prairie with them. And there we were. One afternoon, a gopher came up out of a hole and looked at us. Simon didn't leap for him, David didn't kick him, and I didn't shoot him. There we were, all four of us together. All I was thinking was, I can be happy sometimes. And I'd forgotten that. And with those animals I remembered then. And that is what that book is about, the rediscovery. I didn't hate my body at all. I liked myself very much. Simon is lost. David, with what Robert called his beautiful and sensitive face, has gone to the knacker's. I wish I knew how to tell you. My son Marsh, the musician, is in love with animals.

What effect do you feel your role as translator—the sort of work you did with Bly—has had on your own poetry?

It's led me into some further possibilities of saying something that I think I wanted to say from the beginning. And that, unfortunately, being damned as I consider myself, I felt that I had to say or I would die. I think that most of the people who are alive in the world right now are very unhappy. I don't want people to be unhappy, and I'm sorry that they are. I wish there were something I could do to help. I'm coming to face the fact that there isn't much I can do to help. And I think I've been trying to say that ever since I've started to write books. That's what my books are about.

How do you react to hearing the poems of The Branch Will Not Break *and afterward described as surrealistic?*

They are not surrealistic, they are Horatian and classical. When they sound surrealistic, all that means is that my attempt to be clear has failed. They are not surrealistic, and I am not a surrealist. The crucial element of surrealism is, not a structural and formal matter, but that it is funny. Up to World War I, the ideals in Europe had been ideals of honor, integrity, Mother, apple pie, and the flag. The young men who went into that war suddenly discovered that this was a lie. What it meant was that they were being led to kill each other. The French surrealists responded with comedy, and the only American surrealist we've had who has understood this—no, we've had two of them. One is Malcolm Cowley in the book *Exile's Return*. No, we've had three of them—E. E. Cummings was another one who understood. You know, he went out to urinate on the Paris lawn. Suddenly, a policeman grabbed him, and he immediately found himself surrounded by the French. This was after the war was over, and they shouted at the cop: *Reprieve le pisseur Americain!*—"Let that American pisser go!"

Another thing that happened was that Cowley was sitting, as he tells us in that beautiful book, in a cafe. The waiter pushed him. He pushed the waiter back, and he thought, this is it. You know, *le gendarmerie* will be here in a minute. And so he covered his face with his hands. Suddenly, he found himself lifted on the shoulders of all the people in the cafe, and they carried him down the street singing. The only other American poet that we have had who has understood the principle of French surrealism is our beautiful poet from Ohio—where else?—Kenneth Patchen.

My favorite of your books is Shall We Gather at the River. *And one thing that I really like about it is the fact that it has integrity and coherence. In other words, it's not quite a single narrative poem, but it's not just a collection of separate lyrics either. How do you feel about that in respect to that book?*

It was very carefully written to move in that way. Whether it came off or not is another question, and not for me to judge. . . . Like hell! I know damn well that that book is perfectly constructed, and I knew exactly what I was doing from the very first syllable to the very last one.

Which is what? What were you doing?

I was trying to move from death to resurrection and death again, and challenge death finally. Well, if I must tell you, I was trying to write about a girl I was in love with who has been dead for a long time. I tried to sing with her in that book. Not to re-create her; you can't re-create anybody, at least I can't. But I thought maybe I could come to terms with that feeling which has hung on in my heart for so long. The book has been damned because it is so carefully dreamed.

Do you in constructing your books generally have that idea of coherence in mind?

Every time. Did I mention to you Robert Frost's remark—it is a very Horatian remark—that if you have a book of twenty-four poems, the book itself should be the twenty-fifth? And I have tried that every time, every time.

Well, let's take one more example. What was your principle of order in The Green Wall? *What structural principle were you working with?*

I tried to begin with the fall of man, and acknowledge that the fall of man was a good thing, the *felix culpa,* the happy guilt. And then I tried to weave my way in and out through nature poems and people suffering in nature because they were conscious. That was the idea. I don't think that that book is structurally very coherent, but that was the idea of it.

You know, I left out about forty poems from that book. I had a letter from Mr. Auden about it in which he said, in effect, "I think that you should cut some things, but whatever you cut is up to you." And once I started cutting I got about forty of them out, and ended up with forty. In other words, I write abundantly. And then my next step is to struggle to reduce the ornament, to reduce the abundance—to prune the book, in other words, the way one prunes a tree—so it can grow. This is my idea of a book.

Do you do that with individual poems also—rewrite them and prune them?

Yes. I rewrite my poems so often that I sometimes get mixed up about which version was finally published. I don't want to let a poem go until I think I've got it honed down just to what it should be, and that involves all sorts of weird problems. One of them is that you overwrite it. You've got to know when to stop. Bach is the greatest of the human composers, but in my opinion Mozart is an angel. I think he is the greatest thing who ever . . . he is the spring. I think he was an angel that came to the earth. And that is one thing that makes him angelic—he knows exactly when to shut up. And by knowing that, you sit there, and you realize that your own song is coming awake in music. He can give you your own song. Think of that! God I think that is miraculous, I think that literally is miraculous.

You have said that being a very good craftsman is a problem for you as a poet. How is this so?

Because my chief enemy in poetry is glibness. My family background is partly Irish, and this means many things, but linguistically it means that it is too easy to talk sometimes. I keep thinking of Horace's idea which Byron so very accurately expressed in a letter to Murray: "Easy writing is damned hard reading." I suffer from glibness. I speak and write too easily. Stanley Kunitz has been a master of mine, and he tells me that he suffers from the same problem. His books are very short, as mine are, and he has struggled and struggled to strip them down. There are poets, I have no doubt, who achieve by some kind of natural gift the difficulty that one needs. Because whatever else poetry is, it is a struggle, and the enemy, the deadly enemy of poetry, is glibness. And that is why I have struggled to strip my poems down.

When you sit down to write a poem, what happens? Do you start with an idea, a theme, a rhythm?

In my own case it's usually with a rhythm and not with an idea. And I don't know what I'm going to say, and three-fourths of the time after I've finished I don't even know what I've said. I wouldn't say that I'm a frustrated musician, but I love music, and I think this is why I usually begin a poem that way. Music has given me a much greater sense of the possibilities of quantity in poetry.

But can you do that? Is it really possible to take a musical quality and make it work only in words?

The Elizabethans sure as hell did it. When they figured out blank verse, somehow they learned this was a way you could sing and talk at the same time. And they didn't let it dominate them. Hell, there are about ten thousand examples—Shakespeare poured songs into his plays; Ben Jonson wrote many beautiful songs; Sir John Dowland, one of the great musicians of the world, was at the top of his form right at that moment; Sir John Harrington; Sir John Davies and his "Nosce Teipsum"; George Peele. They were all in there.
Walt Whitman learned how to do it. He didn't understand what he was doing, but he did it. Let me give you just one example, from his poem "I Heard You Solemn-Sweet Pipes of the Organ." He has this line, and you don't have to ham it up to hear the effect: "Winds of autumn, as I walked the woods at dusk I heard your long-stretch'd sighs up above so mournful."

We were speaking of coherence in books of poems. Did you have in mind, when arranging your Collected Poems, *an overall unity?*

Wait till you see my new book. I published the *Collected Poems* because I had a new book going and those other books were getting in my way. I thought that this would be the most practical way of getting them off my neck. Once I've finished something, I've got to be free of it. I also published that book because it was time to get the hell out of America.

The new book is called Two Citizens. *What is the significance of the title?*

My wife, Annie, who means so much to me, introduced me to Europe, which we love. And yet we know that we also love America. We know that at this time Americans, who are good people and a kind of lost people, are suffering very badly. There is so much vitality in this country, there are so many good men—good, kind, intelligent men. Where did it all go wrong? May I quote Mencken? "There are many people in this country, some of whom are handsome, and many of whom are wise, and Calvin Coolidge is President of the United States. It is as though a man, seated before a sumptuous banquet, were to turn aside and regale himself by eating flies."

So Annie, who had taught several years ago in the Overseas School of Rome and in the American school in Paris, introduced me to France and Italy. I'm a Viennese myself—that is, I'm fluent in German. Annie speaks a little French and Italian. We are two citizens. Citizens of the poor old son of a bitch, the United States. But we are also citizens of Europe.

Two Citizens begins with a curse on America. There are some savage poems about Ohio, my home, in that book, poems that I could not have written if I hadn't found Annie. She gave me the strength to come to terms with things which I loved and hated at the same time. And in the middle of that book, between the curse and the final expression of grief, there is a whole long sequence of love poems. I've never written any book I've detested so much. No matter what anybody thinks about it, I know this book is final. God damn me if I ever write another.

Even though I don't love that book, I love what lies behind it, because it grew so directly out of my new life, my life with Annie. We'd planned a trip to Europe, but it was late spring and I was trying to finish up the *Collected Poems*. I felt empty, but Annie kept me going. She even did all the typing. So we finished the book, the contract was signed, the manuscript delivered, and off we went. And for the second time in my life I thought I was done with poetry forever. I always think I am done with poetry forever. We stayed several days in Paris, where we would walk out in the morning. We would go to market, then we would go to a cathedral to see what was going on in town. Then we would go with our cheese, our pâté, our wine, and have lunch. Then we went to bed. Then in the late afternoon we would go out and have an aperitif. And to my utter, miraculous astonishment, I started to write poems again. And they turned out to be love poems, love poems of gratitude. And that went on all summer, all the way drifting down through from Paris to the south of France, and then to Italy.

I told you earlier that I loved *Saint Judas* the best because I came to terms with my own pain then. But the new book is—it's almost a resurrection of *Saint Judas*. In fact, maybe I should have given it one of the titles Don Hall has suggested to me. He's a wonderful man, and he loves to make up titles. One he suggested to me was *Son of Saint Judas*.

Another was *Saint Judas Meets the Wolf Man*. He's a fine man, an excellent poet, and certainly one of our most intelligent critics of poetry. And we have damned few, damned few. That's one thing that's wrong with us, because you can't have a real poetry without a real criticism.

Does your poem "Ars Poetica: Some Recent Criticism" deal with literary criticism?

No, this is a poem about my Aunt Agnes, who is a very suffering woman, and has been dying slowly for many years. I get so damned angry about the difference between literary criticism and real life in this country that I thought I would write an ars poetica of my own, which is about what is really going on in this country.

What would you see as the ideal criticism?

To teach the younger poets the crucial importance of the relation between craft and imagination. Because without craft, by which I mean the active employment of the intelligence, the imagination, that mysterious and frightening thing, cannot come free. We have had to learn so much by ourselves, and you, the younger poets, are in a position to see what Merwin and Dickey and Bly and Kinnell and Stafford and Mary Oliver, with her singular purity and gentleness, and I meant: that the American possibility is a possibility of forms fantastically beyond what we had been taught.

While we've been talking, you have mentioned several very good but almost forgotten poets—Edward Thomas, Rupert Brooke, and others. Of course you've also written a poem indirectly addressed to Edna St. Vincent Millay. Why do we keep forgetting good poets like that?

I have no answer to that. How do you account for the fact that people forgot John Donne for a couple of hundred years? We can't remember everything at once. We do get a few people who understand the intensity and the true beauty of life in the face of death and pain. And what else have we got except love? We've got to have it because the only other thing there is is death and pain. That, I take it, is the meaning of that shocking statement "God is love." Whole cultures have been built to get around that one. Now that we are almost finished, I want to tell you two stories. The first is one of the tales of the Hasidim, from Western Poland.

There was an orthodox Jewish tailor who knew that on the day of atonement he ought to attend the services at the synagogue. He did not go. The next day he met his rabbi. The rabbi said, "All right, let's have the excuse."

The tailor said, "I decided, Master, that yesterday I would go in the back of my shop and talk to God myself."

"All right," said the rabbi, "what did you say to him?"

"Well, I said, 'God, you know everything, and you know all my sins. But for your convenience I will repeat them. Once when I was young, I slapped a child in the face. Once when I was a tailor, I made a pair of pants for a man and instead of giving him back what was left of the material, I kept it myself. I've probably committed a few more and I can't remember them, but God you know everything and you remember them. And as far as I know, that is the extent of my sinning.' "

"Go on," said the rabbi.

"Then I said, 'God, you have allowed children to be born without eyes. You have allowed the human race, whom you created, out of their own unhappiness to kill each other when they did not even know each other. You are all-powerful, you know everything.' "

So the rabbi said, "Go on."

The tailor said, "I told him, 'God, let us compare our sins. If you'll forgive me mine, I will forgive you yours.' "

The rabbi paused, and then shouted, "You idiot! Why did you let him off that easily? Yesterday was the day of atonement. You should have forced him to send the messiah!"

That's a fantastic story.

Yes. Our real life is the most fantastic story. Rabbi Heschel is dead. *Eheu!* Back in Minneapolis I made friends who are Moslems, and they invited me to the first banquet after the feast of Ramadan. Ramadan is a ritual carried on in the spring in which the Moslems remind themselves that there are many poor and suffering on the earth, and from dawn until evening they will not eat or drink. But the Moslems also have their orthodox, their establishment.

In the eighth century, there was a man named Mansar al Halaj who entered the city of Baghdad. He was a Sufi. The Sufi were a Molsem sect who had heard about Jesus, and they believed that Jesus was a saint. There are many of them, but al Halaj is my favorite. This is what he did. He went to the chief authorities of the city of Baghdad and he said, "I am going to try to live as Jesus lived. I know what happened"— eighth century, remember—"I remember what happened to him, and I know that if I try to live as he lived, you will be frightened, and I know what you will do to me. And I want to tell you beforehand that I don't hate you."

Well, they gave him the fish eye and said, "Well, here's another nut."

Then he went out and talked to people, saying, "Why don't we try to love one another?"

Finally, they got him. They crucified him. They cut off his right hand and his left foot and crucified him upside down. And at dawn he was still alive. The vizier—ah, Henry Kissinger—came out and said to him, "Were you flying through the universe again last night?"

And as he died, he said, "No, I was just hanging here, alone with the alone, among the stars."

I've got one more for you. It's a gag, a Moslem gag. You'll like it, it's very nice. One of my best friends in the world is a man named Ghazi Ghalani. He is from Iran, from Baghdad, and I used to see him in St. Paul all the time. There used to be a bar, a piano bar, called the House of Ming. And I would get this phone call saying, "Hello, Jim?"

"Ghazi! Where are you?"

"I am at the House of Ming. Come on down and have a drink."

So I would arrive, and there would be this ninety-year-old woman playing World War I torch songs. And Ghazi would be sitting there. He looked like Danny Thomas. And I would say, "How do you feel, Ghazi?" Now in English, if you ask somebody how he feels and he feels lousy, he'll say, "I feel lousy."

But Ghazi used to do the prayer gesture, and then he would say in Arabic, "If my family traded in shrouds, people would stop dying."

If my boyhood dreams were true, my country would stop dying.

Robert Penn Warren

Robert Penn Warren:
Life's Instancy and
the Astrolabe of Joy

I wish in this chapter to define the questing pattern that is found in the mature poetry of Robert Penn Warren. Critics are in general agreement that Warren's poetry showed a profound change with the publication in 1958 of the volume *Promises: Poems 1954–1956*. Warren had never been what we would call a nihilist, but it is fair to say that before *Promises* he was more a poet of despair and alienation than one of joy and union, a writer influenced (along with his fellow fugitive poet, Allen Tate) by the early T. S. Eliot. With *Promises*, as the title certainly indicates, a sense of hopefulness emerged within Warren's work, and this sense has dominated his poetry since then.[1] What we see in the later work is the poet questing to define, to understand, to apprehend, somehow to seize, the meaning of the joyous promise he senses.

This general quest—which is pursued in all of Warren's most recent work—appears in two slightly different but closely related forms, depending upon the primary goal of the individual manifestation of the quest. One of these versions seeks understanding or hope within a metaphysical realm; it is a quest with quasi-religious implications. The other version is more time-bound and has as its goal an understanding of life within this world. It is my intention to study these patterns by concentrating on representative works. The metaphysical aspect of the quest I will discuss in relation to several poems from the volumes *Now and Then: Poems, 1976–1978* and *Or Else: Poem / Poems, 1968–1974*. In order to illustrate Warren's quest within time (which, to be sure, yearns toward the eternal as well) I will discuss in detail the more recent volume, *Being Here: Poetry, 1977–1980*. Because the latter of these patterns is the more dominant one within Warren's mature work, I will devote most of my attention to it.

Robert Penn Warren is emphatically a philosophical poet, a type of writer that he himself defined in an essay on Joseph Conrad written in 1951.

> The philosophical novelist, or poet, is one for whom the documentation of the world is constantly striving to rise to the level of generalization about values, for whom the image strives to rise to symbol, for whom images always fall into a dialectical configuration, for whom the urgency of experience, no matter how vividly and strongly experience may enchant, is the urgency to know the meaning of experience. This is not to say that the philosophical novelist is schematic and deductive. It is to say quite the contrary, that he is willing to go naked into the pit, again and again, to make the same old struggle for his truth.[2]

As an inductive philosophical poet, Warren does not approach reality with the intention of imposing a preconceived system of values upon it. Rather, he prefers to search through the raw materials presented by the world in the hope of arriving at some understanding, some meaning. With specific reference to his own work, Warren has described this method in an interview: "For me, the process of writing . . . is to grope for the meaning of the thing, an exploration for the meaning rather than an execution of meanings already arrived at. . . . the poem has to start with something concrete and not with an abstract idea."[3] (See "Interview with Robert Penn Warren.") It is for this reason that concrete imagery is so important a component of the poetry of Robert Penn Warren; only by immersing himself within the rich fabric of reality, "life's instancy," does he feel he can arrive at abstract understanding, "the astrolabe of joy."[4]

The same reason—this deep and abiding sense of love for physical reality, for the texture of "the world's body"—also explains why Warren's poems are nearly always narrative in structure; the philosophy is grounded in the telling of a story.[5] Warren has indicated many times that fiction and poetry are closely related in his mind. He has said that between 1943 and 1954 he was unable to finish a single poem because his energies were being devoted almost entirely to fiction. He later came to feel that some of the best ideas he had had—ideas that might have resulted in excellent poems—were rendered into mediocre short stories instead: "Many times the germ of a short story could also be the germ of a poem, and I was wasting mine on short stories." When he found himself once again able to finish poems, he discovered that he was doing so essentially through telling stories, by using a narrative structure: "More and more for me the germ of a poem is an event in the natural world" ("Interview with Robert Penn Warren").[6]

In his long narrative poem *Audubon: A Vision* (1969) Warren rhetorically asks: "what / Is man but his passion?" (*SP*, 85). The passion that gives both emotional force and intellectual structure to Warren's late poetry is a powerful sense of yearning, a longing to understand the meaning of the world that surrounds us. In Warren's most recent novel, *A Place to Come To* (1977), Jed Tewksbury's mentor, Dr. Stahlmann, offers a definition of what it might take to write "the great book":

> "All young men—" he began. Then: "They think they will write the great book. And"—he smiled at me—"I think you will. You have the—the anger, the innocence, the invincible—" He lifted his hand as though to stop me from speaking. "No," he said, "I was not going to say 'invincible ignorance.' No, let me say, with affection and envy, '*sancta simplicitas.*' No—to put it differently—you want something and you do not know its name. Only that—that kind of ignorance, my dear boy—can ever lead to greatness."[7]

To want something, to sense its presence, but not to know its name, is to desire to render a felt truth into language, into literature.

That there is a metaphysical, a transcendent, a quasi-religious dimension to this quest is evident from the definition of his sense of longing that Warren gave in an interview: "I am a creature of this world—but I am also a yearner, I suppose. I would call this temperament rather than theology—I haven't got any gospel. That is, I feel an immanence of meaning in things, but I have no meaning to put there that is interesting or beautiful. I think I put it as close as I could in a poem called 'Masts at Dawn'—'We must try / To love so well the world that we may believe, in the end, in God.' I am a man of religious temperament in the modern world who hasn't got any religion" ("Interview with Robert Penn Warren").[8] I call this sense of yearning "quasi-religious" because it so obviously operates within the realm of the religious—that is, it addresses the same questions that religion sets out to answer, but does so without recurrence to any established theology.[9]

The problem that such a yearner faces, and the avenue he might follow to find a solution, is indicated perhaps most clearly in a series of three poems from the volume *Now and Then: Poems 1976–1978*. "Code Book Lost" (*NT*, 43–44) begins by delineating several images and situations within the natural world that seem to embody some meaning, some "undeclared timbre," the presence of which the speaker feels but which he cannot understand:

> What does the veery say, at dusk in shad-thicket?
> There must be some meaning, or why should your heart stop,
>
> As though, in the dark depth of water, Time held its breath,
> While the message spins on like a spool of silk thread fallen?

Many of the examples that the speaker gives of this sort of thing involve sounds that occur within nature, the indigenous language of the physical world that man cannot decipher: "Yes, message on message, like wind or water, in light or in dark, / The whole world pours at us. But the code book, somehow, is lost." The desire for understanding is as powerful as man's inability to achieve it.

The poem "Waiting" (*NT*, 39–40) seems to move one short step beyond "Code Book Lost" by granting to man the ability, at least occasionally, to speak the truth. Before arriving at this insight, however, the speaker moves through a series of imagined situations that seem to strip life not just of joy but even of the comfort deluded belief might bring:

> You will have to wait. Until it. Until
> the last owl hoot has quivered to a
>
> Vibrant silence and you realize that there is no breathing
> Beside you, and dark curdles toward dawn of no dawn. Until
>
> Drouth breaks, too late to save the corn,
> But not too late for flood, and the hobbled cow, stranded
>
> On a sudden islet, gargles in grief in the alder-brake. Until
> . . . .
>
> You realize, to your surprise, that our Savior died for us all,
> And as tears gather in your eyes, you burst out laughing,
>
> For the joke is certainly on Him, considering
> What we are.

The poem ends by recognizing both man's ability to use language and the fact that, by some miracle, he sometimes uses it correctly, by speaking the truth:

> Until
>
> It grows on you that, at least, God
> Has allowed man the grandeur of certain utterances.
>
> True or not. But sometimes true.

What use man might make of his power of speech is indicated in the third of these poems, "The Mission" (*NT*, 41–42). The speaker awakens from a disturbing dream to the loneliness of the middle of the night. He thinks of the kitchen of his house, then of the dream, then of the moonlight making shadows on the roof above his head, then of a bear hibernating in a northern cave, and finally of the brook down the hill from the cave. The brook

. . . crawls under ice. It has a mission, but,
In that blackness, has forgotten what. I, too,

Have forgotten the nature of my own mission.

As the poem ends, after more thoughts of the nightmare, a tentative
answer occurs to the speaker: "Perhaps that lost mission is to try to
understand / The possibility of joy in the world's tangled and hieroglyphic beauty." The most important word here is *hieroglyphic*, for two
reasons. The word is derived from the Greek roots *hieros*, meaning
"sacred," and *glyphein*, meaning "to carve." One implication in Warren's usage, then, concerns the messages that the "world pours at us"—
apparently, there is a sacred dimension inherent within the beauty of
the world. A second implication concerns the nature of man's understanding, his use of language. A poem is a hieroglyph of something in
the world; the something in the world is a hieroglyph for something
that exists within the realm of meaning.[10] In his attempt to embody
the meaning-bearing beauty of the world within a poem, a man like
Robert Penn Warren is enunciating, however accidentally, something of
that elusive truth that beckons from the veery's song.

Because of his suspicion of purely abstract thinking, Warren will approach the metaphysical realm only on a path that takes him through
the physical world; and when he arrives at the metaphysical, he will
deal with it only through suggestion, never bald assertion. Within Warren's symbology, a fierce brightness is associated with the purely abstract, the realm of infinity and eternity. Not only is it nonproductive
to deal directly with this realm, it is also dangerous—or so Warren
suggests in several poems based upon this kind of imagery. In "What
Day Is," for example, from the volume *Incarnations: Poems, 1966–
1968*, he warns:

> Do not
> Look too long at the sea, for
> That brightness will rinse out your eyeballs.
>
> (*SP,* 103)

And in "Where Purples Now the Fig," from the same volume, it is the
brightness of "the sun" that

> . . . has
>
> Burned all white, for the sun, it would
> Burn our bones to chalk.
>
> (*SP,* 113)

It is the flesh that protects man from the dangers of eternity, as Warren proceeds to make clear at the end of this poem:

> . . . oh flesh, oh sweet
> Integument, oh frail, depart not

And leave me thus exposed, like Truth.

The careful approach Warren makes to the metaphysical is perhaps best illustrated by the poem "Masts at Dawn" (also from *Incarnations—SP*, 115–16), to which he refers in the quotation above from the interview. The poem is narrative in structure and actually tells two stories at once. On its surface, the poem tells of the coming of light with dawn and the darkness it replaces: "Dew whitens in darkness. / I lie in my bed and think how, in darkness, the masts go white." The underlying story emerges from suggestions attached to the images of darkness and light used by Warren. The description of the coming of night begins in an ordinary enough fashion (". . . the English / Finished fornicating in their ketches"), but progresses towards suggestions of death ("The drowned cat") and a loss of belief ("Now is the hour when the sea / Sinks into meditation. It doubts its own mission"). When Warren concludes the poem by saying "We must try / To love so well the world that we may believe, in the end, in God," the two stories fuse; the coming of light within the natural world and the coming of belief within the mind of the man are one action in the end. Warren asserts not just that man must love reality, even at its darkest, its most annihilating, but that only out of this love can a sense of holiness emerge.[11]

The sequence *Or Else: Poem / Poems, 1968–1974* is the fullest, most cohesive embodiment of the metaphysical quest in Warren's work. The perspective that he adopts here is that of an aged man, nearing death, whose mind is filled with questions about time and eternity. In one of the first poems in the sequence, Warren presents a philosophical issue that bears upon both the structure of the volume and its theme. "Interjection # 2: Caveat" (*SP*, 25–26) begins by asserting that "Necessarily, we must think of the / world as continuous." Continuity within the world is a factor of both time and space; without it we could not understand reality:

> . . . if it were not so, you wouldn't know
> you are in the world, or even that the
> world exists at all—
>
> but only, oh, on-
> ly, in discontinuity, do we
> know that we exist.

Discontinuity as used in this passage reflects the existence of human consciousness. Through the use of memory, intellect, and imagination, events may be removed from the process of time, isolated, studied, understood.

From another perspective, however, the effects of discontinuity are not nearly so sanguine. This happens when discontinuity is seen as the ultimate result of the process of time—death, which separates man forever from the world. Thus, the speaker of these poems undertakes a quest in search of a transcendent continuity powerful enough to bridge the gap between time and eternity. Warren expresses this notion at the end of "I Am Dreaming of a White Christmas: The Natural History of a Vision," one of the longer and more detailed poems in the sequence:

> All items listed above belong in the world
> In which all things are continuous,
> And are parts of the original dream which
> I am now trying to discover the logic of. This
> Is the process whereby pain of the past in its pastness
> May be converted into the future tense
>
> Of joy.
>
> (*SP*, 34)

The necessity of discovering the logic of this dream is very great, thanks to the relentless continuity of time: "A clock is getting ready to strike forever o'clock" (*SP*, 43). The sound this clock makes is one "You hear . . . the way a man tied to a post in the yard of the State Penitentiary of Utah / Could hear the mind of the Deputy Warden getting ready to say, 'Fire!'"

The sequence contains two very striking poems that seem to point to a transcendence from the realm of time into that of eternity. "Interjection # 7: Remarks of Soul to Body" (*SP*, 64–65) is an amusing poem that assumes, we notice, the existence of a soul in its title. Early in the poem the speaking soul indicates its interest in the topic of death by saying to the body:

> Keep doing your duty, yes, and some fine day
> You'll get full pension, with your every need
> Taken care of, and not a dime out of your own pocket—
> Or anybody's pocket, for that matter—for you won't have
> Any needs, not with the rent paid up in perpetuity.

As the poem continues, all the bodies present at this party are wined and dined then sent out "for a starlight romp, with the dogs, in the back pasture." The souls stay behind to converse about "the usual topics, /

The death of the novel, the plight of democracy, and naturally, Vietnam." The poem ends:

> But let us note, too, how glory, like gasoline spilled
> On the cement in a garage, may flare, of a sudden, up,
>
> In a blinding blaze, from the filth of the world's floor.

In order to flare up in this fashion, the gasoline must change its form from a liquid to a vapor as it journeys from the earth into the air. The distinction here is analogous to that posited at the beginning of the poem, when Warren separated body and soul. Within the context of a volume so heavily suffused with intimations of mortality, the imagery here clearly suggests a hoped-for transcendence—thanks to the ministrations of "glory"—from time into eternity.

The other poem with these implications is the one that concludes the sequence, "A Problem in Spatial Composition" (*SP*, 80–81). The images in this poem are carefully chosen to create a meaning-bearing landscape. The speaker looks westward through a high window, across a forest toward the setting sun. The time is late—late in the day, late in the year, late in the life. Although eternity is imagistically present in the bright distance of sky—

> . . . pure, pure and forever, the sky
> Upward is. The lintel of the high window, by interruption,
>
> Confirms what the heart knows: *beyond is forever*

—there is a suggestion of its mergence with earth in Warren's description of the mountains:

> Beyond the distance of forest, hangs that which is blue:
> Which is, in knowledge, a tall scarp of stone, gray, but now is,
> In the truth of perception, stacked like a mass of blue cumulus.

In the second part of this three-part poem, Warren begins by describing a tree—"gaunt-blasted and black"—that sends a single barren branch up to the level of the window; its black silhouette can be seen projected starkly against the "dream-blue" of mountain and the "infinite saffron of sky."

At this point, "All is ready" for the action of the poem:

>   The hawk,
> Entering the composition at the upper left frame
> Of the window, glides,

In the pellucid ease of thought and at
His breathless angle,
Down.

    Breaks speed.

        Hangs with a slight lift and hover.

                Makes contact.

The hawk perches on the topmost, indicative tip of
The bough's sharp black and skinny jag skyward.

[3]
The hawk, in an eyeblink, is gone.

As usual, Warren chooses not to explain his meaning, preferring to let
the images speak for themselves—and yet the implications seem clear
enough, given the context of the work as a whole. Reflecting the traditional use of the bird as an emblem for the human soul throughout
English and American poetry (Shelley's skylark, Whitman's thrush),
this poem seems once again to embody the "promise" so often spoken
of in Warren's work:

For what blessing may a man hope for but
An immortality in
The loving vigilance of death?[12]

                                            (*SP*, 78)

The metaphysical concerns so present in *Or Else* are not abandoned
in the later volume, *Being Here: Poetry, 1977–1980*, though they are
reduced in importance. In the more recent book, Warren chooses to
deal with the here and now, hoping to arrive at an understanding of life
as it is lived within the world of physical reality. To the volume Warren
appended an "Afterthought," in which he explains some of what he
intended in these poems. The concluding paragraph is of special
interest:

There is one more thing I may mention. The order of the poems is not the
order of composition (and certain poems composed during the general period
are not included). The order and selection are determined thematically, but
with echoes, repetitions, and variations in feeling and tonality. Here, as in
life, meaning is, I should say, often more fruitfully found in the question
asked than in any answer given. The thematic order—or better, structure—
is played against, or with, a shadowy narrative, a shadowy autobiography, if
you will. But this is an autobiography which represents a fusion of fiction
and fact in varying degrees and perspectives. As with question and answer,

fiction may often be more deeply significant than fact. Indeed, it may be said that our lives are our own supreme fiction. (*BH*, 107–8)

It is characteristic of Warren as philosopher to say that "meaning is . . . more fruitfully found in the question asked than in any answer given"; *Being Here* is a speculative and hopeful volume, incandescent with felt nuances, but without absolutes. No ultimate answer is furnished by these poems—what we find inside is what we are promised on the cover—it is a matter of *Being Here*.[13]

Thus it is appropriate that the "thematic order" (meaning) of the volume should be presented through a "shadowy narrative, a shadowy autobiography." The structure of the volume loosely parallels the structure of life: it begins in childhood (section 1), moves through impetuous youth (2), cynical middle age (3) and speculative, searching middle age (4), then finishes with the summations and vague hopes of old age (5). The question that Warren raises in his phrase "shadowy autobiography"—Just how autobiographical is this book?—he answers both in his "Afterthought" and in the poems themselves. There is a strong sense of distance built into the poems. We never feel (as we so often do when reading the confessional poets) that we are peeking into the secret inmost recesses of the poet's life. The most intimate moments presented are those in which the speaker (certainly Warren himself) feels on the verge of a revelation, generally of a quasi-mystical sort. At such times he is not in the process of getting drunk or seducing someone else's wife; we see him alone instead, in the woods, on the beach, or in the mountains.

In addition to this, certain techniques of narration employed by Warren also have the effect of distancing the reader from a sense of intimacy with what is revealed. Many experiences, for example, are presented as dreams the aged speaker has of his earlier life; we thus are doubly distanced from this material—distanced by the passage of time, distanced by the process of dream. Further, Warren has refined his use of the word *you*—which in the past has often been used to refer to the reader and to other characters in the poems. Here, the word refers almost exclusively to the speaker himself and is used in poems detailing the intimate experiences just mentioned. Warren addresses himself as "you" when speculating on the meaning of an event or questioning his earlier behavior. In either case, the effect is to distance both author and reader from the material. Finally, when Warren refers to the "shadowy autobiography" of the volume as "a fusion of fiction and fact in varying degrees," we are emphatically put off the confessional trail. Warren is not talking only about an individual life—he is talking about the process of life as all thinking people know it. His story thus expands outward to embrace us all, becoming almost mythical, almost, indeed, a "supreme fiction."

The structure of *Being Here* is both linear and circular. As indicated above, Warren approaches time primarily in a narrative fashion, his "shadowy autobiography" moving chronologically toward old age. The "thematic order" is more nearly circular; each of the five sections has its own particular area of thematic concern, but these concerns appear in other sections as well. Moreover, as the book progresses, we see more and more connections between the various concerns, so that ultimately they come to coalesce, forming one large circular pattern. It is my intention here to approach the book through its structure, taking up the thematic concerns as they occur. Once taken up, a given theme will be carried through to conclusion, and its appearance in other sections will be noted.

A central preoccupation of Warren's has always been the nature of time; all three epigraphs to *Being Here* are concerned with this topic. The first is from *Van Nostrand's Scientific Encyclopedia:* "There is in short no absolute time standard." For Warren, this precept operates in two ways. First, he uses memory and dream to foreshorten or even obliterate time; through their agency he is able to make the past present, make it live again. Second, many poems deal with mystic moments, brief in reality but expanding outward into what Warren calls timelessness.[14] The second epigraph is from St. Augustine: "I thirst to know the power and nature of Time." The passage of time is a relentless and powerful force throughout the book, as it speeds us on toward—well, toward eternity, time's other realm, which also has for Warren and St. Augustine tremendous power. The third epigraph is Warren's own definition: "Time is the dimension in which God strives to define his own Being." The process described demands the manifestation of the eternal, the limitless realm of God, within the physical, the limited, the time-bound realm of earth, all of whose rhythms are periodical and end-stopped: "Being" in this sense thus appears precisely "here."

The issue of time for Warren, as we have seen, is not unitary but dual—there is time and there is eternity. *Being Here* as a whole is built upon this polarity, which carries with it several additional paired concepts, paired sets of images, paired settings, situations, experiences, even paired characters. The volume achieves its dynamic, thematic energy from its use of the notion of the quest, which appears on two levels, one aimed at eternity, one rooted within time. The larger or higher quest spans the entire volume, the entire life—it is imagistically described as a path, the metaphorical trail we follow through the thicket (or snowfield) of life. A typical description occurs in these lines from "August Moon":

> The moon is lost in tree-darkness.
> Stars show now only
> In the pale path between treetops.
> The track of white gravel leads forward in darkness.

> > (*BH*, 32)

There is only one path; it moves through time, but its goal, and thus its determining dimension, is eternity. Corresponding to it within the realm of time is the individual or localized quest. There are many of these (particularly dominant in section 2), all having as their goal an apprehension of the truth of the world.

By now it should be clear that we have two approximate locations, approximate places, in this book—one the place of time, one the place of eternity. Eternity is always vague in Warren; it is not where we live, not something we can see or exactly experience in and of itself. As suggested earlier, it is given imagistic, metaphorical representation in the poetry, and exists in contrast to the rather more obvious images associated with the here and now—time, earth, and life as we know it. The places of eternity in *Being Here* are known on earth, but are distant and rarified—the sky, snow, stars, mountains (crags, ledges, scarps), brightness, the color white. This is a silent realm; when birds appear, they are seen against the sky and we cannot hear their song, if any. The realm of time is relatively darker, more colorful. Its places and objects cling to or penetrate the earth—trees, streams, caves, grasses, oceans, lake, and pools. Birds here roost and sing, sometimes mournfully. The settings of time, its landscapes, have movement and tend to flow; the settings of eternity are static, frozen. Each of these realms has its truth or truths; as its goal the path has the truth of eternity, while the individual quests seek the truth / truths of earth.

The volume begins and ends with poems that are separate from the five sections—one a kind of preface, the other a kind of epilogue. Taken together, they measure the distance traveled by the speaker, just as they indicate the direction in which he moves. The first, "October Picnic Long Ago" (*BH*, 3–4), is set in the timelessness of pretime; so young is the speaker that he is not yet aware that time passes and measures our place:

> . . . we *clop-clopped* homeward while the shadows, sly,
> Leashed the Future up, like a hound with a slavering fang.
> But sleepy, I didn't know what a Future was.

The concluding poem, "Passers-by on Snowy Night" (*BH*, 105), is a set piece, almost a parable, and defines as clearly as anything in Warren the notion of the path. Its setting has all the trappings of eternity:

> Black the coniferous darkness,
> White the snow track between,
> And the moon, skull-white in its starkness,
> Watches upper ledges lean,
>
> And regards with the same distant stare,
> And equal indifference,
> How your breath goes white in steel air
> As you trudge to *whither* from *whence*.

Typically, the goal of this journey is rendered only vaguely—it is "the dream of a windowpane's glow," "Where someone presses a face / To the frost-starred glass."

Another aspect of the prefatory poem also demands consideration. The October picnic is a family outing; the people on it who most interest the speaker are his parents, whom he uses to help define his concept of the two sides of time:

> But picnics have ends, and just as the sun set,
> My mother cried out, "Could a place so beautiful be!"
> And my father said, "My ship will come in yet,
> And you'll see all the beautiful world there is to see."
> "What more would I want," she now cried, "when I love
>   everything I now see?"

The mother, and by extension the feminine, is associated with the realm of time, the realm of earth, while the father, the masculine, is linked to the future, perhaps by extension to eternity. The repeated use of *now* in the last line is important in linking the mother to time; also important is how the landscape she loves is described, using the imagery of earth and of time: there is "a stream" and "stones," "A grass circle, and off to one side, by a boulder, a spring / . . . and a crude fireplace of stone."

The time of narration for the poems in this volume is nearly always the time of their writing—that is, now. Within a poem, the speaker will return through memory or dream to the time of the event he relates, and at the end he will carry us forward again into the present. In so doing, he generally speculates both on the meaning of the experience itself and on its relevance to his thinking now. In terms of both time and theme, section 1 picks up where the prefatory poem leaves off—the speaker's thinking is dominated by the figure and meaning of the mother as he reviews certain events from his boyhood. When his two structures—time and theme—conflict with one another, Warren is most likely to prefer the latter over the former; thus, two of these poems relate events rather far removed from the speaker's boyhood, but they are included here because they are concerned with the mother. "The Only Poem" tells of a visit the speaker—now grown—and his middle-aged mother make to see the baby grandchild of a friend. The episode illustrates a newly recognized dimension of this woman's love, as her son sees how strong in her is the mothering impulse—which he knows turns back toward himself. The other of these out-of-time poems is "Grackles, Goodbye," an elegy addressed to the mother, which ends: "only, / In the name of Death do we learn the true name of Love" (*BH*, 21). Two other poems seem, at first glance, alien to the thematic thrust of the section, though their action occurs in its time. However, both "Filling Night with the Name: Funeral as Local Color" and "Recollection in Upper Ontario, from Long Before" are concerned with women—beloved at least by someone, at least one time—who die. We see then that the intertwined concepts of woman and love and death are crucially central here.

Four of the nine poems in the section describe experiences that, in pattern and implication, are virtually the same. "Speleology" (*BH*, 7–8) may not be the best of these poems, aesthetically considered (I prefer "Boyhood in Tobacco Country"), but it does best embody in specific form the generalized or archetypal pattern of this experience. The poem tells how Warren came gradually to know and explore a cave near his childhood house: "I must have been six when I first found the cave-mouth / Under ledges moss-green, and moss-green the inner dark." Summer after summer he returns, but it isn't until the age of twelve that he finds enough courage (not to mention a flashlight) to undertake real exploration. Eventually he finds himself on a ledge that protrudes from the wall of a cavern and hangs over an underground stream. He turns out the light and lies there—

Lulled as by song in a dream, knowing
I dared not move in a darkness so absolute.
I thought: *This is me.* Thought: *Me—who am I?* Felt
Heart beating as though to a pulse of darkness and earth, and thought
How would it be to be here forever, my heart,

In its beat, part of all. Part of all—
But I woke with a scream. The flashlight,
It slipped, but I grabbed it. Had light—
And once more I looked down the deep slicing and sluicing
Of limestone where water winked, bubbles like fish-eyes, a song like terror.

The three most important features of this passage are its location, the state that the speaker briefly enters, and the question of identity. The state of the speaker, physically, is a drowse close to sleep; the experience happens as though "in a dream." There is a loss of individual consciousness, which gives rise to the question of identity—uniqueness (*"This is me"*) is at war with absorption ("part of all"). The concept of union—"part of all"—appears throughout the book, though the identity of the "all" changes subtly as we go along. The imagery of this passage suggests the realm of time rather than the realm of eternity. More specifically, the setting strongly suggests the womb of the mother. Consider the opening stanza, where we enter this place:

> At cliff-foot where great ledges thrust, the cave
> Debouches, soil level and rank, where the stream,
> Ages back, had come boiling forth, and now from alluvial earth
> The last of old virgin forest trees rise to cliff-height,
> And at noon twilight reigns.

The feeling of union experienced by the boy in the cave is designed to remind us of the actual and universal experience of union that the baby has while in the mother's womb. The final tip-off may be the insistent nature of the heartbeat in this and all similar passages. I have said that the feminine in this book is associated with the realm of time. Given this passage, it may be that we should associate the feminine specifically with the past as well. The concept of union with the all is a thematic element present throughout the volume. In its archetypal manifestation, it is linked to the feminine through the strong experience of union that one has in the womb. Later, the physical manifestation of this concept—that is, its appearance within the book's "shadowy autobiography"—will take different forms. Eventually, when it is foreseen in the future, its expression or form will be masculine. Section 1, then, sets up the sense of longing that the speaker will act on throughout the book. It does this by giving him something to long for—that sense of union he once felt, still remembers (however dimly and subconsciously), and wishes to feel again. It becomes the object of his quests, the goal of his journey along the path of life.

In the beginning of the book, it seems to the speaker that union with woman is ultimate and mystical, equivalent to union with God. This notion is expressed in the only poem from section 1 not previously mentioned here—"When Life Begins"—which tells the wonderful boyhood times the speaker spent on his grandfather's farm. We find this stanza:

And the old man, once he said
How a young boy, dying, broke into tears.
"Ain't scairt to die"—the boy's words—"it's jist
I ne'er had no chance to know what tail's like."

                                                                (*BH*, 10)

At this stage in the volume, such lack means an unfulfilled life. Later,
women lose their mystery, their mystical dimension, though there is
one poem in section 2 where the notion of union with or perception of
the all is linked with sex (if not precisely woman). In "Preternaturally
Early Snowfall in Mating Season" (*BH*, 35–36), the speaker camps on a
mountainside and is surprised by an unexpected and heavy snowfall,
which comes during the night. Sometime before dawn, he is awakened
by the furor of two deer mating; it is an impressive experience for him.
The trip out takes "two days, snowshoeing, . . . / And rations short the
second." Malnutrition and exhaustion put the speaker in another
trancelike state, though awake. It is then that he feels he almost sees
"the guessed-at glory"—almost, but not quite. The juxtaposition of the
mating with the near vision is causal and illustrates the power woman
and sex still have over the young man.[15]

Beyond this point, however, the speaker cannot be so swayed by
these paired forces; the most telling poem in this regard is "Part of
What Might Have Been a Short Story, Almost Forgotten" (*BH*, 51–53),
from section 3. The poem is complex, beautiful, and long; briefly, it
tells of the end of a love the speaker finds ultimately and finally (for it
has been a long relationship) unfulfilling. The poem ends with the two
characters moving

Toward what foetal, fatal truth
Our hearts had witlessly concealed
In mere charade, hysterical

Or grave, of love.

The final deathblow is dealt to sex as salvation in these lines of "What
Is the Voice That Speaks" from section 4:

And once, long distance, I heard a voice saying:
"I thought that you loved me—" And I:

"I do. But tomorrow's a snowflake in Hell."
And the phone went dead, and I thought of snow falling

All night, in white darkness, across the blindness of Kansas,
And wept, for I thought of a head thrown back, and the moan.

                                                                (*BH*, 71)

Thus, it is only in section 1 that woman—the mother and the womb—
is used consistently as a means towards and an image for union with
the all. What the speaker takes with him from childhood is the vague
memory of (and consequent longing for) such experience throughout
the rest of his life.

In section 2 of *Being Here* we see the speaker in his youth, restless,
searching for something he can perhaps name but cannot define. The
title of the first poem is indicative of the kind of action that takes place
throughout this section: "Youthful Truth-Seeker, Half-Naked, at
Night, Running Down Beach South of San Francisco." Every one of the
poems here involves a quest and a longing for union or truth. Some
occur within the realm of time and some rely on landscapes that suggest eternity; but none is successful at reaching the goal, which Warren
describes in "Youthful Truth-Seeker . . .":

> You dream that somewhere, somehow, you may embrace
> The world in its fullness and threat, and feel, like Jacob, at last
> The merciless grasp of unwordable grace
> Which has no truth to tell of future or past—
>
> But only life's instancy, by daylight or night,
> While constellations strive, or a warbler whets
> His note, or the ice creaks blue in white-night Arctic light,
> Or the maniac weeps—over what he always forgets.
>
> (*BH*, 25)

Warren's localized quests, those that occur mostly in the middle parts of
the book, always return him to the present moment. There is not the
power here to transcend time in either direction—neither towards
union with the "all" in the past, nor towards eternity in the future. In his
early childhood, the speaker was still close, in time and location, to an
archetypal experience of union (that with the mother in the womb).
Thus, he was able without much effort to create a near approximation of
that satisfying state, as in the cave. When he arrives at old age—in the
final section—we will again see him on the verge of such satisfaction.
Here, however, he is trapped within time, with both consciousness and
understanding consumed by the present moment, "life's instancy."

Another of these poems, "Why Have I Wandered the Asphalt of Midnight?" (*BH*, 29–30), summarizes, through a long series of rhetorical
questions, the questing experience as the speaker knows it during
these years. The middle stanza is typical:

> Why should I clamber the cliff now gone bone-white in moonlight?
> Just to feel blood dry like a crust on hands, or watch

The moon lean westering to the next range,
The next, and beyond,
To wash the whole continent, like spume?
Why should I sit till from the next valley I hear
The great bear's autumnal sex-hoot
Or the glutted owl make utterance?

The time of nearly all of this wandering is night. Darkness is an important aspect of the experience in the cave, just as it is of the experience
in the womb. Likewise, there is a preoccupation in this poem (as in the
section as a whole) with the sound of the heartbeat—nature's rhythm
in the womb; in another stanza we see the speaker standing within
"The spilt-ink darkness of spruces" trying

>   . . . to hear,
> In the soundlessness of falling snow,
> The heartbeat I know as the only self
> I know that I know.

The questing is for a re-creation of the womb experience—but the
speaker is now so far removed from the original that he is unable to re-
create it satisfactorily. He ends up frustrated, hurled back unknowingly
into the light of day:

> Yes, why, all the years, and places, and nights, have I
> Wandered and not known the question I carried?
> And carry? Yes, sometimes, at dawn,
> I have seen the first farmer
> Set bright the steel share to the earth, or met,
> Snowshoed, the trapper just set on his dawn-rounds.
> Or even, long back, on a streetcar
> Bound cityward, watched some old workman
> Lean over his lunch box, and yawn.

Section 3 is, emphatically, the portion of this book devoted to the
pursuits of "day," although a careful distinction has to be made at this
point. I have said that Warren associates darkness with the realm of
time, while white and brightness are associated with the realm of eternity. This is true as far as it goes—that is, when these qualities or tones
are applied to individual images or objects (trees, streams, and fields, as
opposed to snow, stars, and single white clouds). When darkness and
brightness are generalized states (that is, when they refer to the relative
lightness of night or day), then a reversal of sorts takes place. In darkness, things may happen or be achieved that we would naturally associ-

ate with the more metaphysical of the two realms, that of eternity. Conversely, unless the landscape is covered in snow, nothing mystical is likely to occur during day. Ordinary daytime is not just of the realm of time as I have been using the term (for there is a certain exaltedness in that concept); it defines for itself a realm of the mundane, even of the debased. And so section 3 is where Warren attends to the base nature of mankind, including himself. It is a bit disconcerting to find this material at the heart of a book that plays elsewhere so seriously with mystic intonations, sacred undertones. But that is precisely the point—man's life is debased, comical, so far from perfection even in the best cases as to make the word *perfection* laughable. There is no point in promising man redemption if you have to deny human nature to deliver; Warren is a realist, not a dreamer: he justifies the promises he makes by admitting the truth of what we are.

He bares this truth in nearly every poem in section 3, showing the secret stealth of illicit lovers, the "haze," the "personal ambition," the "beast in shadow" that inhabit a "Cocktail Party" (*BH*, 54), even the arrogance of those (the speaker and his friend) who would rid the earth of evil by killing cottonmouth snakes. This is the surrounding reality, and yet Warren can still see the possibility of redemption. In "Function of Blizzard" (*BH*, 45), he explicitly associates snow with eternity ("God's goose, neck neatly wrung, is being plucked") and shows how it can lend grace to man's lowest endeavors: "Black ruins of arson in the Bronx are whitely / Redeemed." Among those in need of grace, he places himself; the poem ends:

> And bless me, even
> With no glass in my hand, and far from New York, as I rise
> From bed, feet bare, heart freezing, to stare out at
> The whitening fields and forest, and wonder what
>
> Item of the past I'd most like God to let
> Snow fall on, keep falling on, and never
>
> Melt, for I, like you, am only a man, after all.

This section also happens to contain Warren's most freely ironic poems. The first line of this poem ("God's goose, neck neatly wrung, is being plucked"), besides creating a metaphor for snowfall, also murders, or at least entraps, the Lord—his goose, after all, is about to be cooked. Later in the poem, Warren puts God into the control of a power (whom we may wish to associate with St. Augustine's all-powerful Time) greater than himself:

Bless God, Who must work under the hand of
Fate, who has no name. God does the best
He can.

And in the last poem of the section Warren apparently wants to take
back the promise of redemption he has made in the name of God. The
poem is called "The Cross (*A Theological Study*)"; in it, the speaker
finds a dead monkey on the beach and erects a crude memorial to it:

And I enough fool to improvise
A cross—

Two sticks tied together to prop in the sand.

But what use that? The sea comes back.

(*BH*, 60)

We seem to end this section with time and death ascendant over man
and God. This shows Warren the realist, Warren the ironist, at work.
Although the volume as a whole comes to a positive conclusion, that
conclusion remains tentative, besieged on all sides by less attractive
but still viable possibilities. It is here, in section 3, that he lays the
firmest grounding for the darker alternatives. We are reminded again
that meaning in this book, "as in life," may be "more fruitfully found
in the question asked than in any answer given."

I want to return briefly to the image of circularity that was posited as
a model for the thematic order or structure of *Being Here*. Sections 1
and 5 of the book blend together on one side of the circle—each suggests a tentative answer, acceptable to the speaker, to the underlying
question of the book. These answers exist, alternatively, within the
timelessness of "part of all" and the womb, and within eternity. Sections 2, 3, and 4 investigate possibilities within the realm of time. Section 3 is farthest from sections 1 and 5—spiritually (there is little or no
spirituality in 3), spatially (on the circle as clock's face, section 1 would
come at 6 A.M., section 5 at 6 P.M., and section 3 at high noon), and in
terms of time / light (morning and evening—the envelopment of near
darkness; noon—the harsh brightness of day). Sections 2 and 4 are
found on opposite sides of the circle, but occupy analogous positions.
Their light is softer—that of day, but with interesting shadows; the
angle of the sun at 9 A.M. and 3 P.M., as it were, lends a teasing texture
to the landscapes of the earth. In terms of theme, these two sections
complement one another much as do question and answer. Section 2
sets out the compulsive habit of questing—within the realm of time,
upon the face of earth. It is the function of section 4 to define the

hoped-for goal (or at least the general area in which the goal might be found) of that kind of questing.

The poems in this penultimate section are all concerned with varieties of sound—most of them natural, some of them human, some from objects or machines. Whereas the process of the quest as presented in section 2 is vague and frustrating (not only because an answer is not found, but also because the speaker is unsure even where he should search), section 4 attempts to solve at least that part of the problem by focusing on the potential of sound. Thus, we find poems with such provocative titles as "Language Barrier" and "What Is the Voice That Speaks?" Even here the search uncovers no ultimate answers and at times is even downright frustrating:

> What grandeur here speaks? The world
> Is the language we cannot utter.
> Is it a language we can even hear?

>   (BH, 72)

However, there is one type of sound that turns out to be more promising than the others. Warren draws it to our attention in a poem that, through its title, is paired in importance with what probably is the central poem in section 2—"Why Have I Wandered the Asphalt of Midnight?"[16]

The new poem is called "Tires on Wet Asphalt at Night" (BH, 68–69), and it presents our speaker once again in a meditative state near sleep:

> As my head in darkness dents pillow, the last
> Automobile, beyond rhododendrons
> And evergreen screen, hisses
> On rain-wet asphalt.

Warren proceeds to imagine a life for the imagined occupants of the car—a man and woman who may later seek truth in the false quest of sex:

>   . . . the old
> Mechanic hope of finding identity in
> The very moment of paradox when
> There is always none.

Then the sound he has heard possesses his imagination and determines the rest of the poem:

> I think of the hiss of their tires going somewhere—
> That sound like the *swish-hiss* of faint but continual
> Wavelets far down on the handkerchief beach-patch
> In a cove crag-locked and pathless, slotted
> Only to seaward and westward, sun low. And I
> Felt need to climb down and lie there, that sound
> In my ear, and watch the sun sink, in its blaze, below
> The blind, perpetual, abstract sea.

The language and action are those of the typical quest—but the importance given to sound in this poem draws our attention to it as a new and potent element.

Of course this isn't just any sound; it is the whisperlike *"swish-hiss"* sound made by tires on wet pavement and waves on a beach. In the poem "August Moon" (section 2) Warren rather baldly states the thematic or conceptual or abstract basis for the importance he places on this particular sound; the setting is yet another quest—

> We walk down the woods-lane, dreaming
> There's an inward means of
> Communication with
> That world whose darkling susurration
> Might—if only we were lucky—be
> Deciphered.

Warren partly hides his concept within the unusual word *susurration*, which means rustle or whisper. But what he is talking about is the goal of all his speaker's quests: he seeks some knowledge of the innermost secret truth of the "world," of earth.

Once this sound has been noticed, we are able to find it in many crucial passages and poems. For example, in "Speleology" the underground stream makes its own sound, "A silken and whispering rustle" (*BH*, 7). In a more complex manifestation, Warren associates this sound with his mother in "The Moonlight's Dream," where the young boy hears his family sleeping and describes their breath sounds: "My mother's like silk or the rustle of lilies that leant / By the garden pool when night breeze was merely a whisper" (*BH*, 17). We recall that both earth and the realm of time are associated with the feminine, and that the cave is akin to the womb. Again, at the climax of a poem treated briefly earlier, "Youthful Truth-Seeker . . . ," we find this same sound. Here the speaker lies down on the beach and imagines that he can hear the inmost whisper of earth:

> Below all silken soil-slip, all crinkled earth-crust,
> Far deeper than ocean, past rock that against rock grieves,

There at the globe's deepest dark and visceral lust,
Can I hear the *groan-swish* of magma that churns and heaves?

(*BH*, 26)

The many individual quests in this book have as their desired end
some apprehension of earth's truth, the meaning of creation. But while
the sound that might contain this knowing is heard, it is not translated
into meaning; our speaker is left again with his questions and longing,
the conviction that something is there—But what is it?

The question or problem of death, just beneath the surface for most
of this book, emerges into prominence in section 5. The power of time,
of course, pushes man relentlessly towards death—and it is with death
in mind that the question of eternity becomes so crucially important.
It is only to be expected that a philosophical poet such as Robert Penn
Warren should, in his seventy-fifth year, devote considerable thought to
this final event. Many images, passages, and whole poems throughout
the volume suggest that this may be the central topic of the book. Even
in the earliest poems, time has its lethal dimension—as shown by an
image that concludes "When Life Begins":

The boy sat and wondered when life would begin,
Nor knew that, beyond the horizon's heave,
Time crouched, like a great cat, motionless
But for tail's twitch. Night comes. Eyes glare.

(*BH*, 10)

Time is elsewhere expressed in this same image, a predatory cat waiting to spring.

There are also entire poems that can be read as the speaker's description of his own imagined death—for example, "Dreaming in Daylight"
and "Better Than Counting Sheep." These poems, which come in earlier sections, do not suggest any solution to the approach of death—
indeed, the speaker ends "Dreaming in Daylight" in a state bordering
on panic. Section 5 attempts to provide some possible solution by
bringing to fusion and conclusion certain thematic and imagistic patterns begun earlier. But first—there is a poem here, one of the most
beautiful in the book, which establishes as rock-bottom fact the existence of death, then longs for some solution. In "Acquaintance with
Time in Early Autumn," the speaker floats in a mountain pool gazing
up at, and meditating upon, a leaf. He imagines how, beneath the life
and strength of summer, time works its way, preparing stem to dry and
leaf to fall. Of course, the image suggests to the old man his own immi-
nent fall, and he meditates on this way of the world:

While ages pass, I watch the red-gold leaf,
Sunlit, descend to water I know is black.
It touches. Breath
Comes back, and I hate God
As much as gravity or the great globe's tilt.

How shall we know the astrolabe of joy?
Shall gratitude run forward as well as back?
Who once would have thought that the heart,
Still ravening on the world's provocation and beauty, might,
After time long lost
In the tangled briars of youth,
Have picked today as payday, the payment

In life's dime-thin, thumb-worn, two-sided, two-faced coin?

(*BH,* 90)

Death is fact, enraging fact—is this to be its day? And is there any answer or solution to the problem it presents, the annihilation of the self? Joy aplenty there has been in the past, for a man so attuned to the "world's provocation and beauty"; is there any joy to come?

A man cannot know, of course, and Warren doesn't pretend to. But he does, through image and statement, raise certain possibilities—possibilities indigenous to the physical world in which he has lived. The posture occupied by the speaker in the above poem—he is solidly upon, within, earth, and gazing up towards the sky—is the same one we find him occupying in nearly all of the "realm of eternity" poems in this volume. In section 4 there is a poem, "Timeless, Twinned," that expresses beautifully the longing the speaker feels for a sense of union with the eternal. He must create such a union himself, and does—despite strong hints of time and mortality behind his back—by staring at, forging union with, a single cloud in autumnal sky:

What if, to my back, thin-shirted, brown grasses yet bring
The heat of summer, or beyond the perimeter northward, wind,
Snow-bellied, lurks? I stare at the cloud, white, motionless. I cling
To our single existence, timeless, twinned.

(*BH,* 70)

More often, given the nighttime nature of most of his longing quests, the speaker gazes upon stars as his emblem of eternity. This line of imagery has its own climax in another of Warren's beach-quest poems, "Swimming in the Pacific" (*BH,* 101–2). Early in the poem he mentions, as the question that has always driven and plagued him,

The vague name of Time,
That trickles like sand through fingers,
And is life.

The poem ends with a kind of summary of the searching years and posits a striking possible answer to this, the ancient question:

But suppose, after sorrow and joy, after all
Love and hate, excitement and roaming, failure, success,
And years that had long trickled past
                    . . .—suppose
I should rise from the sea as of old
In my twilit nakedness,
Find my cairn, find my clothes, and in gathering fog,
Move toward the lights of the city of men,
What answer, at last,
Could I give my old question? Unless,
When the fog closed in,
I simply lay down, on the sand supine, and up
Into grayness stared and, staring,

Could see your face, slow, take shape.

Like a dream all years had moved to.

It is here that we finally meet the manifestation within time of eternity promised by the third of Warren's epigraphs: "Time is the dimension in which God strives to define His own Being." Within this figure emerging from the stars we can see united the idea of eternity and the state of masculinity; thus, a full transfer has been made from the desire for union, to be a "part of all," within the womb, the realm of time, to this desire to unite with the father—associated with the future and with eternity in the very first poem of the book.

There remains a word to say on how this affects the ultimate "payday, the payment"—death itself. The first poem in section 5, "Eagle Descending" (*BH,* 77), a poem "To a dead friend," is an elegy as much addressed to the hopes of the self as to the memory of the friend. Once again, Warren's imagery contrasts the realms of time and eternity; the eagle is emblematic of the dead friend, who has passed forward to eternity from the vale of time:

Beyond the last flamed escarpment of mountain cloud
The eagle rides air currents, switch and swell,
With spiral upward now, steady as God's will.

Beyond black peak and flaming cloud, he yet
Stares at the sun—invisible to us,
Who downward sink.

This one image, this powerful, transcendent bird, embodies once
again—like the hawk in "A Problem in Spatial Composition"—all of
the promises that have filled Warren's work since his own rebirth into
poetry in 1954. The poem ends with earth and its minions in darkness,
and the bird "Alone in glory":

>   The twilight fades. One wing
> Dips, slow. He leans.—And with that slightest shift,
> Spiral on spiral, mile on mile, uncoils
>
> The wind to sing with joy of truth fulfilled.

In line with his questioning method, Warren stops short of absolute
assertion—and of course there are the ironic countermovements noted
above. And yet we know that Warren always presents his greatest
truths through suggestion and image—and this is the logical conclusion reached by all of the various questioning strains in this book: time
is united with eternity, darkness with light, feminine (mother and
womb) with masculine (father and God), sound with silence, the quest
with the path. The circle of theme is closed at the end of the book's
extended biographical line.

Interview with
Robert Penn Warren

●

The original interview was conducted at Warren's home in Fairfield, Connecticut, in March of 1977. The novel *A Place to Come To* had just been published and *Now and Then: Poems 1976–1978* was in preparation. The interview was updated during the summer of 1980, again at Warren's home in Fairfield. *Brother to Dragons: A New Version* had just been published, and *Being Here: Poetry, 1977–1980* was about to appear.

You entered Vanderbilt at an early age, which leads me to think that you grew up in a home where the life of the mind was fully lived. Is that so?

Well, both my father and my maternal grandfather had books everywhere. I've got a lot of my father's books right over there. I recently reread Cooper for the first time since I was a boy, using my father's copies. And each book had the date he finished reading it—1890, 1891, and so on. I spent my boyhood summers with my grandfather on a tobacco farm—he was an old man then. His children used to say, "Poppa," as they called him, "is an inveterate reader"—I thought they meant Confederate—"and he is a visionary." He read poetry and quoted it by the yard. He was wonderful, an idol. His place was very remote and he allowed nobody on it except our family—he was totally cut off from the rest of the world. For one thing, it just didn't interest him. I mean, he read books all the time—Egyptian history or Confederate history or American history or Napoleonic campaigns, and poetry.

But there was nobody to talk to—there were very few people in the community who had any interests like his. Often I wouldn't see another boy for the biggest part of the summer. My grandfather and I were sole companions, except for dinner with my rollicking young aunt—and her husband, when she later married. So I got the benefit of his conversation. I spent hours a day with him, and I found him fascinating. He was against slavery but a good Confederate. He said, "In the end, you go with your people." He was a captain of cavalry under Forrest for several years and fought in many battles. He loved to relive the war with me—under his direction I'd lay it all out on the ground using stones and empty rifle or shotgun shells. That's not the way children should be raised, but it was my way.

Was it the literary activity at Vanderbilt that drew you there?

What I actually wanted to be was a naval officer. I finished high school at the age of fifteen—no great intellectual accomplishment where I went—and later got the appointment to Annapolis. Those were all political appointments in those days, and R. Y. Thomas, our congressman and a friend of my father's, got me the appointment. But then I had an accident. I was struck in the eye by a stone and couldn't pass the physical. So I chose Vanderbilt. I started out to be a chemical engineer, but they taught chemistry primarily by rote—there was no theorizing, no sense of what it was about.

At the same time, I had John Crowe Ransom as a freshman English teacher. He made no effort to court the students, but I found him fascinating—as did many others. He taught ordinary freshman expository writing, but he had other things to say along the way, and he would shine. At the end of the first term he said, "I think you don't belong in here. I think I will have you go to my advanced class." There was only one writing course beyond Freshman English at Vanderbilt. A few people in their sophomore year would study forms of versification, poetry writing, essay writing, things like that, with Ransom, and this is what I did the second half of my freshman year. Ransom was the first poet I had ever seen, a real live poet in pants and vest. I read his first book of poems and discovered that he was making poetry out of a world I knew—it came home to me. Ransom was a Greek scholar by training. He had never taken an English course in his life except Freshman English, which was required at Vanderbilt, where he had gone. And at least once he remarked in a tony way, "I don't see any reason to take a course in a literature where the language is native to you." He laughed at himself for being an English teacher. He said, "I find myself completely superfluous."

Was there much literary activity among the students at that time?

Well, it was a strange situation, and I really can't understand it even today. There was just a tremendous interest in poetry among students. There were two undergraduate writing clubs, junior and senior, where people would read poems and essays to each other. And there was an

informal poetry club—with some overlaps from the other groups—
which met about once a week. We'd read each other's poems and booze
a little—white corn—talk poetry. All kinds of people wrote poems
then—I remember an all-southern football center, a man who later became chairman of the Department of Romance Languages at Wiscon-
sin, and another who later became the only Phi Beta Kappa private in
the Marine Corps.

It is hard to believe now, but this is literally true—when an issue of
the *Dial* came out, people would line up to get the first one. Freshmen
were buying the *New Republic* or the *Nation*, to get the new poem by
Yeats or the new poem by Hart Crane. This didn't last for very long, but
it did last up to the thirties, when I was teaching there and people like
Randall Jarrell were in as freshmen. And all this was going on outside
of the curriculum. That's why I think graduate programs in creative
writing are stupid. Sometimes I've been peripherally involved in them,
but if people want to write they will write. If the community is right, it
is nice if they can show their stuff to their elders, that's natural. But
what we see now is just an attempt to formalize what since the beginning of time has been natural. It is only recently that giving courses
and grades and all that crap has crept into it. In my time it was generally self-propelled among the students.

How did you become a member of the Fugitive group?

The Fugitive group was started before the First World War when
some young professors, including Ransom and Donald Davidson, and
some bookish, intelligent young businessmen got together to discuss
literature and philosophy. But it turned toward poetry after the war.
The moving force was a strange Jew named Mttron Hirsch, an adven-
turer of no education whatever, except that he had read something of
*every*thing. He had been, I was told, the heavyweight boxing champion
of the Pacific Fleet and was a great friend of Gertrude Stein in her early
days. He had also been a model for some of the painters of Paris—he
was an enormously handsome man, very big, perfectly formed in his
way, and he became the center, almost the idol in an odd way, of the
group. He was in his early or middle forties then, and had or claimed to
have a back injury. So he would lie flat on his back on a couch and be
waited on by his kin. I think he made a good thing of it. He was the
wise man of the tribe, and he liked to be able to talk with some learned
friends, so he accumulated people around him. I guess that was the
source of it originally.

I believe Allen Tate and Ridley Wills were the first undergraduates to
be admitted to the group. They were six or seven years older than I.

Tate had been ill and had come back to college, which is why he and I
overlapped. He couldn't pass, or wouldn't pass, freshman math and
freshman chemistry, both of which were required. He had all *A*'s in
everything else, things like Greek and Latin, but he wouldn't do the
others—it bored him too much. So he was around. Then in my junior
year, I guess it was, Ridley Wills and Allen Tate invited me to fugitive
meetings. Greatest thrill I'd had in my life. By then it was mostly a
poetry club—we read each other's poems and argued poetry. Everybody
was an equal in that room—no one pulled his long gray beard. And it
was a good time to be there—Ransom was writing his best poems then,
and Tate was just finding himself. I myself was seventeen, and I said,
"This is what I'm going to do." I had no interest in fiction, though, not
until later.

*John Crowe Ransom must have been a very remarkable man and a
strong presence in the group.*

Well, he was an influence on everybody. For me then he was the
oldest—also at the height of his powers and with a wizardly understanding of poetry. He was a center of this without ever trying to be—
we just automatically looked to him, you see. He was very learned and
a student all his life. And not only that, he was also a great player of
games—a crack golfer and he played tennis, poker, and bridge, sometimes played bridge or poker for the whole weekend. People who didn't
know him well sometimes think he was an unfeeling man, but that
just isn't so at all. I recently had a letter from my goddaughter, who is
Ransom's granddaughter. She said, "He is so often portrayed as being
cold and self-absorbed that I wanted to write and tell you at least one
thing that happened in my presence. When you were ill"—this was in
1972, I had hepatitis and they thought it was cancer—"Pappy either
went or sent someone to the post office three times a day to see if there
was any news, and he telephoned all over the country." He was a man of
great warmth—I wrote an essay in celebration of his eighty-eighth
birthday, and the letter he wrote me in return is incredible. He ended:
"I find myself at last brushing away a furtive tear." He raised vegetables
and flowers, and every morning he would decorate the whole house
with fresh flowers. And he loved to cook breakfast—better breakfasts
than I've had all the rest of my life. He always served them to his wife
while she was still in bed. It was a habit, he said, that he'd fallen into
during her first pregnancy, and he liked it.

Why do you suppose Ransom stopped writing poetry when he did?

Well, I can tell you exactly what he said to me before he stopped
writing. We were sitting by the fireside one night back in the thirties,

when he was at the height of his powers. And he suddenly said, out of silence, "You know, I think I will quit writing poetry." Now he was at his very peak, and I said, "You're crazy." He said, "No, I know what I'm doing." And he did understand himself so well—he had the most systematic mind I ever knew. In everything he did, he was intellectual and introspective—he knew his own mind. But this is one time when he did *not* know what he was doing. "Now Robert," he went on to say—he was a great friend and admirer of Robert Frost—"Robert has fallen to self-imitation, and his poetry has lost its cutting edge. I know I could write a better poem tomorrow than I've ever written in my life; I know how to write my poems. But just writing a better poem is not what I want to do. I want to have the joy of writing the poem of discovery." He said, "If I get a new insight, a new way in, if I grow into something different, I will start again, but I don't want to be the same old John Crowe Ransom. I want always to be the amateur, the poet who writes because he needs to and loves it, and not because it is his profession. I hate the professional poet." That's the way he explained it to me. So I said, "Well, you're crazy," and I still think he was crazy. Randall Jarrell had a different idea, and I think he was right. He said that being a poet is like standing out in the rain, waiting for lightning to hit you. If it hits you once—that is, if you write one really fine poem—you are good; if it hits you six times, you're great. Ransom wouldn't stay out in the rain.

Do you think he was wise to go back late in life and revise his poems as he did?

I think frequently he did harm to the poems. He wanted to be back in touch with it, but he had lost the touch. The last time I went to see him was at the time of his eighty-fifth birthday. I went out there to give a reading and to see him. He was totally himself, not showing any sign of age. After we came back from the reading, we sat down and had a drink, and he said, "I've given myself a birthday present. I've written a new poem." It was a new kind of poem, you see—published in the *Sewanee Review.* He went back into the rain at the age of eighty-five. And that was that.

I want to talk a bit about how you compose your poems. What gets you started on a poem—is it an idea, an image, a rhythm, or something else?

It can be a lot of things. More and more for me the germ of a poem is an event in the natural world. And there is a mood, a feeling—that helps. For about ten years, from 1944 to 1954, I was unable to finish a poem—I'd start one, and get just so far, and then it would die on me. I have stacks of unfinished poems. I *was* writing then—other things, *Brother to Dragons* and some short stories. Many times the germ of a short story could also be the germ of a poem, and I was wasting mine on short stories. I've only written three that I even like. And so I quit writing short stories.

Then I got married again, and my wife had a child, then a second, and we went to a place in Italy, a sort of island with a ruined fortress. It is a very striking place—there is a rocky peninsula with the sea on three sides, and a sixteenth-century fortress on the top. There was a matching fortress across the bay. We had a wonderful time there for several summers, and I began writing poetry again, in that spot. I had a whole different attitude toward life, my outlook was changed. The poems in *Promises* were all written there. Somehow all of this—the place, the objects there, the children, the other people, my new outlook—made possible a new grasp on the roots of poetry for me. There were memories and natural events—the poems wander back and forth from my boyhood to my children. Seeing a little gold-headed girl on that bloody spot of history is an *event*. With the bay beyond, the sea beyond that, the white butterflies, that's all a natural event. It could be made into a short story, but you would have to cook up a lot of stuff around it. All you have to cook up in the poem is to be honest with your feelings and your observation somehow.

This was a new way of starting poems for me—I had been writing two kinds of poems earlier—one kind tended to start from a verbal and abstract point, and the other kind was a sort of balladry, based on an element of narrative. "Billie Potts" was the last poem I wrote before the drought set in. It was a bridge piece, my jumping-off place when I started again, ten years later.

Now my method is more mixed. Some poems can start with a mood. Say there is a stream under your window, and you are aware of the sound all night as you sleep; or you notice the moonlight on the water, or hear an owl call. Things like this can start a mood that will carry over into the daylight. These objects may not appear in the poem, but the mood gets you going.

One poem, "Red-Tail Hawk and Pyre of Youth," which I think is one of my best, was set off by a review of my work. Harold Bloom of Yale is kind enough to like my poetry, and he wrote a review for the *New Leader* in which he talks about the place that hawks occupy in my poetry. When I read it, I realized that it is all true. You don't know your own poetry—working on it so closely, you see it differently. And so I thought about the fact that I had killed a hawk, a red-tail, in my woodland boyhood. I brought him down with what was a record shot for me. I was then a practicing taxidermist, among other things, and I stuffed the hawk and carried him with me for many years—I used to keep him over my bookshelf. This is the key to the poem, a factual event, a memory. It can be like that, but I never know how the next poem will start— I don't want to fall into a formula.

You have said, in reference to both fiction and poetry: "For me the common denominator is always an ethical issue." This is clearer, I think, in fiction than in poetry.

Yes, for me at least, it is much more obvious in fiction. But the relation between the abstract and the concrete is different in more recent poems. The germ of a poem for me now tends unconsciously to be something I might call a "moralized anecdote." I don't mean that the poem will preach a sermon, but I don't want to be coy about what constitutes the germinal start. I would like to show the problem of the abstract and the concrete in the construction of the poem itself. I don't mean that the "moralization" is a "start"—it is the last thing that happens, and then by suggestion.

Brother to Dragons *is, in some ways, your most abstract or intellectual poem—the balance between the abstract and the concrete seems somewhat different from that in other poems. Were you intentionally putting ideas first there?*

For me, the process of writing, sometimes quite a long process, is to grope for the meaning of the thing, an exploration for the meaning rather than an execution of meanings already arrived at. There are plenty of people who work the other way around, but for me the poem has to start with something concrete and not with an abstract idea. I started *Brother to Dragons* with the tale, the story, which I had first heard from an old great-aunt in a localized and garbled form. Then I read a pioneer version and thought about it in various ways. Whatever idea I had was vague and general, the idea that there are two light-bringers—Meriwether Lewis and his cousin, Lilburne. They think they are bringing the light of civilization into the dark of the wilderness, but they discover that they were carrying darkness all along—the darkness that is in the human heart. They are carrying darkness to darkness. That's where it started, my thinking when I started writing. Now, I have learned a lot since then—there might be some Coleridge in it, and something of Conrad's *Heart of Darkness*, which I have known from boyhood. All this has occurred to me much later, many years later. Perhaps it was there at the start, but it was not consciously in my mind at the time.

Brother to Dragons presents at least a partial portrait of human evil. The action takes place in a virtual wilderness and within a context that is notable in other ways. One of the epigraphs, for example, portrays Kentucky as "the dark and bloody ground." There is also the notion of the annus mirabilis—1811, when the action of the poem takes place—the year in which nature seemed to turn backwards, perhaps becoming evil itself. Are these things presented in any sense as an explanation of or justification for the human deed?

Well, they occurred and it ties in, but there is no place where it is hammered home. To the Indians, Kentucky was an evil spot—they hunted there and fought there, but they would not live there. And there are times of disaster in the world's history. I think of the great disaster which destroyed the Mediterranean world at the time of Crete, and of what is probably behind the Atlantis myth. There are times of tremendous disaster in the world. Plagues, the black death, God knows what else. And this really occurred, the annus mirabilis, and it was called that back then. The Mississippi River flowed uphill for three days, knocking down settlements, destroying towns, making new lakes. There was an earthquake that did much damage to Louisville and many other places; the squirrels all dove into the river, killing themselves; horses turned carnivorous—nature was unhinged. But it isn't a moral thing—nature has no awareness of itself, it is neither good nor evil because good is something that somebody chooses. Behind the great disasters in nature there are causes that are wholly natural. So it is a question of the disorder of the human heart—you see, they all could occur.

What is nature? That's the question that is involved here. Is nature naturally good? Is man naturally good? Or does man have to earn his goodness bit by bit?—civilize himself and humanize himself, a long-term process. So the question of nature as good, nature as subject to bursts of inexplicable evil and destruction, is simply a metaphor for the human condition. And in this case the metaphor isn't made up. It is nice when history gives you a metaphor—you don't have to make one up. It has a degree of authority no made-up metaphor ever had. Just like the snake I saw as I climbed the bluff to the Lewis house. That snake is true—a great big snake, big as I ever saw, rose out of the rock and looked me right in the eye. Sometimes you have a lot of luck. I never would have thought of putting that snake there.

If nature is morally neutral in your view, then what about man? Do you subscribe to the doctrine of original sin, as many critics claim you do?

I would not want to be too rigid about this. A man has to learn to be good—he is not born "good" as a baby. St. Augustine was right about that. So in this sense I would say yes, there is original sin—man has to learn virtue; otherwise his sin is original. Certainly there *is* such a thing as evil. It exists in the world and we live with it every day; just look around you. I don't oppose the theological view, but I must say I am not interested in proving the theological point. It doesn't need proving. What I am interested in is the drama of the theological point—put it that way.

"The drama of the theological point"—that phrase must come from the side of you that is the storyteller—not the philosopher, but the man who loves to tell a powerful tale.

I know a million stories, everybody knows a million stories—you've seen them, you've heard them, and you know all about them. But how many do you write? Well, every once in a while, one of them catches on to you, gets in your hair or gets in your pants, and you have a hard time getting rid of it. That is the one that has some special meaning for you—it creates a disturbance or an upset somewhere inside. And it is that upset that gives you the poem or the novel or the germ of one— especially if you are uncomfortable because you don't quite under- stand all that it means. I play a novel ten years, fifteen years some- times—one more then twenty. The germ of *The Cave* was the en- trapment of Floyd Collins in Kentucky in 1925, when I was a junior or senior in college. I didn't even bother to go up there—I was too busy with Shakespeare and John Donne and Baudelaire. I couldn't become a southerner until after I got away from the South.

All the King's Men is another book that was years in the writing. It changed its form, from poem, to play, to novel, but it still isn't quite right. The one thing I regret about the book is that I have no real scene that catches the moment that would explain what Stark gives to Ann that she needs. What emptiness does she feel? That scene never occurs. I faced the question at the time, but I flunked it. I just couldn't see a way to do it. Now I see a perfectly good way. Jack would wonder about it; he would wonder and wonder, and then he would suddenly visualize the possible scene. He would do this in his room in Long Beach, Cal- ifornia. We would take that as the answer. Then he would come home. But I just wasn't up to it at the time—I was still learning. I know more about writing novels now than I knew about writing novels then.

Earlier you explained that you don't start a poem with a theme in mind, that the theme emerges from your groping into your materials.

Is something like this also true of your use of images, symbols? Do you, when writing, consciously and intentionally attach meanings to your images—to the birds, for example, or to the mullet in Incarnations?

Many things that I haven't noticed have been called to my attention by critics. I have gone past such obvious things as the motion of a bird in the sky, the relation of the bird and the man in things like *Audubon*, and the hawk—my fascination with hawks, which Bloom pointed out. I never had noticed this pattern of birds in the poems, though I notice it in my life all the time—that freedom and wonder in the sky, you know, it's something I have to look at. I look at gulls by the hour, hawks, buzzards, anything. But I never noticed about their place in the poems until it was called to my attention in print. You feel earthbound and your aspirations thwarted, while birds have that freedom and totality of being. I don't want to try to interpret it, but that's there.

Another question like this, but a little more personal, concerns the eye, the place of the eye in my work. Well, I'm blind in one eye. I had an injury when I was fifteen, and the eye gradually lost sight until it was completely blind. I spent several years thinking I was going to be totally blind. You see, sympathetic blindness can set in, where the uninjured eye can also go blind. Nobody knows why. So finally they had to remove the injured eye, and that seemed to solve it. But I had been living in horror of this for years, since I was in college. So the "eye" in the poems is very important, but I didn't even know that it was until some critic called attention to it. And this would be true of a great many things. I happen to remember those two things, but there are other things too, I just can't remember them offhand, where critics have caught hold of something significant which I had just walked past, and probably had some very good reason to walk past, something deep in the poems. I blocked it somehow, the business of the eye. But I can't see any reason for blocking this watching the birds. I spent a lot of time as a boy with glasses, identifying birds. I just liked the woods—I was out in the woods a lot.

Do you write your poems in longhand or at the typewriter?

Practically in my head. I do a lot of them when I am exercising. I find that regular exercise, any kind of simple, repeated motion, is like hypnosis—it frees your mind. So when I am walking or swimming, I try to let my mind go blank, so I can catch the poems on the wing, before they can get away. Then when I have a start and am organized, I will sit down with pencil and paper, but never—or rarely—at the typewriter. I once had a bad shoulder injury and must swim or exercise very heavily every morning in order to keep it functioning freely. And this I find is very conducive to writing my poetry.

Do you revise your poems heavily?

Very heavily. I read them and read them, and do draft after draft. And I retain the drafts—often if I am stuck I will go back to an earlier version to refresh myself—I may have been on the right track and taken a wrong turn. Sometimes, after ten or more years, I go back to old fragments and suddenly see what I was after.

Have you ever had an experience some poets speak of, where a poem just comes to you in a burst, as though by inspiration, and all you had to do was write down the words?

The best parts of a poem always come in bursts or in a flash. This has been said by many people—Frost said in a letter, "My best poems are always my easiest." My notion is this, that the poet is a hunter on the track of an unknown beast and has only one shot in his gun. You don't know what the beast is, but when you see him, you've got to shoot him, and it has got to be instantaneous. Writing a poem is like stalking the beast for the single shot. Then, you can labor on the pruning, and you can work at your technique, but you cannot labor the poem into being.

As you've reprinted your collections, you have often left poems out, sometimes many of them. Why is this?

Sometimes I think they are bad, and sometimes other people think they are bad. For instance, when I was preparing my *Selected Poems* of 1966, I consulted with Allen Tate, William Meredith, and Cleanth Brooks. If two of them were strongly negative about a poem, I would take it out, unless I had my own strong reasons for leaving it in. And my editor for thirty years, Albert Erskine, is an honest man and an honest critic, who doesn't mind hurting your feelings for your own good; he is a man of extraordinary intelligence and judgment.

Do you feel that your two creative activities, fiction and poetry, are complementary to one another?

I feel this—they have the same germ; they are very different in the way they manifest themselves, but they spring from the same source. I always put the poem first—if a poem falls across a novel, I will take the poem first. I will stop the novel and go whoring after the poem, as I have done several times. I mentioned earlier how writing short stories kept me away from poetry. Well, *All the King's Men* is a novel, but it started out as poetry, a verse play. The original idea was implicit in a single word, the name Talus, my first name for Willie Stark and also the name of the groom in Book V of *The Fairy Queen*. I was thinking that people like Hitler or Huey Long are machines, executing the will of Justice. Now reducing it to one word is highly poetic, but it is purely private. As for the verse play, some years later, looking back on it for revision, I saw that, as a play, it left out the action and the complications needed to show that power, the man of power, flows into a vacuum—a vacuum in society, government, or individuals. So my man Talus became Stark in a novel—a man whose power fulfilled the weaknesses of others. Stark's gunman, for example, his bodyguard and chauffeur, is a stutterer. When Stark is dead, this man pays him his ultimate tribute: "He t-t-t-talked so g-g-g-good." Stark fulfilled this man's desire to speak.

Now many of my poems have an implicit story or narrative line—I don't feel these generic divisions so sharply as some people do. At a certain stage your feeling moves in the direction of a certain form. Way down there early, your feeling determines what it is going to be. But it can be wrong on a first try.

Some critics feel that poetry has displaced fiction as your most important concern in recent years. Do you think that is true?

I don't know—I still try to roll with the punch and write what needs to be written on a given day. But I started as a poet and I will probably end as a poet. If I had to choose between my novels and my *Selected Poems*, I would keep the *Selected Poems* as representing me more fully, my vision and my self. I think poems are more *you*. Another thing about fiction. When you undertake a novel, you are selling three years in hock, and time, I should certainly say, makes a difference. And, although you can't tell about your financial future, I would have to say I don't need to write a novel right now. Ultimately, I guess I just feel that I like writing poems.

How did you come to write your beautiful poem on Audubon?

There is a little story about that. I never research a book, except if I get in a pinch on some detail, then I will look that up. But when I was thinking about writing *World Enough and Time*, I began to soak myself in Americana of the early nineteenth century, histories of Kentucky and Tennessee, that sort of thing. Well, Audubon appears in that history, so I went ahead and looked at his *Journals* and so forth. I got interested in the man and his life, and began, way back in the forties, as I said, to write a poem about Audubon. But it was a trap—I was trying to write the wrong kind of poem, I had the wrong style for it. I was thinking of it as a narrative poem, but that wasn't right for me. I did write quite a bit, but it wouldn't come together, so I set it aside and forgot about it.

Then in the sixties I was writing a history of American literature with Dick Lewis and Cleanth Brooks, and I did the basic section on Audubon to offer for their comment and criticism. We all read everything, then one person would write up a given section and the others would rewrite the first draft to their hearts' desire—a continuing process. So I got back into Audubon. Then one day, when I was helping my wife make a bed, there suddenly popped into my mind a line that had been in the first version of *Audubon* that I had abandoned, and this became the first line of the new version—"Was not the lost Dauphin, though handsome was only." I never went and hunted the rest of it up, so I only had that one line to go on. I knew then that that was all I needed. I suddenly saw how to do it. I did it in fragments—snapshots of Audubon. I began to see him as a certain kind of man, a man who has finally learned to accept his fate. The poem is about man and his fate—all along Audubon resisted his fate and thought it was evil—a man is supposed to support his family and so forth. But now he accepts his fate. Late in his life he said, "I dream of nothing but birds." Audubon was the greatest slayer of birds that ever lived—he destroyed beauty in order to whet his understanding and thereby create beauty. Love is knowledge. And then in the end the poem is about Audubon and me.

I wrote that poem mostly at night, between sleeping and waking, or early in the morning, or shouting it out loud in the Land Rover going to Yale two days a week, scribbling all the way. Then when I got a draft, I sent it to I. A. Richards. He didn't answer right away, but two weeks later I saw him at a cocktail party in Boston, and he said, "Let's go talk." He said he liked the poem, but there was one thing wrong with it—it needed some more lyricism or lyrical sections, to give a kind of relief. I thought about that for a while, and decided he was right. So some of the lyrics, like the one on the bear, were composed after I talked with him and then inserted.

Do you have a sense of change, of evolution, as you go from book to book of poems?

Well, I would rather answer it this way—I have a horror of self-imitation. I don't want to repeat myself. I want and need (Who doesn't?) a basic continuity. But—if I didn't feel that I was onto something a little bit new, a little bit different from what I had been doing, I think I would stop. Poetry comes to me in phases, fits of a few weeks or a few months, perhaps a half-year, and then there is a break. I know pretty thoroughly when I have finished a phase—every book is based on a curve, and I know when the curve is closing in and the book of poems is over—or even a general phase of poetry. For years now I've worked that way. It is purely intuitive. When I finished the book *Promises*, I was completely through with poems like that. Now the next book—*You, Emperors, and Others*, has no real center. I was groping for a center—there may be some good poems there but no center. But after that I feel that each book is somehow a long poem. Each has one center, a feeling, and I know when that center feeling is over. Then in the next book I will discover some new body of feeling, implying experience. And that's true I think of all the books.

Now the latest book, for instance—*Being Here*—is quite different from the last one. Basically, it is a kind of autobiography. It didn't start out that way, but when I was well into it and began to set the true chronology of the poems, I discovered that it is a kind of shadowy autobiography. Not straight autobiography—it shouldn't be taken as a source of information. But that book is closed, and the one I'm in now is very different. I've written about forty poems since that book was sent to press, and I'll probably keep about thirty. I'm also writing a longish poem, which is going to be a book by itself—it'll be about thirty or forty pages—on Chief Joseph. I've always had in my mind a book like that, so I thought I'd go ahead and find the time this summer.

This notion of change from book to book—do you see that as a stylistic thing as well?

I think that you could find similarities in the style from early to late poems of mine, but I don't make a study of this—it's a problem, but I don't take it as my problem. For me, it's a question of working along and doing the best you can. You must try to approach each poem as a new problem, and try not to fall into the trap of thinking you have found the perfect answer, a formula for how to write a poem. This becomes more acute the older you get, and when you are seventy-five, it becomes very acute. The tendency is to imitate yourself, to repeat something that seemed to work. What I do is, if I get into a poem and find the form is going sour for me, I just throw it into a folder of old poems. Now and then I read the old stuff over and find something there which can be said and seen afresh—it could be a phrase, a line, a group of ten lines. I've done that for years.

Could you apply the idea of your essay "Pure and Impure Poetry" to your poetry?

I would say that I write an impure poetry. Sometimes the lines are almost prosaic, a limited breakoff of a lyrical process. Some poems contain prosaic lines alternating with lyrical passages, and this deliberately produces a poetic tension. I could take for example my three poems on Dreiser—well, they're really one poem. I'm a great admirer of the fiction of Dreiser—I've read him over and over again. So I wrote these three poems. One is in terza rima—a few high-flown poetic bits, but looking like a prose lyric, and ending with this line: "May I present Mr. Dreiser? He will write a great novel, someday." That line has a different flow entirely. The second poem is in yet another style—open and free. Then the third is three tight stanzas, short lines. So they are all about Dreiser, but in very different styles—three different ways of going at him. Almost all of the composing of those poems was done in the bathtub. I was in Vermont in the winter, and would go on long hikes, getting very cold. I would warm up with long baths, so that is where the poem was written, in the bathtub.

You have some reputation as a critic and editor, though in more recent years you seem to have turned away almost completely from this type of writing.

Those are ways of being in contact with things that interest me—I never wanted to make a career of it, although I did enjoy the work. I could spend my life very happily studying Coleridge, studying Dreiser, and so forth. I just like something else better. I have more need for something else. Writing criticism is a little bit like teaching. I like to talk about books I have read, and I always liked the association with the students. I think that only in the university can you find a certain kind of humanistic temperament to deal with—I don't mean that everybody who teaches has it, but some people are quite wonderful. They know something disinterestedly, and know how to apply it, and it is a privilege to associate with them. But I couldn't have stood teaching beyond a certain point—I got sick of hearing myself, for one thing. And I have ceased to have any interest in writing criticism, even though there is a new edition of my *Selected Essays* in preparation. I have sworn that I will never write another line of criticism of any kind. I will write some fictional prose, I want to write a couple of more novels that are in my head, but I really enjoy writing poetry more now.

How do you feel about the common designation of you as a New Critic?

I think it's a label of convenience—a great big tent trying to cover a vast and varied menagerie. Yvor Winters is a New Critic, and I'm a New Critic, but we couldn't be more different. He believed that a firm pentameter line indicates moral strength; I think it indicates a firm pentameter line. Winters I admire, but I think he commited suicide as a poet by theorizing himself out of poetry. Cleanth Brooks is another New Critic—a devout and studious Christian, a theologian, and a historical literary scholar. He was trained at Oxford as an eighteenth-century specialist, and with his tutor, Nichols-Smith, he edited twenty-five volumes of eighteenth-century letters. Well, history and theology are supposed to have nothing to do with New Criticism. Richards is another New Critic, but he and Cleanth have both nothing and everything in common.

Ransom wrote an ontological criticism, and I am a pragmatic critic—I'm just trying to make sense of what is in hand, not trying to prove a theory. All my criticism is basically drawn from social conversation or from teaching—trying to deal with a text with a friend or a small group of students. I do believe in exegesis—poetry has to be gone into, has to be studied. I don't mean just grammatically; there's also the question of the nature of metaphors involved in poetry. And you have to pay attention to the historical context. But you can't be responsible for everybody's foolishness—your own's enough. There's more bullshit with regard to the subject of New Criticism than any other you could name, except transubstantiation.

You have lived through a whole tragic generation of American poets, people like Delmore Schwartz, John Berryman, Sylvia Plath, Randall Jarrell—poets suffering from alcoholism, neurosis, and so on. Do you have any explanation for that whole phenomenon?

I think you can very easily cook up romantic explanations, as some of them did, and blame it on the age. It is true that there was a time when poets had a firmer place in society, performed a clearer function. But I don't think any competent psychiatrist would say the age killed these poets—I think they would find some other explanations, closer to home. I wouldn't undertake to do a psychoanalysis of these cases. I don't know enough about them, for one thing, though it is clear that there were difficulties in their lives. Berryman was an alcoholic, Crane was an alcoholic and a homosexual, very unhappy—losing all his friends.

And Randall's life was a life of tension and torment. I was very fond of Randall, I often had him to the house when he was a freshman or a sophomore, and we became good friends for life. He was very depressed the last time I saw him. But then in the last letter I had from him, just before his death, he said, "I feel very happy now. I will teach again, I have new things to say and new poems to write. I feel better and more like myself than I have for years." But he was having a mess of trouble too. I think poets and artists in general tend to be a little more precarious of balance in certain ways than other people. But many of them are very tough customers and know how to take their punishment; and many of them are people of great energy.

Since the fifties, your own poetry has been mostly optimistic and affirmative, emphasizing the glory of the world and its promises. And yet you also have poems on ugliness, death, racial violence, and so on. How do these poems fit into your general vision?

Well, that's all part of the picture, just the other side of it. You have people like Dreiser, who are humanly monsters but who make great things. There is Flaubert, whose main reward in going to Egypt was to get syphilis, and yet he had his inspiration for *Madame Bovary,* and he thanks God to be alive, appreciating the curve of the wave on the river. It is the complication of life—nothing more complicated than that.

Harold Bloom has written of certain similarities between your thinking and Emerson's. You are also the author of a poem called "Homage to Emerson." Are you an Emersonian thinker?

Bloom has kidded me about this. We are good friends, and I admire his work greatly. Some of it leaves me far behind, but I am ready to take the fault for that. But I just don't see Emersonianism. Emerson evolved a style which allowed him to say great-sounding things, but I really think he suffers from a modern disease—self-righteousness, the idea of natural virtue. I think he just has a basic idiocy in him, the old Emersonian disease. Then there is Emerson's Platonism—I'm just not a Platonist. He would say, "We have to carry the wood into the house as though it were real." Well, wood is real—I've cut and carried too much not to know.

What about the transcendental side of Emerson, as opposed to his more social or political commentary?

I'm not a transcendentalist. I find that kind of talk just doesn't make any sense to me—well, in some ways. I'll put it this way: I *hope* we can find meanings in nature, in the viewing of nature, and I am a lover of nature. I've spent a lot of time alone in the woods just watching. I've long since stopped my systematic looking at things, being scientific about it. Now it's just watching streams or something. And I think there is a rapport of man in nature, but the rapport is man regarding nature as metaphor, nature as image in emotional response. I put nothing mystic in that. Nature presents an image of meaning, it carries all of our force in itself—a hawk on the wing or a tree on the cliff. The meaning is there, but not as a god-sent message. The object is there as what it is, but its imagery can carry this vague, certainly unintended, metaphorical sense. I wouldn't go any further than that.

There is in Emerson a tremendous sense of man's potential for joy, and this seems to be an idea that you also have.

I do think man has a potential for joy. Some are lucky and some are not, and I've been lucky—knock on wood right quick. We all have troubles and difficulties in life, but I am fortunate in having a happy marriage, children to be proud of, and an occupation that can support me and that I love. Of course we don't know what tomorrow may bring, but I feel I've been extremely lucky in parents, in family life, in friends, in so many ways. I feel a very fortunate man. It is just plain joy to look at the sky or a leaf sometimes. This abiding world.

And this sense of joy is, for you, not a mystical thing, not related to any notion of an afterlife, but based on your feeling about the life we live on this actual earth of ours.

Well, I am a creature of this world—but I am also a yearner, I suppose. I would call this temperament rather than theology—I haven't got any gospel. That is, I feel an immanence of meaning in things, but I have no meaning to put there that is interesting or beautiful. I think I put it as close as I could in a poem called "Masts at Dawn"—"We must try / To love so well the world that we may believe, in the end, in God." I am a man of religious temperament in the modern world who hasn't got any religion. Dante almost got me at one stage, but then I suddenly realized, My God, Dante's a good Protestant! If you don't believe me, read about Manfredi in the *Purgatorio*. Where have I gone?! I would prefer to reverse the whole ordinary thing—I would rather start with the world for my theology.

Conclusion

●

Each of the poets discussed in this book sees the world in dualistic terms. Viewing this split from the outside, we might define the basic dualism that concerns them as distinguishing between the realm of the physical and the realm of the metaphysical, between the material world and the spiritual world. Viewing the same split from a slightly different perspective, we would have to distinguish between the objective (physical, material) and the subjective (metaphysical, spiritual). We would be assuming, that is, that the metaphysical or spiritual exists only because of the creating ability or the perceiving ability of the human mind.

A recent book of criticism—*American Visionary Poetry* (Baton Rouge: Louisiana State University Press, 1982) by Hyatt H. Waggoner—bears interestingly upon this issue. Waggoner bases his reading of several poets upon recent laboratory research into the phenomenon of human sight—How is it that the human eye and brain are able to perceive individual physical objects (much less a complex world full of them) through the physical fact that photons of light seem to strike the retina of the eye? Perception, viewed from a scientific perspective, turns out to be an act of creation; what the mind brings to the process of seeing is at least as important as what reality contributes to it. Essentially, we learn to see through a cultural and linguistic process; without the ability to bring this knowledge to bear upon those photons, we would not be able to understand the world at all. The role of the mind, then, is at least equal in importance to the role of the body (by which I mean the world out there, the world of physical objects) in determining our knowledge of the material world on even the most elementary level.

In the work of the poets whom he considers visionary (chiefly Whitman, but also Crane, Williams, Roethke, Ammons, and David Wagoner), Hyatt Waggoner finds a unified conception of the world—a conception, that is, that brings the subjective and the objective, the physical and the metaphysical, the material and the spiritual together into a seamless whole. This is essentially the state of affairs that I have found existing in the work of Richard Wilbur and Robert Penn Warren, the state of affairs deeply desired in the work of William Stafford, Louis Simpson, and James Wright. For Wilbur, of course, the physical and spiritual realms exist most seamlessly—through the use of metaphor he is able to discover in such obviously physical events as the waving of a tree or the flowing of an ocean intimations of the sacred.

Robert Penn Warren is more of a doubter. In his view, man can only come to the unseen by immersing himself deeply within the seen, by experiencing, that is, the worst that life has to offer. Thus, Warren's vision of the sacred is intimately bound up with his perception of a transcendent human soul—a soul able to overcome triumphantly the most tragic realities of life. That he perceives (however dimly) the promise of a further transcendence, from the physical realm to the spiritual realm, further testifies to Warren's faith in the power of the human mind, its creativity and imagination.

James Wright may be the most emphatic dualist among these five poets. The effort he made to live within, and get the most out of, a fallen and hostile physical universe is truly heroic. However, he never lost his belief that there had to be something other, something better— a realm of paradisal happiness from which man came and toward which he might journey. This realm is most clearly perceived in Wright's latest work, but also appears in a poem like "A Blessing," which achieves apotheosis for its speaker in its concluding three lines. The depth of Wright's "envisioning" of this other realm is a measure of how painful the real world generally is in his work.

For William Stafford, the unseen world is to be found away from society, somewhere at the end of a disappearing path, deep within the uncharted wilderness. Like the other poets considered here, Stafford never explicitly defines what he is looking for; our understanding of it has to be intuited from the images that he uses, the implications of his stories and his words. Louis Simpson similarly moves away from society in his early work, but not in the direction either of the wilderness or of an unseen paradise. Rather, Simpson holds in highest esteem the expression of the human spirit within poetry and other forms of art. Late in his work, however, Simpson overcomes the sense of alienation that rules his middle phase in order to identify with the suffering shared by all mankind. Thus, an ideal community of the spirit is finally envisioned in his work.

What sets these five poets apart from the poetic movement that dominated American literature during the time they were writing— the confessionalism of Lowell, Berryman, Plath—is the dual vision at the heart of their work. The failure of the confessional poets resulted from their inability to connect in any meaningful way with the outside, objective world. They projected a solipsistic longing outward, but it was not matched by reality, and a kind of suicide (whether real or metaphoric) was all that could result. The poets of hieroglyphic beauty, by contrast, create a situation of productive and nurturing tension out of the conjunction of their inner vision of the ideal and their outer vision of the real. These components are ultimately fused into a single vision, which is finally the source of their richly traditional poetry.

Notes

Introduction

1. Helen Vendler, *Part of Nature, Part of Us: Modern American Poets* (Cambridge: Harvard University Press, 1980), p. ix.
2. Charles Molesworth, *The Fierce Embrace: A Study of Contemporary American Poetry* (Columbia: University of Missouri Press, 1979), p. ix; David Kalstone, *Five Temperaments: Elizabeth Bishop, Robert Lowell, James Merrill, Adrienne Rich, John Ashbery* (New York: Oxford University Press, 1977), p. 3.
3. Breslin is perhaps the most formally oriented of these four critics. His goal is to study five manifestations of the stylistic discontinuity that occurred in American poetry in the late fifties and early sixties: "My own belief is that this moment saw the emergence of an antiformalist revolt which can best be understood by an historically informed formalist criticism—that is, one concerned with the changing theories and practices of poetic form" (James E. B. Breslin, *From Modern to Contemporary: American Poetry, 1945–1965* [Chicago: University of Chicago Press, 1984], p. xiv). Mazzaro describes his book as "an attempt to isolate recurrent *patterns* and influences in the work and reputations of seven poets" (Jerome Mazzaro, *Postmodern American Poetry* [Urbana: University of Illinois Press, 1980], p. vii; emphasis added). Pinsky combines form and content, but with the latter growing out of the former: "My thesis in this book is that we learn many of our attitudes toward language and reality from the past, and that it takes considerable effort by a poet either to understand and apply those attitudes, for his own purposes, or to abandon them" (Robert Pinsky, *The Situation of Poetry: Contemporary Poetry and Its Tradition* [Princeton: Princeton University Press, 1976], p. 4). Altieri opens his preface by announcing a somewhat more mixed set of goals: "My aims in this book are to explain the logic and implications of the aesthetic of presence that dominates much of the self-consciously postmodern poetry written in the 1960s, and to describe some poetic careers I think representative of styles, values, problems, and achievements basic to the decade" (Charles Altieri, *Enlarging the Temple: New Directions in American Poetry during the 1960s* [Lewisburg, Pa.: Bucknell University Press, 1979], p. 9).

The Sacramental Vision of Richard Wilbur

1. See Stephen Spender's general argument in his *T. S. Eliot* (New York: Viking Press, 1975).

2. Simpson's comment appears in the "Interview with Louis Simpson," below. On the postromantic preoccupation with a literal truthfulness about the self, see Lionel Trilling's *Sincerity and Authenticity* (Cambridge: Harvard University Press, 1972).

3. Robert Boyers, "On Richard Wilbur," *Salmagundi* 12 (1970): 76.

4. Anthony Hecht, "The Motions of the Mind," *Times Literary Supplement*, May 20, 1977, p. 602. On the same subject, and in similarly colorful language, Clive James has commented: "Ten years have gone by since *Advice to a Prophet* and for most of that time the major American poets have been sweatily engaged in doing all the things Wilbur was intent on avoiding. Instead of ordering disorder, they have revealed the disorder in order; instead of cherishing a personal equilibrium they have explored their own disintegration; where he clammed up or elegantly hinted, they have clamorously confessed. To be doubtful about the course American poetry . . . has taken, you do not have to be in entire agreement with Hannah Arendt's warning that those men are making a mistake who identify their own personalities with the battlefield of history. You need only to be suspicious about artists playing an apocalyptic role" ("When the Gloves Are Off," *Review*, no. 26 (Summer 1971): 43).

5. James Dickey, "Richard Wilbur," in his *From Babel to Byzantium: Poets and Poetry Now* (New York: Harcourt Brace Jovanovich, 1976), p. 171. Similarly, Donald Hill has commented that "High spirits, sheer exuberance, pervade all of Wilbur's best poems; and no doubt he would be willing to say with Stevens that 'poetry is the gaiety of language' " (*Richard Wilbur* [New York: Twayne Publishers, 1967], p. 120). Bruce Michelson has also spoken of this quality: "Wilbur is sometimes sniffed at as 'optimistic,' which seems to me another condescending, misleading label. Borrowing an apt phrase from Loren Eiseley, we would do better to call him a 'midnight optimist'; for amid the constant shape-shifting of nature, Wilbur, much like Eiseley, finds cause for a guarded, cautious hope" ("Wilbur's Words," *Massachusetts Review* 23 [1982]: 98).

6. Boyers, "On Richard Wilbur," p. 76. Randall Jarrell, of course, set the pattern for this type of criticism of Wilbur. In his review of *Ceremony*, Jarrell said: "Most of his poetry consents too easily, with innocent complacence, to its own unnecessary limitations. Once an unusually reflective halfback told me that as a run develops there will sometimes be a moment when you can 'settle for six or eight yards, or else take a chance and get stopped cold or, if you're lucky, go the whole way.' Mr. Wilbur almost always settles for six or eight yards; and so many reviewers have praised him for this that in his second book he takes fewer risks than in his first" ("A View of Three Poets," *Partisan Review* 18 [1951]: 693). Donald Hill, author of the only true full-length study of Wilbur's poetry, is more generous in his judgment: "His skills include the ability to achieve a poise and self-assurance beau-

tiful in themselves—what earned his work the ambiguous epithet 'elegant'; an almost unfailingly telling adjustment of thought to the sentence structure; and a constant word-play that is exciting because it requires a constant revaluation of familiar things" (*Richard Wilbur*, p. 18).

7. Richard Wilbur, "On My Own Work," in *Responses: Prose Pieces, 1953–1976* (New York: Harcourt Brace Jovanovitch, 1976), pp. 118–19.

8. Richard Wilbur, "The Bottles Become New, Too," in *Responses*, p. 220.

9. Wilbur, "On My Own Work," pp. 117–18.

10. Richard Wilbur, "Lying," *New Yorker*, January 24, 1983, p. 36.

11. Wilbur, "The Bottles Become New, Too," p. 217. Many critics have, of course, noted Wilbur's love for the "things of this world." Donald Hill perhaps states it best: "Wilbur is an unusually sensuous poet. In his early poems this sensuousness expresses itself partly in the sharpness, justice, and fullness of the descriptive detail. His penchant for seeing scenes and objects (or hearing sounds, or touching things) in the light of general ideas does not prevent his giving close attention to the things observed, and his inferences are well-rooted in his objects" (*Richard Wilbur*, p. 17).

12. Richard Wilbur, "Alatus," in *Seven Poems* (The University of Nebraska at Omaha: Abattoir Editions, 1981), p. 9.

13. Affirming his Christian perspective, Wilbur wrote, apparently in a letter to Paul Cummins: "I have never doubted the existence of God and the radical goodness of the world. St. Paul offends me with his distaste for the body, and I dislike all 'spirituality' which condemns the body or this world." Although these sentences are quoted in Cummins's book, *Richard Wilbur: A Critical Essay* (Grand Rapids: William B. Eerdmans, 1971, p. 40), they are not footnoted, and so we cannot be certain of their exact origin.

14. Richard Wilbur, "A Christmas Hymn," in *The Poems of Richard Wilbur* (New York: Harcourt, Brace & World, 1963), p. 57. Subsequent quotations from this volume and Wilbur's two later books will be documented parenthetically in the text. The title of this book will be abbreviated *PRW*; other abbreviations I will use are *WS* (*Walking to Sleep: New Poems and Translations* [New York: Harcourt Brace Jovanovich, 1969]) and *MR* (*The Mind-Reader: New Poems* [New York: Harcourt Brace Jovanovich, 1976]).

15. Wilbur, "On My Own Work," p. 125.

16. Thomas Traherne, *Centuries of Meditations*, ed. Bertram Dobell (London: P. V. & A. E. Dobell, 1927), p. 121.

17. William Heyen, "On Richard Wilbur," *Southern Review* 9 (1973): 628–29. On the same topic, Ralph J. Mills, Jr., has written: "The natural world in its particular mood and season becomes, through the poet's eye, through a wealth of analogy and allusion, sacramental; though with Wilbur this awareness of the spiritual possibilities inherent in the physical order never reaches to the level of visionary or mystical intuition" ("The Lyricism of Richard Wilbur," *Modern Age* 6 [1962]: 43). Wendy Salinger, similarly, has noted that Wilbur is "a religious poet. . . . Beauty is spiritual for him, as it is for Hopkins. When again and again Wilbur recalls himself to reality, it is the Incarnation, a *spiritual* reality, to which he returns: the incarnate world is 'the spirit's right oasis'" (Introduction to *Richard Wilbur's Cre-*

ation, ed. Wendy Salinger [Ann Arbor: The University of Michigan Press, 1983], p. 11). Finally, and most concisely, there is Edgar Bogardus, who writes: "the things of this world are not in themselves exalted in Wilbur's poetry; it is the god in them" ("The Flights of Love," *Kenyon Review* 19 [1957]: 143).

18. Richard Wilbur, *Twentieth Century Authors, First Supplement,* ed. Stanley Kunitz (New York: H. W. Wilson Company, 1955), p. 1080. In his essay "Wilbur's Words," Bruce Michelson comments on the issue of creating order from chaos through the agency of poetry: "Wilbur's verse is . . . an act of hopeful conjuring, done with a wish that the order created in the poem might somehow become an order perceived" (*Massachusetts Review* 23 [1982]: 99).

19. Wilbur, "Regarding Places," in *Responses,* p. 159.

20. Hecht, "The Motions of the Mind," p. 602.

21. At least two other critics have taken brief note of this facet of Wilbur's art. In her introduction, Wendy Salinger observes that "creation, like history, asks of the poet-observer an analogous act. Only through the poet's own creative labors is the god experienced, incarnated. Art, in this sense, is an act of worship" (Salinger, ed., *Richard Wilbur's Creation,* p. 11). More aphoristically, Charles R. Woodard writes: "Things do not exist for [Wilbur's] mind to make poetry of them, as some critics have charged; rather his mind exists to make poetry, as gracefully as possible, of things whose existence is subject to no final certainty in the 'dream-cache' of the most enlightened head" (" 'Happiest Intellection': The Mind of Richard Wilbur," *Notes on Modern American Literature* 2 [Winter 1977], item 7).

22. Kenneth Johnson, "Virtues in Style, Defect in Content: The Poetry of Richard Wilbur," in *The Fifties: Fiction, Poetry, Drama,* ed. Warren French (Deland, Fla.: Everett / Edwards, 1970), p. 211. Among other critics who have written of the role of the mind in Wilbur's poetry, two stand out. Charles R. Woodard points out that "Between the two poles of sensation and knowledge, Wilbur's mind functions as mediator" ("Richard Wilbur's Critical Condition," *Contemporary Poetry: A Journal of Criticism* 2 [1977]: 24). In his more recent essay, Brad Leithauser similarly notes that "it is significant that the major tension in [Wilbur's] work is the contrary, dissociative tug between the ideal and the actual, and the shuttling role the mind must play between the spirit's hunger for visions and the body's physical hungers" ("Richard Wilbur at Sixty," in Salinger, ed., *Richard Wilbur's Creation,* p. 284).

23. Hyam Plutzik has alluded to this poem while making a general observation about Wilbur's propensity to mingle the material and the spiritual: "Mr. Wilbur . . . walks among the devils that his fellow poets keep pointing out to him, but he doesn't see them. Instead, he persists in seeing angels. Other poets would see angels if they could. They peer, they squint, they turn about quickly sometimes to catch an unwary angel that may be wandering about" ("Recent Poetry," *Yale Review* 46 [1956]: 295).

24. Hecht, "The Motions of the Mind," p. 602.

25. After writing the preceeding sentence associating Wilbur's "l'acacia" with

the mythological and paradisical Arcadia, I wrote the poet asking whether such an association had been in his mind while he was writing the poem. His reply follows:

"As for your question about 'Part of a Letter' I feel a little of the hesitancy one is bound to feel about what was meant by any long-ago work. What the poem conveys to me now is a charmed moment, a condition of happiness 'easy' and 'cheerful'; there are various sensuous things which contribute,—sound, fragrance, the sun-spangles which evoke pebbles, shells, and coins and which make me think of an animated Impressionist painting . . . a painting of a cafe-scene put into motion. Then there is the remarkable series of sounds in the last line, in which French becomes something like birdsong. The girl has gold on her tongue because of 'minting,' 'coins,' and 'spangles,' and because any kind of eloquence is golden-tongued. Was I also thinking of the Golden Age? Did 'acacia' make me think of Arcadia? As to those questions I can't swear; 'acacia' has a Greek root, the poem describes a near-paradisal moment, the pleasure of it is chaste and thus nearly 'spiritual.' I guess what I feel is that no one could be blamed for sensing Golden Age or Arcadian overtones, though I should not want those overtones to diminish the immediacy of the poem" (letter from Richard Wilbur to Peter Stitt, 28 May 1984).

26. This is an aspect of Wilbur's work that I have not found discussed by other critics—though it is certainly possible that I have missed an important consideration of it. John P. Farrell does veer close to my subject in his article "The Beautiful Changes in Richard Wilbur's Poetry," when he says: "[Wilbur's] poems present to the *open eye* a procession of constantly changing forms. And they are, or at least can be if the eye is educated, beautiful in their actuality" (*Contemporary Literature* 12 [1971]: 76). After this passage, however, Farrell focuses upon his real interest, which is Wilbur's use of history.

27. Wilbur, "On My Own Work," p. 125.

28. Wilbur, "Edgar Allan Poe," in *Responses*, p. 49.

29. The poem was published in *Ploughshares* 8, nos. 2–3 (1982): 11–12.

30. Wilbur, *Seven Poems*, pp. 14–15.

William Stafford's Wilderness Quest

1. William Stafford, "Making a Poem / Starting a Car on Ice," in *Writing the Australian Crawl* (Ann Arbor: University of Michigan Press, 1978), p. 66.

2. Stafford, "A Way of Writing," in *Writing the Australian Crawl*, pp. 17–18.

3. Ibid., pp. 20, 18. Writing specifically about the function of myth in Stafford's poetry, George S. Lensing has noted as well the poet's "free-associative" method: "Stafford's poetry does not begin with a preconceived 'message' or even a formal method. To 'stumble' on myth necessitates a complete openness to the resources of the imagination" ("William Stafford, Mythmaker," *Modern Poetry Studies* 6 [1975]: 6).

4. Stafford, "A Way of Writing," pp. 18–19.

5. James Dickey, "William Stafford," in his *From Babel to Byzantium: Poets and Poetry Now* (New York: Farrar, Straus and Giroux, 1968), p. 139.

6. From the "Interview with William Stafford" in this volume. The poet William Heyen, a strong admirer of Stafford's work, has expressed his own reservations about the casual way Stafford writes his poems: "It may be . . . that Stafford has come to trust his way just a little too much. 'To me,' says Stafford, 'poetry is talk that is enhanced a little bit.' To me poetry is talk that is enhanced quite a bit. . . . Maybe the poet is less of an instrument, less of a receiver, and more of a shaper than Stafford believes him to be. Maybe just a little bit more critical consciousness, consciousness coming out of the cortex, would go a long way" ("William Stafford's Allegiances," *Modern Poetry Studies* 1 [1970]: 317). Similarly, Roger Dickinson-Brown has complained that "The quantity of what [Stafford] publishes is out of proportion to the really few things he has to say. . . . the excess has created a need for severe editing. Someone other than the poet will have to produce a 'definitive' Selected Poems, or he will be buried in the clutter . . . " ("The Wise, The Dull, The Bewildered: What Happens in William Stafford," *Modern Poetry Studies* 6 [1975]: 32–33).

7. From the "Interview with James Wright" in this volume.

8. Those wishing further information on bibliographic matters are referred to James W. Pirie's outstanding *William Stafford: A Primary Bibliography, 1942–1979* (New York: Garland Publishing, 1983). Mr. Pirie is librarian emeritus of Lewis and Clark College, where Stafford taught for many years and where Mr. Pirie assembled what is by far the most extensive Stafford collection in existence.

9. On the way Stafford has collected his poems into books, George S. Lensing has written: "Stafford's finest poems are scattered almost indiscriminately over his career. One has little sense of major evolution and change in his work; both method and matter are relatively consistent from volume to volume" ("William Stafford, Mythmaker," p. 3).

10. William Stafford, "An Introduction to Some Poems," in *Stories That Could Be True: New and Collected Poems* (New York: Harper & Row, 1977), p. 201. Subsequent quotations from this volume will be documented parenthetically within the text, using the abbreviation *STCBT*. The other such abbreviation that I will use in this chapter is *GFR*, which stands for *A Glass Face in the Rain: New Poems* (New York: Harper & Row, 1982).

11. Stafford, "Finding What the World Is Trying to Be: An Interview with Sanford Pinsker," in *Writing the Australian Crawl*, p. 124.

12. The poem was first published as part of the essay "Making a Poem / Starting a Car on Ice," in *American Poets in 1976*, ed. William Heyen (Indianapolis: Bobbs-Merrill, 1976), p. 374. Stafford has since reprinted it (along with the essay) in *Writing the Australian Crawl*, p. 75.

13. In the only book-length critical study devoted to Stafford's work, Jonathan Holden makes a point similar to mine: "*Coldness* is . . . a metaphor by which Stafford measures his sense of Nature's otherness. The cold aspect of the world is its threatening aspect, threatening because it is indifferent to human life" (*The Mark to Turn: A Reading of William Stafford's Poetry*

[Lawrence: The University Press of Kansas, 1976], p. 18). Holden's point about the cold is part of his larger idea that there is a profound distance between man and nature in the poems of William Stafford. I do not think there is so radical a separation—indeed, I think the primary motivating passion in Stafford's poetry is man's desire to merge into the mysterious sacredness of nature.

14. The poem appeared first in Heyen's *American Poets in 1976* (pp. 373–74) and has since been reprinted in *Writing the Australian Crawl* (p. 74).

15. John F. Lynen, *The Pastoral Art of Robert Frost* (New Haven: Yale University Press, 1960), p. 13.

16. Ibid., p. 9. In their book *Four Poets and the Emotive Imagination: Robert Bly, James Wright, Louis Simpson, and William Stafford,* George S. Lensing and Ronald Moran point out the negative poles of what I am calling Stafford's essentially pastoral vision: "The precarious world in which the poet finds himself is described through three principal categories. The first is composed of the dangers of the wilderness and nature itself, dangers that existed as much in the past as in the present, though they seem more acute now. The second category is made up of specific descriptions of modern, technological society. The poems here are concerned with the threats of nuclear war, of a ravaging industrial society, and of a mechanical existence that divorces the individual from authentic human values. Finally, some poems form a category which exposes the sham and vapidity of modern social behavior" ([Baton Rouge: Louisiana State University Press, 1976], p. 194). Lensing and Moran's discussion of Stafford is the best that I have seen in print.

17. Lynen, *The Pastoral Art of Robert Frost*, p. 11.

18. "Representing Far Places" illustrates in a mild way how easy it is for a pastoral poem to turn didactic. As long as Stafford makes his points primarily through the manipulation of images, he manages to avoid this failing. It is when he yields to the temptations of bald statement—overt sermonizing, some would call it—that a poem will go sour. Thus, the reader cannot help but feel that the homily with which this poem ends ("It is all right to be simply the way you have to be, / among contradictory ridges in some crescendo of knowing") is an unfortunate mistake. Roger Dickinson-Brown has described essentially the same failing as "a complacency of tone . . . that kills perception and what might be called perfectly true feeling." Too often, Dickinson-Brown continues, "I see a man seduced by his own habit of being very simple and very wise" ("The Wise, the Dull, the Bewildered," pp. 34–35).

19. Stafford, "I Would Also Like to Mention Aluminum: An Interview with William Heyen and Al Poulin," in *Writing the Australian Crawl*, p. 129.

20. Holden, *The Mark to Turn*, p. 6. Indeed, Holden sees the imagination as the primary concern of Stafford's poetry: "The imagination—its resilience, its stubborn and playful instinct for deriving meaning and awe from the world—is the central theme of Stafford's work" (ibid.).

21. Stafford, "Writing and Literature: Some Opinions," in *Writing the Australian Crawl*, p. 12.

22. The comparison is certainly a startling one. Because of the country-bump-kinish stance he adopts in his poetry, Stafford is assumed by some readers to lack the cultural sophistication we generally expect from our authors. Jonathan Holden obviously disagrees: "In fact . . . his poems and his conception of poetry are extremely sophisticated. A deft, alert intelligence exhibits itself everywhere in his work—through his frequent etymological use of words, through puns, through the construction of deliberate but carefully limited ambiguities and through a scrupulous New-Critical attention to consistency" (*The Mark to Turn*, p. 6).

23. Lensing and Moran, *Four Poets and the Emotive Imagination*, pp. 187–88. Similarly, John Lauber has written of the relationship between father and son in Stafford's poems: "Adolescent rebellion is absent; the father appears not as rival or oppressor, but as teacher, initiator, gift-bearer, and the gift he brings is a way of perceiving or of being in the world" ("World's Guest—William Stafford," *Iowa Review* 5, no. 2 [1974]: 90).

24. In his article on the importance of myth in Stafford's poetry, George S. Lensing has commented on the poet's use of narrative: "It is significant that Stafford's search for myth is conducted within the frame of 'some story.' His poems, though occasionally surrealistic in part, are founded on narrative, the imparting to the reader a human event in time" ("William Stafford, Mythmaker," p. 4).

25. The closely related notions of the path and the quest in Stafford's poetry have been noticed by other critics. Jonathan Holden, for example, has suggested that "Stafford's most common image for process is the image of a 'path.' This metaphor interlocks closely with both his metaphors of distance and place" (*The Mark to Turn*, p. 41). William Heyen introduces this idea into his discussion of Stafford's use of poetic form, which he metaphorically describes as "a road of words." He continues: "Stafford is fond of using what he calls 'an organized form cavalierly treated.' The room to follow impulse within outer strictness. The second line of Thomas Gray's 'Elegy Written in a Country Churchyard': 'The lowing herd winds slowly o'er the lea.' 'Winds,' the sense of a path, not necessarily the shortest, straightest line to the stable, but still a path within infinite possibilities of paths. The cattle of the imagination graze all over the place but, finally, the path winding homeward" ("William Stafford's Allegiances," p. 308). Finally, Dennis Daley Lynch points out that, in Stafford's poems, "undoubtedly the most striking thematic metaphor . . . is the motif of the journey. Trips of varying length and importance occur throughout [the] canon" ("Journeys in Search of Oneself: The Metaphor of the Road in William Stafford's *Traveling through the Dark* and *The Rescued Year*," *Modern Poetry Studies* 7 [1976]: 122).

26. Stafford, "Some Arguments against Good Diction," in *Writing the Australian Crawl*, p. 58.

27. In any case, other critics have paid adequate notice to this component of Stafford's work. Dennis Daley Lynch, for example, notes that "Much of William Stafford's poetry contains a painful, nostalgic longing for the way things were. . . . The remembrances usually center on the most basic and

important elements of the past—namely, parents and the hometown" ("Journeys in Search of Oneself," p. 123). John Lauber makes essentially the same point, though more inclusively: "The poetry of William Stafford is rooted in a series of natural pieties rare in contemporary life or literature: piety toward the earth itself, toward the region, the home, the parents, toward one's total past" ("World's Guest—William Stafford," p. 88).

28. For George Lensing and Ronald Moran, the two quests for home become one, as they explain in a passage that states the thesis of their essay: "Stafford's poems reveal thematically a singular and unified preoccupation. The voice of his work speaks from a sheltered vista of calm and steady deliberation. The speaker looks backward to a western childhood world that is joyous and at times edenic, even as he gazes with suspicion and some sense of peril upon the state of modern American society. The crux of each volume by Stafford involves the search for that earlier age identifiable by certain spiritual values associated with the wilderness, values which can sustain him and his family as well as the whole of the technological and urban society which surrounds him" (*Four Poets and the Emotive Imagination*, p. 178).

29. As an introduction to their discussion of "Bi-Focal," Lensing and Moran comment on the hidden nature of the truth as Stafford presents it: "Stafford's depiction of the essential wilderness is set up through images—almost always in terms of a vertical hierarchy. The outer world is one of surfaces and shadows; it is available to everyone and yields many precious moments. The other world, concealed and far less accessible, is underground; its perception becomes the abiding vocation of the poet" (ibid., p. 204).

30. Speaking of the search conducted in Stafford's poems, Lensing and Moran point out that "while the journey involves the physical world of the wilderness, its reality is spiritual" (ibid., p. 193).

31. Robert Coles, "William Stafford's Long Walk," *American Poetry Review* 4, no. 4 (1975): 27. Lensing and Moran have also commented cogently on the role of the Indian: "Another character-type who corresponds to the father in the poetry of Stafford is the American Indian. Like the father, the Indians and their chiefs are dead; and their wisdom also derives from intimacy with the wilderness. . . . The qualities by which the Indian is most consistently defined are not ferocity and warfare, but reticence and concealment. . . . His life is enacted according to rituals and symbolic patterns which bring him into harmony with the wilderness" (*Four Poets and the Emotive Imagination*, p. 192).

Louis Simpson: In Search of the American Self

1. The theme of the individual's sense of alienation from society has been noticed by other of Simpson's critics. C. B. Cox, for example, writes: "Always something of an alien, his criticisms reflect personal dissatisfaction because he can never completely associate his own cosmopolitan literary

inheritance with the brash and expansive landscapes of America. For him, the real search is not for new lands, but for one's true identity and the meaning of one's death" ("The Poetry of Louis Simpson," *Critical Quarterly* 8 [1966]: 77). Karl Malkoff has expressed much the same notion using slightly different terms: "Simpson has reconstructed the romantic myth of the conflict between innocence and experience, between the infinite possibilities of childhood and the narrow confines of adulthood, between romantic optimism and existential despair" (*Crowell's Handbook of Contemporary American Poetry* [New York: Thomas Y. Crowell, 1973], p. 297).

2. Louis Simpson, *North of Jamaica* (New York: Harper & Row, 1972), p. 199.

3. Simpson, "As Birds Are Fitted to the Boughs," in *People Live Here: Selected Poems, 1949–1983* (Brockport, N.Y.: BOA Editions, 1983), p. 14. Subsequent quotations from this volume will be documented parenthetically within the text, using the abbreviation *PLH*. The other abbreviation that will be used is *BHN*, for Simpson's *The Best Hour of the Night* (New Haven and New York: Ticknor & Fields, 1983).

4. Many critics have commented on the change in Simpson's style. In fact, as early as 1958, before the change had occurred, Robert Bly was already calling for it: "the spectre appears of a war between content and form, with the form acting so as to render the content innocuous, or as a sort of protective camouflage to conceal exactly how revolutionary the content is. . . . he should avoid his fault, which is a tendency in form to do what has already been done. He should search for a form as fresh as his content" ("The Work of Louis Simpson," *The Fifties*, no. 1 [1958]: 25). As for the change itself, Ronald Moran (in the only full-length critical study yet devoted to Simpson's work) ascribed it to Simpson's 1959 "move to California [that] marked the beginning of a significant stylistic change in which the conventions gave way to the freedom inherent in colloquial expression and in meterless lines" (*Louis Simpson* [New York: Twayne, 1972], p. 59). While William H. Roberson has taken note of the connection between the change in style and an increase in personal subject matter—"The increased flexibility of the poetry also marked a movement away from the impersonal toward a more personal quality" (*Louis Simpson: A Reference Guide* [Boston: G. K. Hall & Co., 1980], p. x)—Richard Howard has explained the connection more fully: "*At the End of the Open Road* appeared to jettison all the scrimshaw-work which had been such a typical and such a reassuring aspect of Simpson's verse. . . . The poet [came to rely] more on *personality*, his own awareness of his voice . . . as a mortar to hold his lines together, dispensing him from certain evidences, certain cartilages in his text" (*Alone with America: Essays on the Art of Poetry in the United States since 1950* [New York: Atheneum, 1969], pp. 465–66). The new style itself has been accurately characterized by Duane Locke: "In *Open Road*, the style loosens, the lines become uneven, and the movement of the natural voice and phrasal breaks replace [*sic*] preconceived measurement. The imagery tends toward inwardness, and the result is a more phenomenal poetry, one in which the subjective imagination transforms by its own operations the objective into what constitutes genuine reality" ("New Directions in Poetry," *dust* 1 [1964]: 68–69).

5. Simpson, "Capturing the World as It Is: An Interview with Wayne Dodd and Stanley Plumly," in his *A Company of Poets* (Ann Arbor: University of Michigan Press, 1981), p. 225.

6. Simpson, *A Revolution in Taste: Studies of Dylan Thomas, Allen Ginsberg, Sylvia Plath, and Robert Lowell* (New York: Macmillan, 1978), pp. 169–70. That the created Simpson protagonist has an inevitably subjective basis is made clear by Yohma Gray, who wrote in 1963 that Simpson's "point of view is more subjective than objective; the reader is aware of the intrusion of the poet's private, inner life in the poems rather than the insertion of an invented character from whom the poet is detached. He does not demonstrate what Keats called 'negative capability,' or what has been more recently called aesthetic distance. Although he sometimes writes in the third person, the reader senses a subjective 'I' in the poem" ("The Poetry of Louis Simpson," in *Poets in Progress*, ed. Edward Hungerford [Evanston, Ill.: Northwestern University Press, 1967], p. 229).

7. Several critics have noticed Simpson's preoccupation with an American subject matter. Writing in 1965, James Dickey commented: "His *Selected Poems* shows Louis Simpson working, at first tentatively and then with increasing conviction, toward his own version of a national, an American poetry. . . . He demonstrates that the best service an American poet can do his country is to see it all: not just the promise, not just the loss and the 'betrayal of the American ideal,' the Whitmanian ideal—although nobody sees this last more penetratingly than Simpson does—but the whole 'complex fate,' the difficult and agonizing *meaning* of being an American, of living as an American at the time in which one chances to live" (*From Babel to Byzantium: Poets and Poetry Now* [New York: Farrar, Straus and Giroux, 1968], pp. 195–96).

8. Simpson, "Walt Whitman at Bear Mountain," in *A Company of Poets*, p. 34.

9. James Wright, "The Delicacy of Walt Whitman," in *Collected Prose* (Ann Arbor: University of Michigan Press, 1983), p. 19.

10. Simpson, "Rolling Up," in *A Company of Poets*, p. 314.

11. Another opinion on this poem (one with which I obviously disagree) is expressed by Ronald Moran: "The last line, 'My life that I hold in secret,' is actually a lament for the speaker's inability to feel—for his inability now to become involved with any degree of commitment with a woman" (*Louis Simpson*, p. 104). This interpretation is repeated almost verbatim in a book that Moran later wrote with George S. Lensing: " 'Summer Morning' . . . ends with the line, 'My life that I hold in secret.' This is the speaker's lament for his own inability to feel any degree of commitment with a woman now" (*Four Poets and the Emotive Imagination: Robert Bly, James Wright, Louis Simpson, and William Stafford* [Baton Rouge: Louisiana State University Press, 1976], p. 157).

12. Simpson, "Dogface Poetics," in *A Company of Poets*, p. 17.

13. It is interesting that Robert Bly should have pointed out, as early as 1958, this same quality in Simpson's early poems: "The poet's strength is great love of humanity . . . " ("The Work of Louis Simpson," p. 25). Early reviewers were more likely to see Simpson as misanthropic than humane.

14. Speaking specifically of the poems in *Searching for the Ox* (1976), Dave Smith noted that Simpson "has come to a certain unfashionable narrative base, to a poetry that unabashedly employs the devices of prose fiction" ("A Child of the World," *American Poetry Review* 8, no. 1 [1979]: 11).

15. Simpson, "Rolling Up," p. 316.

16. Simpson, *Three on the Tower: The Lives and Works of Ezra Pound, T. S. Eliot, and William Carlos Williams* (New York: William Morrow & Company, 1975), p. 35.

17. Simpson, "Lowell's Indissoluble Bride," in *A Company of Poets*, p. 199.

18. Simpson, "To the Jewish Book Council" (unpublished address: May 3, 1981), ms. p. 3.

19. Simpson, "Rolling Up," p. 316.

20. On the role of personality in Simpson's poems, Dave Smith has commented: "Like Whitman, he contains many selves who go adventuring within the letter I" ("A Child of the World," p. 12).

21. Indeed, a common reaction to much of Simpson's poetry has been that it is satirical. Certainly there is a bitter edge to many of the anti-America poems of phase two; however, as Robert Bly pointed out in the passage quoted above, in general it is Simpson's humanistic impulse that is dominant. Thus, when Karl Malkoff writes, of "Hot Night on Water Street," that "It is a satire of small-town America" (*Crowell's Handbook*, p. 295), it seems to me that he is wrong. The poem instead intends to present the feelings of loneliness experienced by its speaker.

22. Nikki Stiller, "Shopping for Identity: Louis Simpson's Poetry," *Midstream*, December 1976, p. 66.

23. Writing in 1966, C. B. Cox was already able to see Simpson moving towards mystery: "In his most recent work his rhythms have become more free, less tied to iambic norms, and he makes increasing use of mysterious imagery whose total effect is beyond rational appraisal" ("The Poetry of Louis Simpson," p. 83).

24. The best critical discussion of the spiritual dimension in Simpson's recent work is that by Dave Smith in *American Poetry Review*, where he suggests: "Simpson, I believe, would argue that there is no division between inner and outer life except for those who have gone 'astray' and that what poetry must do is find a direct and clear way of making this life, its Oneness, fully visible as it was in whatever tropics we came from" ("A Child of the World," p. 14).

25. Simpson, "The Sound of Words for Their Own Sake—an Afterword," in *People Live Here*, p. 203.

James Wright: The Quest for Home

1. Criticism on the poetry of James Wright most often deals with the poet's style, particularly the change in style that he effected in the early 1960s. With regard to content, most critics see several themes and general concerns in the poetry, but no overall pattern to hold these together. For exam-

ple, James Seay—writing in the *Georgia Review* in 1973—points out that "there are several concerns which have been manifest in Wright's poetry right from the start." At various points in his essay, Seay mentions four specific issues: (1) "Probably his most abiding concern has been loneliness" (p. 117); (2) "Another related theme has to do with Wright's compassion for what Auden, in his foreword to the first edition of *The Green Wall*, called 'social outsiders'—criminals, prostitutes, drunks, and social outcasts in general" (p. 118); (3) "It would be a mistake, however, to conclude that because of loneliness and thoughts of death and despairing humanity Wright is incapable of experiencing and expressing joy" (p. 120); (4) "There has always been in Wright's work this strong desire to find a closer union with the natural world—even a desire to escape corporal limitations and merge with some spirit that encompasses all nature, not just the human realm" (p. 121). (My quotations are taken from the essay "A World Immeasurably Alive and Good: A Look at James Wright's *Collected Poems*," as it appears in *The Pure Clear Word: Essays on the Poetry of James Wright*, ed. Dave Smith [Urbana: University of Illinois Press, 1982]. In the notes that follow, this book will be referred to as *Clear Word*.)

2. James Wright, "Introduction: The Quest for the Child Within," in *Breathing of First Things* by Hy Sobiloff (New York: Dial Press, 1963), p. xix.

3. Ibid., pp. xxii–xxiv.

4. William Wordsworth, "Ode: Intimations of Immortality from Recollections of Early Childhood," in *Romantic Poets: Blake to Poe*, ed. W. H. Auden and Norman Holmes Pearson (New York: Penguin Books, 1978), p. 199.

5. Other critics also have noticed Wright's affinity with Wordsworth's way of thinking. Leonard Nathan, for example, suggests that the unhappiness so pervasively present in the work of Wright and other contemporary poets becomes clear "if one understands the dialectic of romantic poetic: children have direct contact with nature (nature by now has become the key to understanding and appreciating other humans, the world, and God). But innocence is lost in growing up, in the corrupting artificiality of society. This loss leads to a paralyzing melancholy which can only be escaped by a restoration of the lost connection with nature, at which time, the poet achieves something like a religious joy and the power to bless. A record of this achievement is found in Wordsworth's 'Lines Composed a Few Miles above Tintern Abbey'" ("The Tradition of Sadness and the American Metaphysic: An Interpretation of the Poetry of James Wright," in *Clear Word*, pp. 164–65).

6. James Wright, "Father," in *Collected Poems* (Middletown, Conn.: Wesleyan University Press, 1971), pp. 15–16. Subsequent quotations from this volume will be documented parenthetically within the text, using the abbreviation *CP*. The other abbreviation that will be so used is *TJ*, for Wright's *This Journey* (New York: Random House, 1982).

7. Robert Bly, "The Work of James Wright," in *Clear Word*, p. 78.

8. Ibid., p. 79. The quotation from "A Fit against the Country" appears in *CP* on p. 8. Critics in general agree with what Bly says here. Dave Smith, for

example, begins by seeing traditional American poetry of the 1950s as "beyond passion, rather than made of passion. The contemporary poets responded by beginning to write what Donald Hall described as 'the poetry of a man in the world, responding to what he sees: with disgust, with pleasure, in rant and in meditation' [Hall in the Introduction to his *Contemporary American Poetry*, 2nd ed. (New York: Penguin Books, 1972), p. 30]. If the result was art it would be the art of personal experience from which might rise a forged self, an empirical wisdom, a more tested vision of the real. The choice is, in retrospect, clear: the art about nothing at all or the life-roughened poem" (Introduction to *Clear Word*, p. xvii).

9. Leonard Nathan has also commented upon the connection between death and the sense of separation in Wright's early poetry: "he is surely preoccupied with melancholy and often visits the grave in his poetry, chiefly to define at its darkest edges what he finds to be a basic human condition, loneliness" ("The Tradition of Sadness," p. 159).

10. W. H. Auden, Foreword to *The Green Wall* by James Wright (New Haven: Yale University Press, 1957), p. xii.

11. James Dickey, "New Poets of England and America (I)," in his *The Suspect in Poetry* (Madison, Minn.: Sixties Press, 1964), p. 42.

12. The subject of love in Wright's poetry is also touched upon by Dave Smith in his essay "That Halting, Stammering Movement": "Wright's myth of creation and redemption from human cruelty is based on the single absolute which allows the self to grow toward recognition, acceptance, and consolation. Love is the only possibility for reconciling ourselves to ourselves and the world" (in *Clear Word*, p. 187).

13. James Wright, "The Stiff Smile of Mr. Warren," in *Collected Prose* (Ann Arbor: University of Michigan Press, 1983), pp. 240–41.

14. Ibid., p. 242.

15. D. H. Lawrence, "Introduction to *New Poems*," in *Selected Literary Criticism*, ed. Anthony Beal (New York: Viking Press, 1956), pp. 85, 86, 87.

16. Most of the criticism devoted to Wright's poetry concerns the question of style, specifically the dramatic change in style effected between the second and third books. James Seay defines the changes in leading up to a point very similar to the one I have just made: "[Wright] had . . . begun concentrating on simplifying the individual line, sharpening the imagery within a given line, making it more obviously receptive to the irrational, and reducing exposition to a minimum. In this new spareness there was no room for rhetorical impulses. In general the imagery took on a more luminous nature and a dreamlike fluidity. As for the development of the total poem he gave himself more freedom to depart from a strictly 'logical' progression and introduce the unexpected, the unpredictable. . . . Wright became more concerned with the question of how the poetic revelation in its unfolding could more closely approximate the actual sequentiality of images and ideas that led the poet to a given conclusion" ("A World Immeasurably Alive," p. 114). Similarly, Karl Malkoff has noted that Wright's "growth in poetic technique has been accompanied by a shift in his conception of the artist's relation to reality, from confidence in the poet's abil-

ity to perceive reality from a coherent and consistent point of view to acceptance of a multiplicity of perspectives that he can no longer order"
(*Crowell's Handbook of Contemporary American Poetry: A Critical
Handbook of American Poetry since 1940* [New York: T. Y. Crowell Co.,
1974], p. 331). Dave Smith's view is similar to these (Introduction to *Clear
Word*, pp. xviii–xix), while William Matthews quarrels with the premise of
all these arguments: "I . . . suggest that Wright did not abandon, in a dramatic move similar to religious conversion, an early career as a glib poet in
traditional forms. Like most young poets, he began in the currently accept-
ed style. I think not only that he found it wanting, but also that it found
him wanting. . . . Wright used traditional forms clumsily. . . . I believe that
Wright is a profoundly traditional poet, but that he discovered his personal
uses for literary tradition through rhetorical forms, rather than through
stanza forms or rhyming patterns" ("The Continuity of James Wright's
Poems," in *Clear Word*, p. 101).

17. Among the critics disliking and / or misunderstanding the poem is Thom
Gunn, who suggested in 1964 that the poem is made up of several images
"loosely connected by situation, followed by a general observation that
may well have occurred to the poet after he perceived the images, but is for
us connected with them neither by logic nor association. . . . the final line
is perhaps exciting because we are surprised to encounter something so
different from the rest of the poem, but it is certainly meaningless. The
more one searches for an explicit meaning in it, the vaguer it becomes.
Other general statements of different import could well be substituted for
it and the poem would neither gain nor lose strength" (quoted in Robert
Bly, "The Work of James Wright," pp. 90–91).

18. Robert Bly's understanding of this poem, published as early as 1966, is
exemplary, quite up to the general standard of his excellent essay: "The
question the poem never asks directly is this: how is it possible for there to
be so many spiritual emblems, signs, reminders of the path, everywhere,
and yet for the man who sees them to have gotten nowhere, to have
achieved none of the spiritual tasks that those emblems suggest?" ("The
Work of James Wright," p. 90).

19. Wright, "A Note on Trakl," *Collected Prose*, pp. 83–84. For some critics,
Wright's idealization of animals—and of nature in general—occasionally
goes too far; so Robert Bly felt when writing about *The Branch Will Not
Break* in 1966: "the poems about animals tend to be weak. The animals are
often unreal. Evidently what happens is that, tired of his own vision of the
hostility of things, Wright assumes in animals a gentleness that is not
there. . . . the bulls are too delicate; even the ants are well-read" (Bly, "The
Work of James Wright," p. 96). We must bear in mind, however, that such
idealizations do serve an important thematic function in Wright's work, as
was noticed by Hank Lazer, writing about *This Journey* some years later:
"Wright clearly belongs to the American tradition, from Bradstreet to
Emerson to Frost to Roethke, that makes nature a symbol of spirit, what
James Breslin terms 'visionary pastoralism' " (" 'The Heart of Light,' " *Vir-
ginia Quarterly Review* 59 [1983]: 721).

20. The interpretation Richard Howard gives to this poem is somewhat differ-
    ent from mine. After quoting the concluding three lines, he writes: "By a
    sensitive enjambment, Wright indicates both the breaking *and* the
    blossoming here, the surrender of perfection necessary to achieve . . . iden-
    tity" ("James Wright," in Howard's *Alone with America: Essays on the Art
    of Poetry in the United States since 1950* [New York: Atheneum, 1969], p.
    585). Speaking of Wright's work in general, Charles Molesworth more or
    less agrees with Howard: "This central, personal myth—that the poet
    must lose himself in things, for only there will he find his tongue, the only
    agency of his true survival—lies pervasively installed in all of Wright's
    poetry" ("James Wright and the Dissolving Self," in *Contemporary Poetry
    in America: Essays and Interviews*, ed. Robert Boyers [New York:
    Schocken Books, 1974], p. 274). Shirley Clay Scott carries this argument in
    favor of the secular even farther, seeming even to deny Wright the quest for
    self-identity noticed by Howard and Molesworth: "Whether he likes it or
    not, Wright's poetry demands of him continual return to a world of ug-
    liness and potential defeat. However attractive various escapes and releases
    may be—death, nature, states of consciousness less wearisome than
    human awareness (which is to be differentiated, of course, from tiresome
    self-awareness), he comes to resist them as seductions that will not answer
    to his desire" ("Surrendering the Shadow: James Wright's Poetry,"
    Ironwood 5, no. 2 [1977]: 61).
21. When *Shall We Gather at the River* was first published (1968), James
    Wright said of Jenny, in answer to a question I had asked: "She was a real
    person, but that's not her name." Critics (as opposed to biographers) are
    certainly on firmer ground approaching her, not as a real person, but as a
    composite, even a mythological, figure—as Robert Hass does: "She is the
    secret inside the word *secret* which appears so often in the book: the dis-
    covery of his spirit and of the beauty of the body and of the desire for love
    which grew up in Ohio and was maimed there" ("James Wright," in *Clear
    Word*, p. 213).
22. James Wright, "To the Creature of the Creation," *Two Citizens* (New York:
    Farrar, Straus and Giroux, 1973), p. 59.
23. Wright, "Theodor Storm: Foreword," *Collected Prose*, pp. 75–76.
24. Wright, "Translator's Note on Herman Hesse," *Collected Prose*, pp. 88, 90,
    89.
25. Wright, "The Pure Clear Word: An Interview with Dave Smith," *Collected
    Prose*, p. 199.
26. Wright, "Ohio Valley Swains," *Two Citizens*, p. 19.
27. Writing at a time when Wright's own attitude towards Ohio was still am-
    bivalent—that is, after the publication of *To a Blossoming Pear Tree* (1977)
    but before *This Journey*—Dave Smith was still able to see Ohio as the
    answer to Wright's search for home: "His poems tell only one story, the
    great story of finding the way home, and on the right terms. . . . We find
    him again and again standing in the place of darkness where the dream has
    died. Trying always to assume his individual responsibility for life, he
    leans like a compass needle toward the true place which is inside but

which in the poems is Ohio, the place named after the river that is life itself" (Introduction to *Clear Word*, pp. xxiii–xxiv). Writing somewhat earlier than Smith, Jane Robinett addresses this subject in commenting upon the versions of the poem "At the Executed Murderer's Grave": "[Wright's] 'dead Ohio' becomes a kind of hell filled with criminals, the 'bewildered mad' of the St. Claire Sanitarium, 'crying drunks,' and 'revolting Ohio animals,' mostly the two-legged kind. The poet's first-hand knowledge of this hell is authenticated for the reader by the fact that this is the country in which he was born, where his father worked all his life as a 'slave' in a factory" ("Two Poems and Two Poets," *Ironwood* 5, no. 2 [1977]: 39). Finally, Robert Hass sees Wright turning against Ohio as early as 1968, when *Shall We Gather at the River* was published: "Suicidally beautiful: the poems have suffered from that temptation and the poems from this point on, the best of them I think, reflect a determination to face 'the black ditch of the Ohio' and not be killed by it" ("James Wright," p. 212).

28. Lazer, " 'The Heart of Light,' " p. 722.

29. In 1966, even as he was arguing that the dominant direction in Wright's poetry was *out* of the garden, Robert Bly still was able to recognize the strength of the opposing tendency: "It is difficult for Wright actually to live in the present. He sees himself surrounded by a world so entirely hostile that writing poetry becomes for him at times a sort of step sideways into another dimension—the dimension of beauty, rather than a wrestling with ugliness" ("The Work of James Wright," p. 95). In his essay "James Wright," Robert Hass takes as one of his central concerns the way Wright attempts to escape the harshness of the real world through aestheticism, an exaggeration of the beauty within his poetry. Hass even suggests that, late in his life, Wright came to feel that one important function of the artist is precisely to show the way out of man's earthly vale of tears. The poem Hass discusses concerns the Italian artist Giotto: "[It] has that stubborn preference for animals and angels, that wish to cut out the middleman, but it is about the mature artist Giotto who must, if anyone is going to, lead both shepherd and the sheep out of the dark" (p. 220).

30. For Hank Lazer, it is the lizards who are most important among the small creatures of *This Journey:* "For Wright, as for Roethke, creatures such as the lizard offer analogies for the poet's spiritual journey. The lizard is a form of attention, the uncompromising uplifting of a face toward the light's blessing, representing the very stance that Wright seeks" (Lazer, " 'The Heart of Light,' " p. 719). In a much earlier essay, Alan Williamson spoke of the same impulse as it appears in Wright's "strong desire to transcend the bodily self into a delicacy intuited from animals, stones, dreams" ("Pity for the Clear Word," *Poetry* 119 [1972]: 298). Finally on this topic, I would like to take note of lines written by James Wright in the spring of 1964, but not published until 1977 and never collected into a book. He ends a poem entitled "Four A.M.":

> I can hear the cricket's whisper, I can hear paradise
> In the fluttering pulse of the astounded bird

Rise[n] from the dead.
But I cannot yet hear so much as a cricket's whisper
Of my own name.

(*Ironwood* 5, no. 2 [1977]: 67)

It was not, in fact, until the poems of *This Journey* that Wright was able to associate directly his own name, the Peaceable Kingdom of the animals, and the notion of paradise.

31. Wright, Introduction to Sobiloff's *Breathing of First Things*, p. xxvii.

Robert Penn Warren: Life's Instancy and the Astrolabe of Joy

1. For the most complete discussion of the change in Warren's work, see *The Poetic Vision of Robert Penn Warren* by Victor Strandberg (Lexington: The University Press of Kentucky, 1977), particularly pp. 21–33.

2. Robert Penn Warren, " 'The Great Mirage': Conrad and *Nostromo*" in *Selected Essays* (New York: Vintage Books, 1966), p. 58.

3. In that interview, Warren also says: "the relation between the abstract and the concrete is different in more recent poems. The germ of a poem for me now tends unconsciously to be something I might call a 'moralized anecdote.' I don't mean that the poem will preach a sermon, but I don't want to be coy about what constitutes the germinal start. I would like to show the problem of the abstract and the concrete in the construction of the poem itself. I don't mean that the 'moralization' is a 'start'—it is the last thing that happens, and then by suggestion."

4. The phrases appear respectively on pages 25 and 90 of Robert Penn Warren, *Being Here: Poetry, 1976–1980* (New York: Random House, 1980). Subsequent quotations from this volume will be documented parenthetically within the text of the chapter, using the abbreviation *BH*. Other abbreviations that will be used are *SP* for *Selected Poems: 1923–1975* (New York: Random House, 1975) and *NT* for *Now and Then: Poems, 1976–1978* (New York: Random House, 1978).

5. *The World's Body* (1938) is the title of the volume of criticism in which Warren's teacher, John Crowe Ransom, testifies to his own devotion, within literature, to the physical world. In the interview in this volume, Warren comments upon the importance of Ransom to his own development as a writer.

6. Among other critics who have noticed the prominence of narrative within Warren's poems is Calvin Bedient, who has written: "Warren is so constituted that he needs incident to build a vital image. Narrative steadies his language, holds back passion, . . . and incites his dramatic sense of syntax. In his best poems limiting circumstances and lyrical feeling mingle in a live reaction" ("Greatness and Robert Penn Warren," *Sewanee Review* 89 [1981]: 341).

7. Robert Penn Warren, *A Place to Come To* (New York: Random House, 1977), p. 60.

8. "Masts at Dawn" appears in *Selected Poems*, pp. 115–16.

9. Among other critics, Samuel Thames Lloyd III has also recognized that Warren's sense of longing operates within the religious realm. He says that Warren's intense love of the physical world "seems to impel the speaker towards an awareness of another dimension, the one he associates with whiteness and in 'Masts at Dawn' even calls God. But little can be known of this other dimension, and concern for it, turning the world into a 'parable,' can be a means of evading the pain and joy of life within the osmosis of being. This God is profoundly immanent; 'God' is a word for the sense of awe and holiness the speaker feels in his experience of the world. Beyond that he cannot and will not go" ("Robert Penn Warren: In the Midst of the World," Ph.D. Diss., University of Virginia, 1981, p. 242).

10. The argument that I here abstract from Warren's poem will be familiar to reader's of Ralph Waldo Emerson's *Nature*. Although Warren has vigorously denounced Emersonian thinking many times (as he does in the interview that follows), critics persist in finding parallels between his thinking and Emerson's. Harold Bloom speaks of this ("The Sunset Hawk," *New Leader*, January 31, 1977, pp. 19–20), while Samuel Lloyd is especially persuasive: "Emerson's impact is unmistakable throughout [Warren's] later career. . . . Warren's Romanticism stands surprisingly close to the tradition Emerson initiated: the poet as sayer, as representative man, searching through his experience for glimmers of transcendent truth" ("Robert Penn Warren," p. 213).

11. There is no question that the language and the imagery of Warren's poetry are often religious in their derivation and implication. There is also no question that Warren, especially in his interviews, sometimes goes out of his way to deny that his message is otherworldly or religious. Several critics have chosen to emphasize the latter half of this contradiction—for example Stanley Plumly, in his discussion of the volume *Incarnations:* "The title of the volume is ironically poised, for it is precisely the lack and / or denial of *spirit incarnate* that motivates this book. The *incarnations* represent manifestations of the flesh as flesh only, of the body as self-contained embodiment. The Word, therefore, becomes the poet's word made into the tentative flesh of the poem" ("Robert Penn Warren's Vision," *Southern Review* n.s. 6 [1970]: 1203). Others who agree with Plumly are Monroe Spears ("The Latest Poetry of Robert Penn Warren," *Sewanee Review* 98 [1970]: 350, 355–56) and Guy Rotella (" 'One Flesh': Robert Penn Warren's *Incarnations*," *Renascence* 31 [1978]: 33). Samuel Lloyd moves away from these views, in the direction of the transcendent, while still carefully grounding Warren's vision in the real: "To discover patterns of meaning which yield a capacity for peaceful acceptance and joy in one's life is the fundamental spiritual quest for the later Warren" ("Robert Penn Warren," p. 33). Victor Strandberg, however, quotes Warren himself in proving that, in fact, the implications of Warren's language and imagery are sacred after all, and that we might as well admit it: "[Warren] speaks approvingly of 'a central fact' in *The Ancient Mariner*, 'that the world is full of powers and presences not visible to the physical eye, . . . that there is a spiritual

order of universal love, the sacramental vision, . . . that nature, if understood aright—that is, by the imagination—offers us vital meanings.' Most
significantly, those vital meanings ascend to the theistic: 'the world of
Nature is to be read by the mind as a symbol of Divinity. . . . It might be
said that reason shows us God, and imagination shows us how Nature
participates in God'" ("Warren's Poetic Vision: A Reading of *Now and
Then*," *Southern Review* n.s. 16 [1980]: 20).

12. In his reading of this poem, Harold Bloom (though his review is entitled
"The Sunset Hawk") prefers to emphasize the importance of the "gaunt-
blasted" tree branch rather than the bird: "The emphasis is upon the immanent thrust of the natural object, rather than its transcendent possibilities" (p. 20). Victor Strandberg sees birds in general in Warren's work
as the anima, "a deeper, purer self, or 'soul'" that "relays some glimmers
of light, 'vision,' or 'uncharted Truth' to its forsaken *alter ego* lost in
darkness" ("Warren's Poetic Vision," pp. 22–23). Samuel Lloyd's reading is
closer to my own than to these: "That stub, thrusting skyward, perceived
by the imagination, is the best that the finite world and the human mind
can do. But sometimes, as here, a moment of grace occurs, the infinite
bestows itself on the finite, the eternal comes into time, and the work of
the imagination makes contact with the beyond" ("Robert Penn Warren,"
p. 294).

13. On the importance of elemental being in the volume, Calvin Bedient has
written: "Being for Warren, as for Heidegger, is what time immediately
discloses. His awareness of 'being here' as a tragic investment of pleasure,
is 'ammoniac.' . . . Warren follows Heidegger in calling the taking of Time
full in the face, in 'heart's hilarity,' *instancy* and entitles the volume in
which the word appears *Being Here*" (" 'One Flesh,' " p. 335).

14. Speaking of Warren's poetry in general, A. L. Clements has commented
upon these timeless moments: "The ultimate symbolizandum [sic] of Warren's poetry, as of all religious language, is the mystical or transcendental
or peak experience" ("Sacramental Vision: The Poetry of Robert Penn Warren," in *Critical Essays on Robert Penn Warren*, ed. William Bedford Clark
[Boston: G. K. Hall, 1981], p. 224). Later in the essay, Clements goes on to
explain: "At times the divine is seen as incarnate in the world. In such
perfect moments, or epiphanic spots of time, ordinary, everyday events and
entities appear extraordinary and transcendent, become charged through
the creative imagination with enormous physical, emotional, and spiritual
meanings, are more fully created or brought into fuller being" (pp. 230–31).

15. Victor Strandberg has noticed the general role of sex in Warren's poetry
with regard to an earlier poem; he speaks of "the One Flesh of sexual inter-
course ('sweat-grapple in darkness'), but this mode of self-transcendence,
like that associated with the dance and the music, proves so fleetingly
evanescent that 'I can't now even remember the name' of the dancer–sexual partner. Again, the quick fix of sensual experience, though it has an
undeniable integrity of its own, will not suffice as a substitute for philosophical insight" ("The Long Foreground of 'Old Nigger on One-Mule
Cart,' " in *Robert Penn Warren: A Collection of Critical Essays*, ed. Richard

Gray [Englewood Cliffs, N.J.: Prentice-Hall, 1981], p. 148). Guy Rotella similarly has spoken of "sex as solution" in Warren's poetry as one of several "false visions of meaning and value" ("Greatness and Robert Penn Warren," p. 31).

16. In his essay on *Now and Then* Victor Strandberg recognizes the general importance of the language, the sound, of nature in the recent poetry: "Increasingly in Warren's later poetry, the healing of the fallen self depends upon its grasp of a language that operates outside the realm of rational consciousness, disclosing a wholly different impression of reality" ("Warren's Poetic Vision," p. 20).

Index